THE 1995 MURDER YEARBOOK

Brain Lane is an expert in the field of true crime, and is the author of *The Encyclopedia of Forensic Science* (Headline, 1992), *The Encyclopedia of Women Killers* (Headline, 1994) and (with Wilfred Gregg) *The Encyclopedia of Serial Killers* (Headline, 1992). He founded The Murder Club in 1987, and compiled the formidable six-volume series of *Murder Club Guides* to Great Britain.

Brian Lane came to writing via fine art, theatre and experimental music and also spent a number of years with the United Nations in Geneva and Vienna. Now living in London, he continues to research, write and lecture on true-crime subjects.

Also by Brian Lane

The Murder Club Guides (6 vols.)
The Murder Guide to Great Britain
The Murder Guide to London
The Butchers
Murder Update
The Encyclopedia of Serial Killers (with Wilfred Gregg)
The Encyclopedia of Forensic Science
The Encyclopedia of Cruel and Unusual Punishment
The Murder Yearbook
The Murder Yearbook: 1994 Edition
Chronicle of 20th Century Murder
The Encyclopedia of Women Killers
The Encyclopedia of Mass Murder (with Wilfred Gregg)

The 1995 Murder Yearbook

Brian Lane

HEADLINE

First published in 1994
by HEADLINE BOOK PUBLISHING

10 9 8 7 6 5 4 3 2 1

ISBN 0 7472 4537 1

Typeset by
Letterpart Limited, Reigate, Surrey

Printed and bound in Great Britain by
Cox & Wyman Ltd, Reading, Berks

HEADLINE BOOK PUBLISHING
A division of Hodder Headline PLC
338 Euston Road
London NW1 3BH

Contents

Updates in Brief

Appendix 2: Mass Murder Update

Case Studies

Updates in Brief

Acknowledgements

In many ways the *Murder Yearbook* has evolved over the few years of its existence. At first it was one person's project – mine. One person's view of recent international crime; and yes, one person's 'soap-box'. However, I had always wanted and intended *Yearbook* to go beyond this almost parochial outlook to include the views and opinions of others, as capable in their analysis as me, as proficient in their literary skills (and often more so) as me. Readers of the last edition of *Yearbook* will already have noted this slight shift with the inclusion of material by my collaborator (on *The Encyclopedia of Serial Killers* and *The Encyclopedia of Mass Murder*) Wilfred Gregg, and my old friend and colleague John Bevis; their respective contributions, I firmly believe, enriched the book though the cover carried my name only.

And so this year we have been a little bolder. The name of John Bevis is more prominent, and we have been joined by another excellent writer and commentator, Trisha Reed, who has lent her own very individual approach to crime in the late twentieth century. As for the future of the *Murder Yearbook*, I would like to think that could develop even further – into a multinational collaboration; next year I would like to see contributions from friends and colleagues in many different parts of the world – whether talking about their own national crimes or other people's. Perhaps it is time that the *Murder Yearbook* became an orchestra rather than a one-man band.

That said, I must for this edition thank not only Wilfred, John and Trisha, but someone else familiar to discerning readers of true crime, the Canadian columnist Frank Jones, my friend and partner in crime – without his regular dispatches where would we be?

It is in the nature of any book analysis such as this, which is in many cases an assessment of what the world's media has contributed to our understanding of human-kind's darker side, that the researches and conclusions of some of the finest national and international reporters has been one of our valuable sources of reference – too many to mention, thank you nevertheless to those men and women who provide us with the NEWS.

Writers alone do not make books, any more than journalists alone make newspapers and magazines, films and television. That function of 'making' is fulfilled, in the case of *Murder Yearbook*, by a loyal and supportive team who, over the past years I have grown to admire and respect – after all, what use is my manuscript if nobody gets a chance to read it. My agent Julian Alexander has helped me more over the years than his modest stipend could ever repay, and his ability to shield me from the harsher realities of commercial publishing is a treasure beyond price. For Headline, my editor Sarah Hughes has never failed to turn up with the right response to any situation – encouragement, sympathy, enthusiasm, good humour, and yes, a little necessary but gentle bullying as deadlines pass. I am luckier than I deserve in having had over the course of so many books my consistently watch-ful and supportive copy editor Bela Cunha, whose eagle-eye has for so long saved me much potential embarrassment, and but for whose keying skills of *Year-book* I might not have had a manuscript at all. Most importantly, as always, I would like to express my sincere thanks to Headline's Editorial Director Alan Brooke for his unfailing enthusiasm for this and many other projects. His is indeed a door that is always open.

Brian Lane
July 1994

Author's Introduction

Regular readers of Brian Lane's *Murder Yearbook*s will remember that they were originally titled *Murder Update*, in the hope of conveying the fact that very few of the most notable homicides are over and forgotten with the end of the trial. Aside from the fact that, in Britain, it takes at least one year from the solution of a crime to the trial, and then perhaps several more years to win the right to appeal, many murders have an intrinsic interest which extends beyond the simple ethic of crime and punishment. In other words, contain elements greater in their implication than the fact of killing – science, for example, where techniques such as DNA profiling help solve not just one crime, but revolutionise the whole of criminal investigation; another area in which advances are solving crimes is psychological profiling. Justice is a further concept which frequently keeps a crime in the news; or in this instance, perhaps we should be speaking of *in*justice, a problem which seems to have dogged the British legal system increasingly over recent years. Another factor which contributes to the longevity of a murder case is the almost legendary status awarded to some killers – the brothers Kray come to mind, and Peter Sutcliffe, the 'Yorkshire Ripper', Brady and Hindley, the 'Moors Murderers', and mad Charlie Manson, whose fan club would be envied by most film stars. These 'monsters' seem rarely to be out of the media spotlight, and if proof were needed, what better example than Jack the Ripper? Sometimes crimes enter popular folklore because of their sheer scale – either in terms of numbers or gruesomeness; some, like the cannibal killings of Jeffrey Dahmer, embrace both.

One of the functions of the *Yearbooks*, then, is to act as a cumulative collection of case studies, updating some of the major crimes which have been covered in previous editions. Another virtue of their format is that it is flexible enough to examine not only individual crimes of violence, but also issues of contemporary concern as they are reflected in the homicide statistics. It is hoped, therefore, that although *Murder Yearbook* can be read as a number of individual cases of international interest and importance, it can also take a look behind the façade of a crime at the background problems from which it arises.

The Appliance of Science

One of the major breakthroughs in the increasingly desperate war waged by law enforcement officers against the serial killer has been the emergence of that branch of forensic psychiatry known as 'offender profiling'. That is, the evaluation of such elements of a killer's *modus operandi* as victim trait, location, degree of violence, favoured weapon, and so on, to construct a profile of the *sort of* person who might be responsible for a series of related murders. It is important to stress *sort of* person, because no degree of accuracy in profiling will ever produce a name. It is equally important to stress that, although a profile is invaluable for comparison with a suspect list, it would be a short-sighted officer indeed who discarded a suspect simply because he did *not* fit the psychological offender profile. A more detailed discussion of the background and development of psychological profiling will be found in the Introduction to Appendix 1 (page 265). It is also a technique which was employed to classic effect in the hunt for the serial killer Colin Ireland whose trial for the brutal murders of five homosexual men in London took place in 1993 (see page 63). The English psychologist Mike Berry assembled a profile of the 'gay killer' which proved accurate, as did his American counterpart Professor Jonas Rappeport.

Justice Delayed

One of the surest ways of keeping a case in the public eye via media coverage is the suspicion of a miscarriage of justice. And judging by the number of convictions overturned on appeal in recent years, Britain is enjoying something of an epidemic. However, in the year covered by this edition of *Yearbook*, the two most interesting cases of miscarriage took place in France and in the United States. In Nice, Omar Raddad was tried in January 1994 for the murder of his elderly employer and was convicted on mainly unreliable circumstantial evidence. Although Madame Marchal was found beside a cellar door on which '*Omar m'a tuer*' had been written in blood, the likelihood of the message having been the victim's last words is remote, and not only are legal and media observers anxious for a retrial, but a national poll taken in France revealed that 64 per cent of the population believe Raddad was wrongly convicted (see page 88).

In a curious reversal to the release of all the people whose convictions were found to be unsafe, Byron de la Beckwith (see page 95) was convicted of a murder he committed thirty years earlier. On the night of 12 June 1963 Beckwith shot dead foremost civil rights leader Medgar Evers. Despite clear forensic evidence of his guilt, self-confessed racist and segregationist Beckwith was tried twice and on both occasions all-male, all-white juries in Jackson, Mississippi, failed to agree and mistrials were declared. In February 1994 'Deelay' Beckwith was finally convicted by an equally comprised black/white jury and sentenced to life imprisonment.

One English case that has refused to be forgotten is the

savage and pointless murder of PC Keith Blakelock during the riots at Broadwater Farm estate in north London in 1985.* The officer was literally hacked to death after tripping over and being pounced upon by the mob of blood-crazy demonstrators. Although three men were tried and convicted for PC Blakelock's murder, police conduct in handling interviews with the prisoners and tampering with confession evidence led to the convictions of Winston Silcott, Engin Raghip and Mark Braithwaite being declared unsafe and unsatisfactory by the Court of Appeal in 1991. Indeed, shortly after this manuscript was delivered to the publisher, two senior police officers involved in the inquiry, Superintendent Graham Melvin and Detective Inspector Maxwell Dingle found themselves in the Old Bailey on 22 July 1994 charged with perverting the course of justice and Mr Melvin with a further charge of perjury. Both men were acquitted on 26 July by a unanimous decision.

Recent news, too, of Winston Silcott. Although his conviction on the Blakelock case was reversed, Silcott could not be released as he was already serving life for a killing committed in 1984. At a party in east London, it was said that Silcott stabbed to death Anthony Smith. According to his lawyers, Silcott was attacked first and only acted in self defence. In January 1994, Home Secretary Michael Howard rejected an application for the case to be referred back to the Court of Appeal. However, in July 1994, Mr Justice Schiemann granted Silcott leave to challenge the Home Secretary's refusal, and called for the case to be dealt with urgently. In a statement from prison, Winston Silcott said: 'I did not expect the Home Secretary to look at my case impartially; perhaps now he will be made to do so by the courts.

* See *Murder Update*, Brian Lane, Robinson Publishing, London, 1991 and *Murder Yearbook* 1993 Edition, Brian Lane, Headline, London, 1993.

If any court takes the trouble to look at the full facts of my case they can only come to one conclusion – that I was attacked and did no more than defend myself. It is not a crime to act in self defence.'

There were updates, too, in one of the most tragic, most unpardonable cases of miscarriage of justice ever to disgrace British legal history. In 1976 Stefan Kiszko, a twenty-four-year-old clerk with the Inland Revenue, was convicted of the murder of eleven-year-old Lesley Moleseed and sentenced to life imprisonment.* Due mainly to the determination and courage of Stefan's mother and a small group of local supporters, he was released on appeal in 1992 after serving sixteen years in prison, humiliated and vilified by press, public and fellow prisoners. There was little chance of the appeal failing because it could be *proved* that Stefan Kiszko could not possibly have committed the murder. Forensic evidence was available that due to a physical disability he was *incapable* of producing the semen which it was claimed was deposited on Lesley Moleseed's clothing. What's more, *this evidence was available to the prosecution at the time of the trial; it was never passed on to the attorneys acting for the defence*. Of course, there was the usual clutch of mealy-mouthed non-apologies, and some mention of compensation. Sadly, the horror of his unnecessary ordeal took a grave toll of Stefan Kiszko's mental and physical health. In Christmas week 1993 he died of what is thought to have been a heart attack.

Less than five months later, in early May 1994, Stefan's mother Charlotte also died. It is supremely ironic that just one day after Charlotte Kiszko's funeral the Crown Prosecution Service announced that it was to charge Detective Superintendent Richard Holland and Ronald

* See *Murder Yearbook* 1993 Edition, Brian Lane, Headline, London, 1993.

Dutteridge with 'acts intending and tending to pervert the course of justice'. Mr Holland, who retired from the West Yorkshire police force in 1983, and Mr Dutteridge, a forensic scientist, also retired, were involved in the investigation into the killing of Lesley Moleseed.

Another of the classic miscarriages of justice in which forensic evidence is vital also got its regular airing during the spring of 1994. There can be few, even among those too young to remember the trial, who have not encountered the controversy over James Hanratty's guilt for the shooting dead of Michael Gregsten and the serious maiming of Gregsten's mistress Valerie Storie at the appropriately named Deadman's Hill on the A6 in 1961. Despite doubtful identification evidence and in the face of another more suitable suspect (Peter Alphon) who subsequently confessed to the shootings at length, James Hanratty was convicted and hanged. Like many other cases which have refused to die, the Hanratty conviction has been contested by lawyers, solicitors, investigative journalists and members of the Hanratty family for more than thirty years. The reason for the revival of interest in the case in 1994 is that it has for some time been known that, as a result of a sexual attack on Miss Storie at the time of the incident, samples of semen were collected from her clothing. In those days, of course, DNA profiling or 'genetic fingerprinting' was still a quarter of a century away. But the samples were preserved and could now be subjected to DNA testing. Clearly poor James Hanratty is no longer able to give blood samples for comparison, but his brother is more than willing to co-operate, and Professor Alec Jeffries, who developed DNA profiling, has offered to carry out the tests in his own research laboratory. There is just one snag to all this – the Home Office refuses, under any circumstances, to release the original samples, in spite of numerous requests from the Hanratty family. In early 1994, their legal representatives applied again for access. It will look strange indeed if the authorities, who maintain the correctness of Hanratty's execution, fail to take advantage of this opportunity to once and for all time vindicate their stand.

The seemingly endless battle for a posthumous pardon for Derek Bentley took one hesitant step forward during 1993. Like the so-called 'A6 Murder', the shooting of PC Sydney Miles during a gun battle between police and two youths has become an English *cause célèbre*. On the night of 2 November 1953 Derek Bentley and Christopher Craig (armed with a gun) climbed on to the roof of Barlow and Parker wholesale confectioners at Croydon intent on burglary. A conscientious neighbour called the police and in the skirmish that followed it was thought that Craig fired his weapon and killed PC Miles; Bentley was already under arrest. Their trial before Lord Goddard, the Lord Chief Justice, was a model of bigotry and both youths were convicted of murder. Because he was too young, Christopher Craig was reprieved from the death sentence, but Bentley who was already in police custody and had never touched a firearm that night was hanged at the age of nineteen. From that date the whole of the Bentley family began a campaign which was to last forty years and more. And when Derek's parents died, it was his sister Iris who maintained a tireless fight for his posthumous pardon. After decades of disappointment, after forty years of laying a wreath at the gate of Wandsworth Prison on the anniversary of Derek's execution, Iris Bentley, now sixty-one years old, achieved a kind of breakthrough. In October 1992 the then Home Secretary, Kenneth Clarke, refused to grant a posthumous pardon (again). (To give him some credit, the Home Secretary had admitted that had he been Home Secretary in 1953 he would have reprieved Derek Bentley.) However, it was the claim of Mr David Pannick QC, acting for Iris, that Mr Clarke had acted unlawfully in suggesting that it was only possible to consider a pardon when he was satisfied of 'technical and moral innocence'. The three High Court judges before whom the claim by Miss Bentley was being heard in May 1993, described it as 'a very unusual matter'. Nevertheless, their verdict, given at the beginning of July, was that Bentley should have been reprieved because he did not pull the trigger. Lord Justice Watkins said: 'There is compelling argument that even by the standards of 1953, the then Home Secretary's decision was clearly wrong.' It was in many ways a triumph – after all it was the first time that any member of the judiciary had conceded that Derek Bentley should have lived. But it was only a partial triumph for Iris Bentley. She and her advisers still had to convince a new Home Secretary (Michael Howard) to grant that final elusive posthumous pardon. Typically, he did not. Still hiding behind legal jargon and political delaying tactics, Howard could not bring himself to admit that Derek Bentley was wrongly charged, wrongly convicted, wrongly sentenced . . . and wrongly hanged. He did, though, concede that he personally would have granted a reprieve. What was offered was a sort of half-measure, a kind of 'partial pardon'. The Home Secretary, it turned out, felt that a full pardon was 'inappropriate' and in his recommendation to the Queen, suggested she address herself to the issue of Bentley's *sentence*. And so the indomitable Iris Bentley fights on: 'Derek was in my prayers last night, and he will be in them tonight. I've kept my promise, and I've a few years left in me. His name shall be cleared before I die [Iris is at present battling courageously against cancer].'

One man who has enjoyed rather more success with the appeal process is Edward Browning. In June 1988, twenty-two-year-old Mrs Marie Wilkes, seven months pregnant, was found battered and stabbed to death on an embankment of the M50. It is known that Mrs Wilkes had broken down in her car and walked to the nearest motorway emergency telephone to call for help. A number of other motorists reported seeing a silver-grey car parked on the hard shoulder to the telephone. On 3 June thirty-five-year-old Edward Owen Browning, a night club bouncer from south Wales, was charged with the murder. It would be significant that his car which was also impounded was later found to be forensically unconnected with the murder, and there had been no attempt to clean it. During October and early November 1989 Eddie Browning stood his trial at Shrewsbury Crown Court. On 8 November he was found guilty and sentenced by Mr Justice Turner to life imprisonment with a recommendation that he serve at least twenty-five years. Browning, not unusually in such cases, continued to protest his innocence and applied for leave to appeal. The appeal, based on the accusation that the trial judge did not warn the jury strongly enough to be cautious over evidence about the identification of the killer's car and his appearance, was rejected and on 24 May 1991 Browning lost his appeal. In November of the same year he went on hunger strike at the Gartree maximum security prison to draw attention to his case. Although the gesture made little enough impact, newspapers were reporting in May 1992 that Home Secretary Kenneth Clarke had reopened the M50 case with specific reference to the videotape of a key police witness who underwent hypnosis in order to retrieve information which had dropped from his immediate memory. It was never shown by the police to either the defence lawyers or the Crown Prosecution Service. Campaigning journalist Paul Foot in his days at the *Daily Mirror* was more specific: 'It shows him [Inspector Peter Clarke] describing the car – both before and during hypnosis. Pretty well every single detail clashed with the facts about Eddie Browning's car.' It was just the evidence Eddie Browning's defence needed, and the videotape was the main witness in Browning's new appeal in May 1994. It showed Inspector Clarke describing the killer's vehicle as a silver-grey non-hatchback Renault with chrome bumpers and the registration number C856 HFK. Browning's car was a hatchback with plastic bumpers and the registration number C754 VAD. This clearly clashed with the police story and was suppressed as evidence. The result was that the Lord Chief Justice Lord Taylor was obliged to note that this 'plainly constituted a material irregularity' and 'was a failure to disclose evidence which would have been of great value to the defence'. On 13 May 1994 Eddie Browning walked from the court a free man.

Living Legends (And a Couple of Dead Ones)

But it was not only the miscarriages which attracted media attention during 1993–4. Most of the old familiar faces were there, the bogey-men (and -women) who are staple fare across the years. The Menendez brothers, Lyle and Erik (see page 111), accused of murdering their parents for the inheritance, and who have kept the American television audience glued to the screen these past few years, finally came to trial – two trials in fact – and still no jury managed to convict them. All that happened was that they walked into court as two heartless familicides who rendered their parents unrecognisable with a couple of shotguns, and emerged the touching picture of abused innocence reducing Court TV audiences to tears. This one will run and run.

On this side of the Atlantic, Jeremy Bamber was rattling the bars of his cell in the cause of proving his innocence before the court of appeal. The first rumbles were heard in September 1993 when campaigners seeking his release sent a submission to the Home Office listing grounds for an appeal against his conviction on charges of shooting dead five members of his family. A month later Jim Shelley, no stranger to controversial journalism and a man with a keen eye for the details others miss, wrote an intriguing piece for the *Guardian* weekend supplement under the headline 'Who Killed Bambi?' It would do an injustice to the article to try to precis it in two lines, but it does, with gentle persuasion, at least own to the possibility that the answer is Bambi did. Whether Sheila 'Bambi' Caffel was really capable of such savagery as was committed at White House Farm in October 1986 may never be known, but her estranged husband Colin Caffel, who wrote a long letter of rebuttal against the Shelley article in the following week's *Guardian* supplement was at pains to point out to readers 'a number of blatant lies told about Sheila Caffel – mainly by her brother Jeremy – that I can clearly refute'. And what of Jeremy? Jeremy was within a whisker of getting leave to appeal approved according to some of the popular press. But there was just one problem. While members of the Justice For All Group were putting together material for an appeal, the ITV television broadcasting company was putting together material for a drama-doc of the White House Farm Murders in their regular 'Crime Story' strand scheduled for 22 December and starring Bamber lookalike Neil Roberts as Jeremy. For what it was worth, retired detective Stan Jones, who led the Bambi inquiry, was urging 'misguided do-gooders' to watch the programme which, Mr Jones believed, would be the 'final nail in Bamber's coffin'.

Jeremy Bamber was not the only convicted killer to be immortalised on the small screen. The irrepressible Nick Broomfield assembled a wonderful portrait of serial killer Aileen Wuornos and her abominable new 'family' (see page 331), and the cannibal killer Issei Sagawa also featured in a drama-doc as part of Channel 4's 'Witness' strand. Sagawa it was who, in 1981, as a Japanese student in Paris, became obsessed with fellow student Renee Hartvelt and, when she failed to respond to his unwelcome advances, shot her, committed necrophilia and then dismembered her body, taking time out to photograph his progress and to eat slivers of his victim's flesh. In his autobiography, *Excuse Me for Living*, the tiny oriental describes with evident delight how 'I touched her hip and wondered where I should eat first. I took a meat knife and when I stabbed it went right in. I could see a red colour, it looked life beef, red meat. A little came out and I put it into my mouth. It had no smell or taste. It melted in my mouth like raw tuna in a sushi restaurant.' And nobody should know better than Issei Sagawa. The television programme broadcast in November 1993 revealed that, following a derisory four years in a French asylum, he was packed off back to Japan where he became a restaurant critic!

A more recent cannibal, Jeffrey Dahmer, also had his own television documentary, and a book about his early life written by his father. As well as Norman Mailer's *Executioner's Song* and its accompanying made-for-TV mini-series, the Utah killer Gary Gilmore, who insisted on dying in front of a firing squad for his murders, was immortalised in June 1994 by a book about his early life; this one was written by his brother Mikal Gilmore. Mikal is a rock journalist for *Rolling Stone* and his *Shot in the Heart* is reputed to have earned an advance of $700,000.

Two long-dead members of the 'aristocracy' of England's murderers also found popularity in prose in 1993–4. Letters written by Dr Crippen to his mistress Ethel Le Neve were made public at the Public Record Office at Kew. Crippen, celebrated for killing his domineering actress wife Belle Elmore, wrote many of the letters while he was in the death cell at Pentonville Prison awaiting execution. Other documents in the Crippen collection included a memo from the prison governor describing Crippen's last hours before he was hanged on 23 November 1910. On one occasion, the governor writes, Crippen 'broke down and was crying for fully ten minutes'.

Another document with far less reliable a pedigree was what purported to be the personal diary of Jack the Ripper. Announced as the find of the century, the text was written in longhand in what appeared to be a Victorian scrapbook. What was so extraordinary was that it identified Jack as none other than James Maybrick, the prosperous Liverpool cotton merchant who was supposedly poisoned with arsenic by his wife Florence in 1889. The manuscript had arrived on publishers Smith Gryphon's desk via a man named Frank Barrett, who alleged he had been given it by a friend (now deceased). That a large number of crime historians considered the work a fake was never in question; what gave the whole charade interest was the way it set earnest Ripperologist against earnest Ripperologist, expert against expert. Threats of legal action were flying about like confetti on a windy day as these eager folk sought to authenticate or debunk the claims made for the 'diary'. In the end the book was published and became a bestseller, despite the fact that the majority of forensic science experts had by that time become suspicious of the manuscript's provenance. By July 1994, the debate was all over. Mr Frank Barrett had confessed to a local newspaper that he had faked the diary and gave details of where he obtained the authentic ink and paper. And a great sigh of relief emanated from the world of Ripperology – no spoilsport had killed off the passionate pastime of squabbling over Jack's identity.

And on that cautionary note, it is time to return to the present, where, sadly, humankind is still capable of equally gruesome slaughter as that perpetrated by Jack the Ripper. However, it is my sincere hope that the contents of this book are balanced and above all fair. It is always my intention to inform, if my words can also entertain, then so much the better.

Brian Lane
July 1994

The Statistics of Homicide

THE STATISTICS OF HOMICIDE

Difficult as it may be to believe, the number of cases initially recorded as homicide in Britain during 1992* (the latest year for which figures are available) *dropped* by 6 per cent, the first fall in five years. The figures were:

1991	726	(includes murder, manslaughter and infanticide)
1992	**683**	**(includes murder, manslaughter and infanticide)**

of which 382 victims were male and 240 female. Once again an alarming 45 per cent of female victims were killed by current or former spouses, cohabitees or lovers, and for both genders the majority of victims were acquainted with their killer. Following the yearly trend, the most common method of killing was with a sharp instrument, and the most common circumstance (motive) was following a quarrel or flash of anger (more than 50 per cent).

Overall figures for the United States, also for the year 1992†, are as follows:

1991	24,703	representing 9.8 per 100,000 inhabitants
1992	**23,760**	**representing 9.3 per 100,000 inhabitants**
% change	*–3.8*	*–5.1*

* Derived from *Criminal Statistics for England and Wales 1992*, published by the Home Office Research and Statistical Department, London, 1993.

† Derived from the Uniform Crime Reports *Crime in the United States 1992*, published by the US Department of Justice, Washington DC, 1993.

These figures are customarily broken down into the four regions of the nation:

Region	*1992 (per cent)*	*Per 100,000*
Southern States	41	11
Western States	23	10
Midwestern States	20	8
Northeastern States	17[1]	8

[1] Decrease over the previous year of 3 per cent

Tables and charts on the following pages present more specific details of these overall trends.

The Growing Threat of Firearms

Home Office figures show that crimes involving a firearm rose to around 13,000 in England and Wales in 1992 – or one every thirty-five minutes. And they are increasing at a rate of 8 per cent every year. The pettiest of criminals now goes armed, and robberies netting trivial amounts of cash are often committed with the aid of a gun. The 1980s saw the number of incidents of weapons used in robberies soar from 1,893 to 5,200 a year, while in the same period the statistics for weapons used in acts of violence leapt from 277 to 861. Of the total number of recorded homicides – fairly constant at around six or seven hundred a year – between 7 and 10 per cent are caused by shootings.

There are suspected to be 2.5 million illegal firearms in the UK. Weapons are coming into the country from Russia and eastern Europe – where the collapse of communism has led to a flood of Eastern bloc weapons on the market – as well as from countries such as Israel. In 1992, 437 weapons and 21,519 rounds of ammunition were seized at customs. Ex-army weapons are also available on the black market,

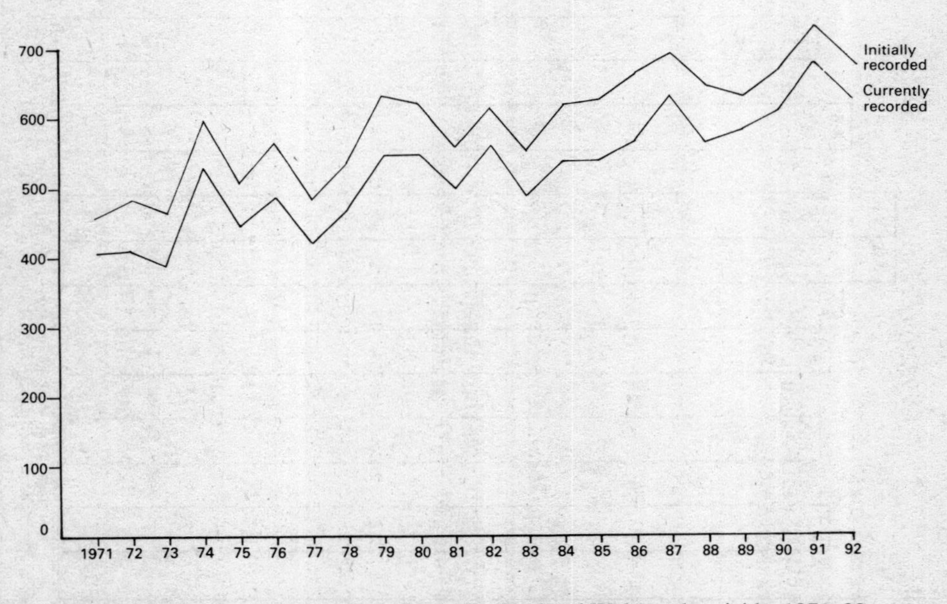

Chart 1 Offences recorded by the police in England and Wales as homicide, 1971–92

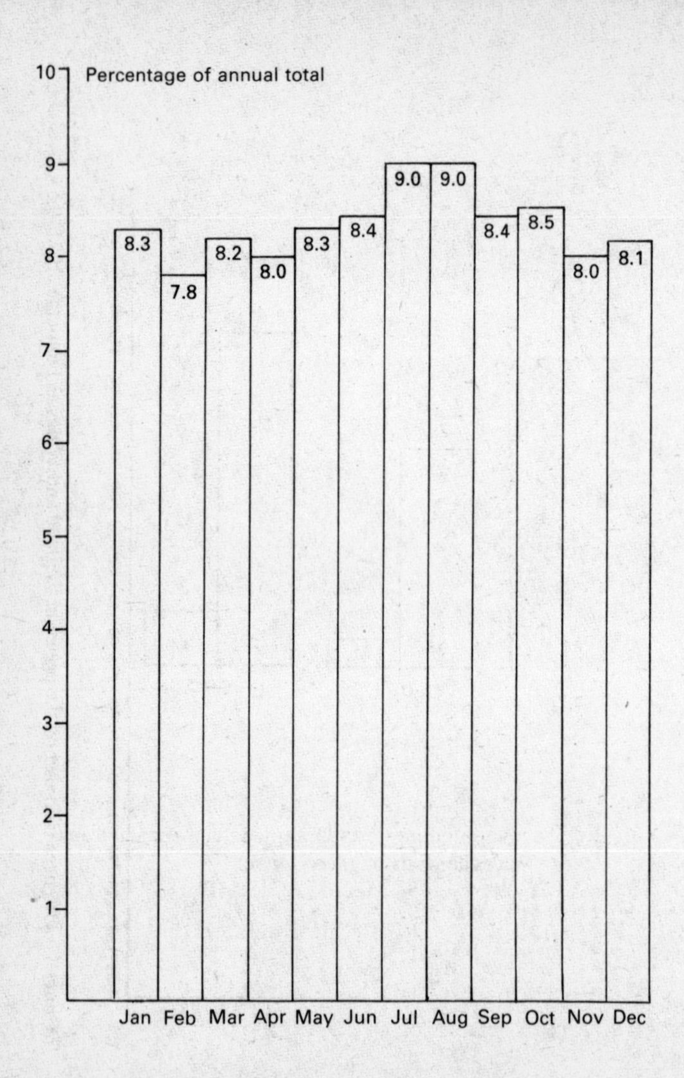

Chart 2 Murder in the USA, 1992, by month

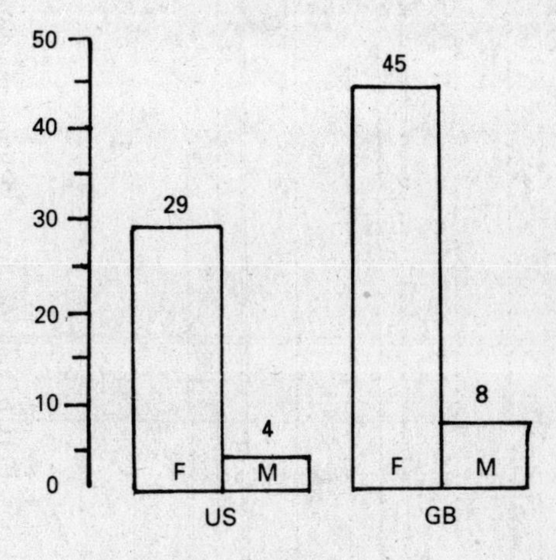

Chart 3 'Spouse-killing'*, 1992, United States/England and Wales comparison (*percentage*)

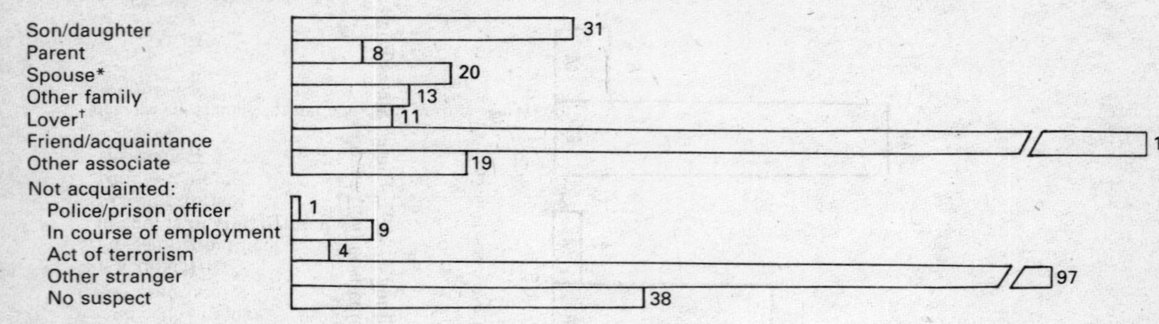

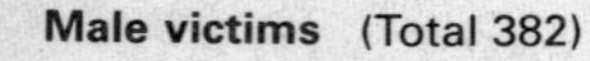
*Includes cohabitant, former spouse or former cohabitant
†Or former lover

Chart 4 Murder in England and Wales, 1992, by relationship of victim to main suspect (*number of offences*)

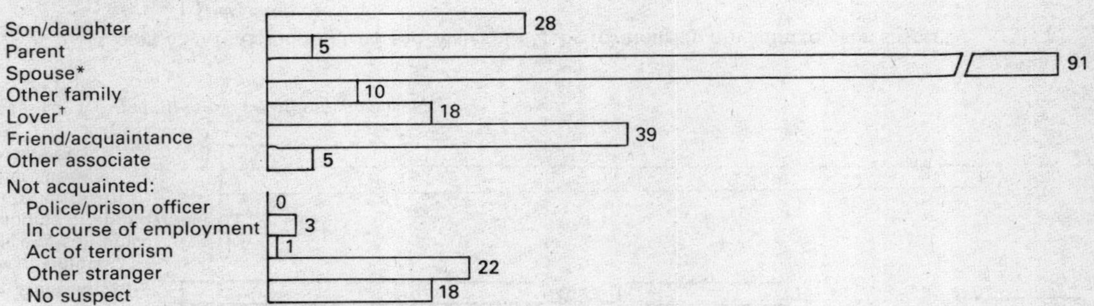

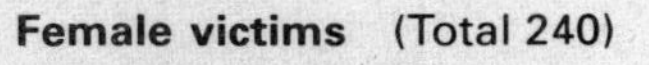
*Includes cohabitant, former spouse or former cohabitant
†Or former lover

Chart 5 Murder in England and Wales, 1992, by relationship of victim to main suspect (*number of offences*)

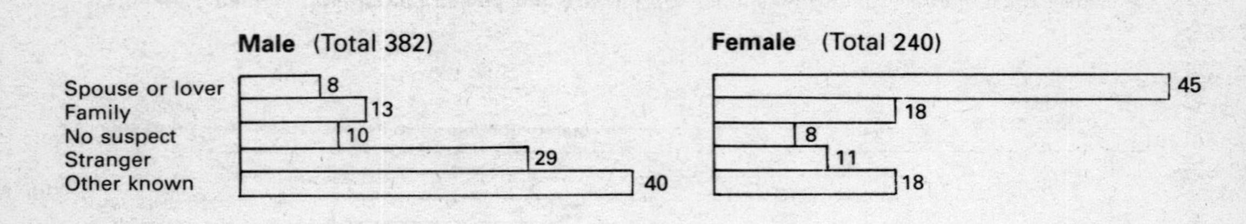

Chart 6 Murder in England and Wales, 1992, by relationship of victim to main suspect (*percentage*)

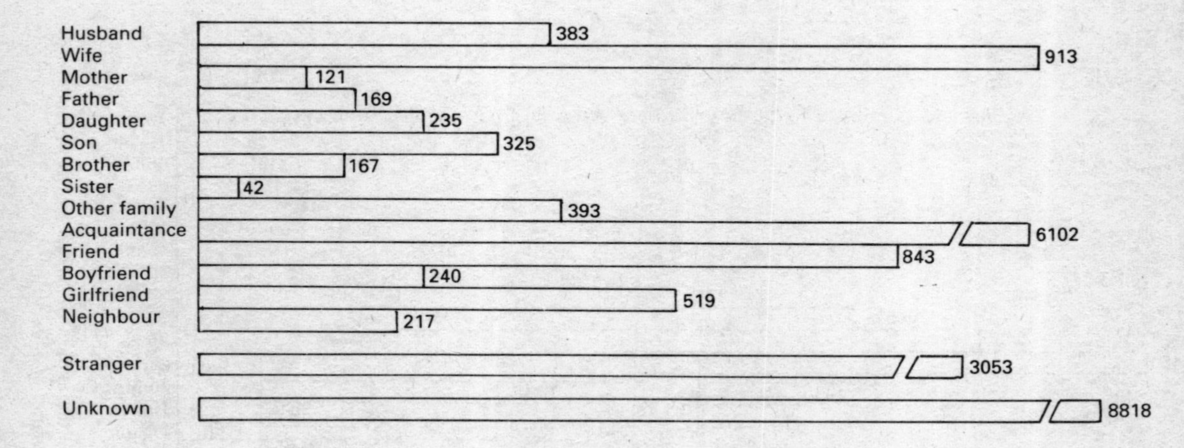

Chart 7 Murder in the USA, 1992, by relationship of victim to main suspect (*number of offences*)

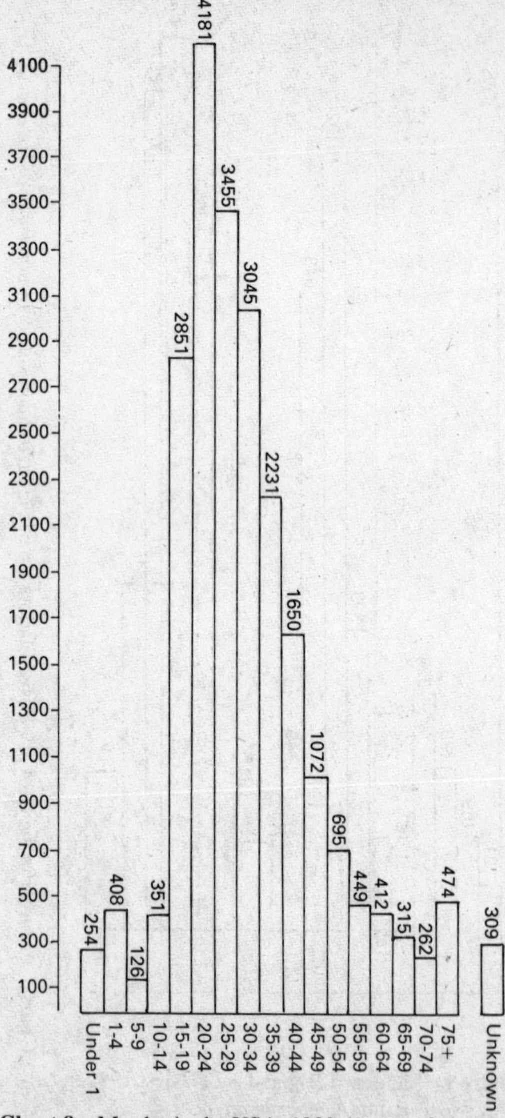

Chart 8 Murder in the USA, 1992, by age of victim (*number of offences*)

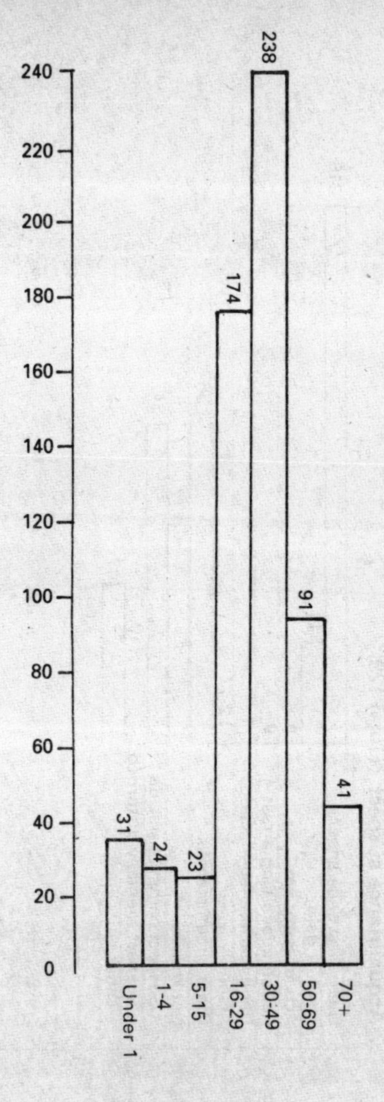

Chart 9 Murder in England and Wales, 1992, by age of victim (*number of offences*)

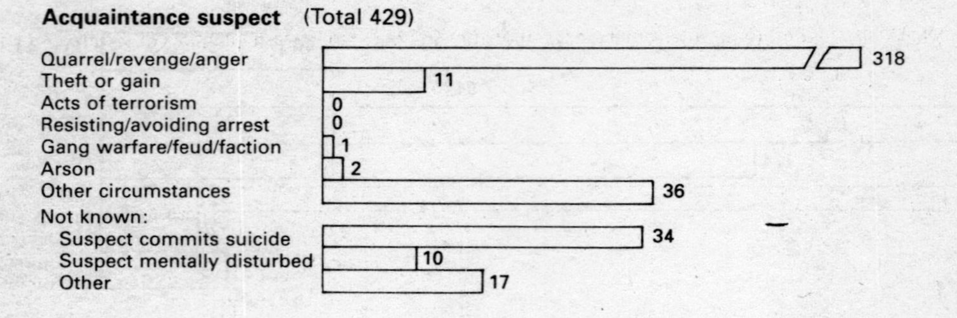

Chart 10 Murder in England and Wales, 1992, by apparent circumstances (motive) (*number of offences*)

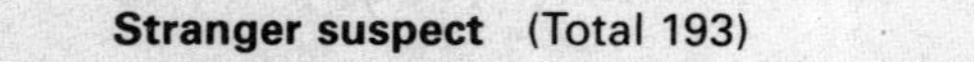

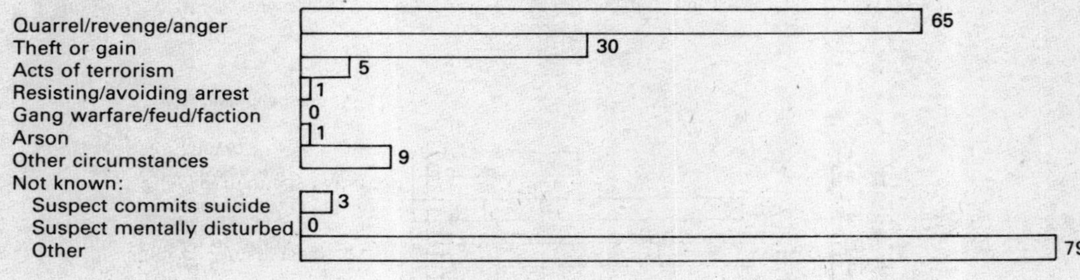

Chart 11 Murder in England and Wales, 1992, by apparent circumstances (motive) (*number of offences*)

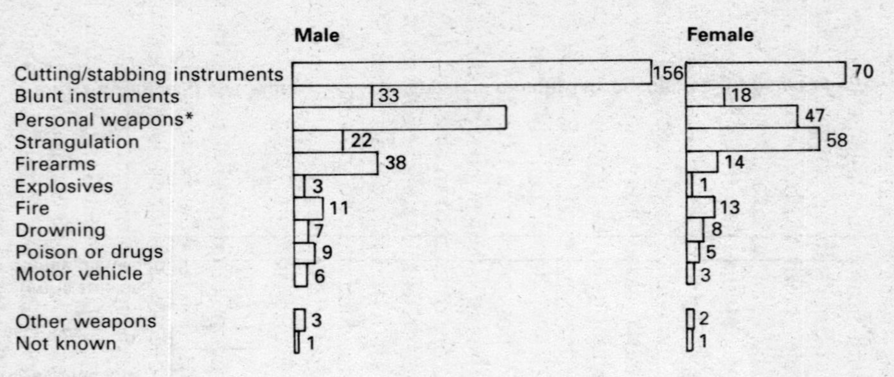

Chart 12 Murder in England and Wales, 1992, by type of weapon used (*number of offences*)

brought back by soldiers as trophies after the Falklands and Gulf wars. And guns stolen during burglaries are sold on for use in armed robberies – some of them antiques as much as ninety years old. With nearly one million shotgun and firearms certificates in Britain this is obviously a plentiful source. The certificates cover weapons used for sport, gaming and 'collectables'; most semi-automatic weapons were outlawed in 1988 after the Hungerford massacre.

The central figure in the underworld arms trade is the armourer: there are thought to be as many as twenty in the East End of London alone. They will sell anything from a sawn-off shotgun to a hand grenade, with prices rising to £800 for a machine pistol, and £1,500 for an AK47. Guns are often made available for rent, as no villain wants to be in possession of a firearm for longer than necessary, but the full selling price is payable if they are fired. Fired guns are often thrown away, as they can incriminate by being forensically matched to spent cartridges. For this reason too, some contract killers favour revolvers, which are compact and powerful and, of course, do not spill their shell cases. Gun-hire customers are predominantly armed robbers, drug dealers, and contract killers.

Outside of London, one of the most notorious districts where the gun holds sway is Manchester's Moss Side. Here fourteen-year-old Benji Stanley was shot dead as he queued for food in Alvino's Pattie and Dumplin' take-away shop in January 1992, in what was believed to be a case of mistaken identity. And here, four months later, college student Andrea Mairs was shot in the stomach by a stray bullet when she pulled back the curtains of the family home in Carlton Street, having heard screeching tyres and the sound of gunshots. She survived after surgery, but injuries have forced her to give up her studies. Moss Side is controlled by two rival gangs of black drug dealers: the 'Goochies' and the 'Doddies', identified by red and blue bandannas respectively. Both gangs use children on mountain bikes to deliver heroin and crack; and both gangs are armed with revolvers, Sten guns and AK47 assault rifles. The walkways and rat-runs of the grim Alexandra Park tower-block estate provide the perfect environment for their gun-controlled intimidation.

In the USA, of course, the tradition of ordinary citizens carrying guns is strong, but in 1990 alone no fewer than 16,000 people were shot dead – the numbers checked off on a three-storey digital 'clock of death' in New York's Times Square. President Clinton has faced strong opposition to his attempts at gun control from the powerful National Rifle Association of America, which insists the right to bear arms is guaranteed under the US Constitution. On 24 May 1993 Rodney Peairs was acquitted of shooting dead Yoshi Hattori, a Japanese student who mistakenly entered his house at Baton Rouge, Louisiana, looking for a party. Mr Peairs's lawyer told the court: 'You have the absolute right to answer your door with a gun.'

But the Brady Bill, which passed before Congress in November 1993, stipulates a five-day waiting period for gun customers, and bans the sale of handguns to anyone under twenty-one. If this amendment seems modest, it should be seen in the context of a society where more than 250,000 children own guns; in 1992, for the first time, more young Americans died of gunshot wounds than in car accidents. A 'toys for guns' exchange initiative in New York over the Christmas period in 1993 netted a 'spectacularly successful' 1,502 weapons, and is likely to be repeated in other high-crime areas. But there is a long way to go: the newest terror on the New York subway is a gang which robs passengers at the point of TEC-9 machine guns, which can fire up to 100 rounds at a time.

Los Angeles is just one other American city among

many with a huge gun problem. The city is home to no fewer than 570 Latino gangs and 315 black gangs, whose 200,000-odd members committed 800 murders in 1992. Children as young as eleven years of age are initiated, and there is, distinct from many gangs, a large female membership. In 1992 a quarter of the 3,500 drive-by shootings were undertaken by women.

In fact, women have become the target for firearms advertisements sponsored by the NRA, promoting weapons such as Smith & Wesson's .22 Ladysmith revolver. The adverts suggest that gun-ownership is a necessary act of women's equality and independence, and show guns juxtaposed with photographs of small children with captions like: 'Self protection is more than your right – it's your responsibility' and: 'There is no freedom for women who are afraid to walk alone.' The monthly *Women and Guns* boasts a readership of 25,000, 80 per cent of whom have a gun for personal protection. As Kate Muir has written in *The Times*: 'The proliferation of guns, legal and illegal, has resulted in the general feeling that killing in self-defence by both sexes is absolutely justifiable, and that guns cannot be controlled.' And it is not only self defence which in popular opinion warrants the use of a gun: Ellie Nesler, a mother who walked into Tuolumne County Courthouse, California, on 2 April 1993 and shot dead the man accused of sexually molesting her son, has become a national heroine.

June 1994 brought new fears of an influx of automatic weapons into Britain. According to an article by the *Observer*'s political correspondent Andy McSmith, the problem is that laws introduced in the wake of the Hungerford massacre prohibiting the sale of automatic weapons exempt firearms which have been deactivated – that is to say, they have been rendered unfirable, usually through having the firing pin removed. The problem is that firing pins are by no means difficult to replace, and deactivated weapons which can be bought freely over the counter in gunshops (even by mail order) are being restored to working order. That these weapons are finding their way on to the market in increasing number is testified by the number seized by the Greater Manchester police during their crack-down on the activities of the city's rival drug gangs.

One City's Sadness

At the end of April 1994 the *Chicago Tribune*, making use of Chicago Police Department figures, announced the alarming statistic that the murder rate in the city had risen to one every ten hours. Between 1 January and 25 April, 291 people were killed; in the same period in 1993, 241 people were slain.

One worrying aspect of the increase was identified by psychiatrist and president of the Community Mental Health Council, Dr Carl Bell. Dr Bell, who has made a long-term study of urban violence, told the *Tribune* that traditionally homicide resulted from 'interpersonal altercations' – in other words, where the victim is known to the killer, both often being members of the same family or circle of friends. However, he is now beginning to witness a sharp rise in gang-related homicides; this has proved particularly tragic when innocent bystanders, often children, are killed in the cross-fire between feuding gangs warring over drug territories. Victims such as ten-year-old Jamone Ross, who was shot while sitting on his bicycle in the South Side district. Rodney Collins was another ten-year-old, shot on 29 March 1994 when he was caught in cross-fire while he was riding his bicycle just yards from where Jamone Ross died.

Given the escalation in gang warfare, and the predilection for guns as a rapid means of 'solving' problems it is no surprise that shooting is the most favoured method

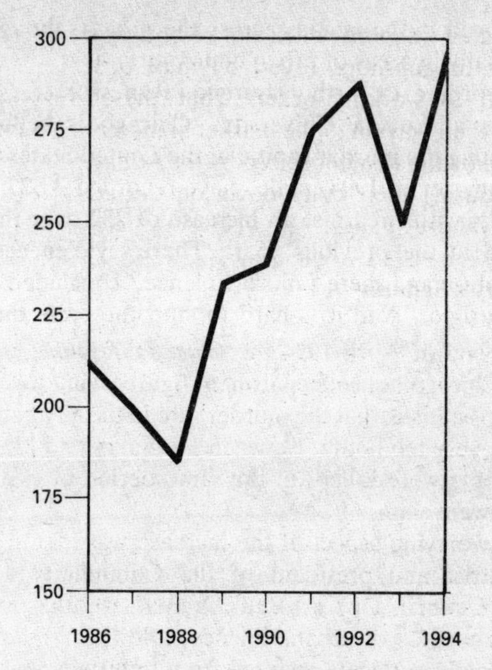

Chart 13 Number of people killed in Chicago (January–April for the years 1986–94)

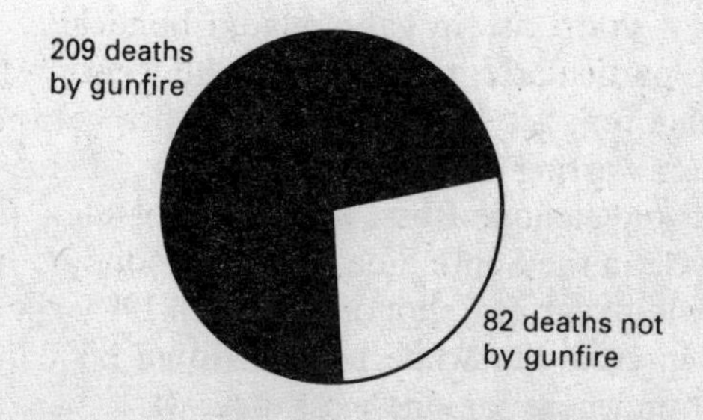

Chart 14 Deaths by shooting in Chicago (January–April 1994)

employed by homicides across the nation, though most especially in areas of urban deprivation.

According to Arthur Lurigio, Professor of Criminal Justice at Loyola University: 'Chicago is hellbent on becoming the murder capital of the United States.' In the first quarter of 1994, police have recorded 2,823 serious assaults with firearms, an increase of 232 over the same period in the previous year. 'There's violence, there's retaliation and there's more violence,' concluded Professor Lurigio. 'And it is hard to stop the cycle once it is started.'

Notable Modern Trials

Canada

'A WARPED, TWISTED AND DEEPLY TROUBLED MAN . . .'
The Trial of Valery Fabrikant

Professor Valery Fabrikant was a disgruntled man. A specialist in mechanical engineering, he had emigrated from what was then the Soviet Union in 1979 and was currently on the staff of Concordia University, Montreal. For reasons either real or imaginary, Professor Fabrikant was convinced that his academic colleagues were exploiting students and researchers by adding their own names to scientific papers in which they had played no material role. He had already taken out lawsuits against two staff members, in which he insisted both men withdraw their names from upwards of thirty published papers and make a public admission that they had made no contribution to them. The two accused responded with counter lawsuits of their own. A storm, indeed, was brewing over the groves of Academe.

Valery Fabrikant next made use of some truly twentieth-century wizardry – a system of transmitting information internationally through a computer network accessed by most universities around the world. The professor's exposé began: 'Dear Colleague, the events I will tell you about are so outrageous that you will have to see it to believe it . . .' he concluded: 'I have little time left, because on 25 August I will be in jail for contempt of court and must do the mailing fast . . . I cannot fight the battle without your help. Speak up.' Far from arousing moral outrage on his behalf, Fabrikant's electronic campaign, supported by copious bundles of printed documentation which purported to expose a conspiracy against him within the university, was greeted either with knowing winks and taps on the forehead, or irritation. Thus did the sword become mightier than the pen – or in this case the gun became mightier than the word processor.

On 24 August 1992 Professor Valery Fabrikant took a collection of guns with him to the ninth floor of Concordia University where he opened fire on his colleagues; not, it should be added, with any great attention to target selection. Fabrikant killed four people, wounded another and took a couple of hostages. Twenty-six-year-old student Peter Lawn later recalled: 'We were in Professor John Saber's office, Saber was on the phone to his wife at the time. Then we heard noises. I looked out and saw this man walking towards us, a gun in each hand.' As Fabrikant strode calmly into the room John Saber told him: 'Don't point those at me. I'm not joking.' At which the gunman fired twice and left. Saber fell to the floor, his shirt covered in blood. As the student hurried to alert the security staff he passed Dr Fabrikant's office, where Michael Hogben was lying face-down on the floor, very still. As he was making his way to the ground floor Peter Lawn heard more shots fired. One of the victims turned out to be Professor Matthew Douglass, who was alive on arrival at hospital but died later of gunshot wounds to the head. When the final reckoning was made, when the hostages had been released and Professor Fabrikant taken into custody, it was revealed that the five victims were John Saber, Michael Hogben, Matthew Douglass and Phoivos Ziogar, all dead, and secretary Elizabeth Horwood, wounded. The two hostages were student/receptionist Maria Benavente and a security officer. Only one was even mentioned on Fabrikant's list of 'miscreants', and the two men who were the targets of his greatest venom (and lawsuits) were not harmed.

Much of this information was presented by witnesses at a preliminary court hearing conducted before Quebec Court Judge Gilles Cadieux in October 1992. Professor Valery Fabrikant elected to act as his own defence attorney, and he cut a not entirely sympathetic figure as he scorned and derided the witnesses, frequently accusing them of lying.

The country had to wait until the middle of March the following year for another glimpse of the eccentric Professor Fabrikant. His trial opened at the Quebec Superior Court, where he faced four charges of murder, one of attempted murder and two of forcible confinement. Evidence was given by one of the first police investigators on the scene of the killing spree that victim Michael Hogben, the president of Concordia's faculty association, was still clutching a letter requesting Fabrikant to stop pestering the academic staff. As he was found with three bullet wounds in Professor Fabrikant's office, it seems clear that he was delivering the letter when he was shot dead. In part the message read: 'Visit the [faculty association] office only at specific times of the day with an appointment. Discuss your case [the association was trying to sort out Fabrikant's grievances] only with Hogben. Your personal conduct and behaviour cause considerable distress to [union] staff. The frequency of your visits constitutes harassment.' The correspondence was signed by Michael Hogben and bore the date 21 August.

Four weeks after the trial started, in mid-April, it was fifty-two-year-old Valery Fabrikant's opportunity to address the jury under oath. By way of explaining his lethal outburst he told the court: 'Just imagine if a peaceful person like me, who cannot even hit someone, just shot several people, something very wrong must have happened.' The professor concluded that: 'Either I am insane in which case everything is OK; but, if a normal person shot four people, questions have to be asked, and the answers are terrifying.' Clearly preferring to be considered mad rather than bad Fabrikant went on: 'I didn't want to kill anyone. I had no control over myself when all this was going on . . . No one in his right mind would want to kill secondary people. Everyone who was put in the situation I was can become violent; you cannot destroy human dignity indefinitely.' He added, with a curious lack of logic: 'The main reason I decided against an insanity defence is that I want the truth to be known.' And Professor Valery Fabrikant got his way because, on 11 May 1993, after being declared 'fit to stand trial' by two out of the trio of psychiatrists who testified, he was formally found fit by the jury.

It proved to be a major error of judgement, because such was Fabrikant's subsequent performance in the Superior Court at Quebec that Justice Fraser Martin announced that the defendant's 'disruptive behaviour' in court made it all but impossible to continue with the trial. The result of this action was that no more witnesses were heard and Fabrikant was given no further opportunity to testify to the court. Instead it was left to him to make a brief defence summation before the jury retired to consider their verdicts. Judge Martin observed wryly: 'There is not much precedent for this, but then there isn't much precedent for much of what has gone on during this trial.' But if nothing else it gave spectators the laugh of their lives and was described in the press as 'the best theatre Montreal has seen in ages'. Judge Martin had already gritted his teeth twice at being described by Fabrikant as a 'little low crook', but his patience finally snapped when, on the morning his trial was dismissed, the professor announced to the open court: 'Welcome to the Muppet Show; Mr Martin is the presiding Muppet.' It earned him his fifth citation for contempt of court and he was sentenced to three months' imprisonment to be served consecutively with the sentences for other citations. By way of reply Fabrikant squared up to the judge and said: 'Do not scare me. I could not care less. If you want to do another illegal thing, do it. Never again try to scare me,' adding as a final gesture of bravado: 'I repeat again – you are a little low crook.' Having banished a smouldering defendant from the court, Justice Fraser Martin told the jury by way of explanation – if any were needed: 'In this country we hear over and over again the word "rights". Particularly in criminal law, we hear of the right to a full answer in defence. Yes, it is a right, but it carries with it a duty to exercise it within the rules that apply to the running of a criminal case . . . This morning was but a culminating event.'

Having been effectively deprived of a stage, Professor Fabrikant made use of his limited summation platform to declare that the judge had behaved in a 'lawless' fashion, and insisted the jury bring in a verdict of mistrial. 'This kind of thing didn't even happen in the Soviet Union,' he reminisced. 'I am not allowed to tell you what happened.' Rambling on about conspiracies in the groves of Academe, Valery Fabrikant, despite his own protestations of sanity, was beginning to look very dangerously unbalanced, an impression which was not lost on Judge Martin, who promptly cut off the mad professor's polemic on justice.

In his own summing up the jury chief prosecutor Jean Lecours reminded the court, if they needed their memory jogged, that: 'A university is a place to study and learn – it is not a shooting club. When someone goes there with three fully loaded handguns and extra ammunition one can conclude there is premeditation [to murder].'

It was a view which the jury obviously shared because, following a five-month trial and a retirement of seven hours, on 11 August 1993 they returned guilty verdicts on each of the seven charges – four counts of first-degree murder, one of attempted murder and two of forcible confinement. As Supreme Court Justice Fraser Martin sentenced Fabrikant to four mandatory life terms he told the prisoner: 'The events of 24 August 1992 at Concordia University boggle the mind . . . The least one can say is that you are a warped, twisted and deeply troubled man. Today your credentials are firmly established as a vicious murderer, a wretched man puffed up and transformed by the power of the gun into an artificial giant.' Handcuffed and surrounded by four police officers Valery Fabrikant sprawled across the dock with a grin on his face which turned into a smirk as each of the verdicts was pronounced. For the attempted murder he received a further twelve years and for each of the forcible confinement convictions seven years to be served concurrently. The six citations for contempt of court, amounting to two years, will also be served concurrently. Effectively this should mean that Professor Fabrikant is not eligible for parole for twenty-five years.

England

'A MURDERER FOR ALL SEASONS'
The Trial of Robert Black
(Guest contributor: Trisha Reed)

It was a balmy summer's day in July 1982, the sort of weather when children find it impossible to stay in the house. Pretty, freckle-faced Susan Maxwell had been playing tennis with her friend Alison Raeburn at Coldstream in the Scottish Borders. The pair were evenly matched, with Susan eventually winning by a single game.

Alison planned on spending what remained of the

afternoon window shopping, so at 4.10 p.m. eleven-year-old Susan set off to walk back to her home at Crammond Hill Farm in nearby Cornhill-on-Tweed. It was the first time she had ever been allowed to walk home alone from the tennis club across that bridge over the River Tweed which marks the border between Scotland and England. Susan, still dressed in the yellow T-shirt, shorts, white socks and sand shoes in which she had been playing, and holding her tennis balls and a small blue flask which had been filled with orange juice before she set out from home, swung her racket as she walked happily along the busy A697, enjoying the summer sunshine.

She passed a group of youngsters bathing in the river, and was seen ambling across the bridge. Seconds later she had simply vanished into thin air. Back at Crammond Hill Farm, Susan's mother Liz was becoming anxious. It was not like Susan, the eldest of her three children, to be so late, and before long Liz Maxwell had set out to look for her. To her dismay, the tennis club was locked and deserted when she arrived and, after an hour of further fruitless searching, a distraught Mrs Maxwell telephoned the police.

Two weeks later, Liz could be heard making an emotional appeal for her daughter's safe return on Jimmy Young's Radio Two programme. But, 264 miles from Coldstream, at a lay-by in Loxley on the A518 Uttoxeter to Stafford road, thirty-two-year-old lorry driver Arthur Meadows had solved the mystery of Susan's disappearance; there, in thick undergrowth, he found the body of a young girl. She had her tennis shorts on, but her head rested on the pants she had been wearing underneath them.

Susan Maxwell's body was too badly decomposed for forensic pathologists to ascertain either how she had died or whether she had been sexually assaulted, and when an inquest was finally held, in July 1983, the jury returned an open verdict. But Susan's death, tragic and humble as it was, marked the beginning of what was to become the biggest investigation ever carried out by the British police.

At first it was thought that Susan had been dragged into a maroon-coloured Triumph by at least two men, after a passer-by reported seeing a girl answering her description struggling with the men and 'banging around with a tennis racket'. He had assumed at the time that he was witnessing nothing more ominous than a family squabble. Considerable police effort was expended on trying to trace the car but, three months after Susan disappeared, investigators seemed very little nearer to finding the killer. The *Daily Express* reported that detectives were increasingly pinning their hopes on an informer – or on 'the million to one chance that the killer will be caught striking again'. A million to one chance it may have been. But on a hot day in July 1990, that is exactly what did happen. By then, however, at least two more children had died.

It was another of those hot days, almost a year after the abduction of Susan Maxwell, when five-year-old Caroline Hogg from Portobello, near Edinburgh, begged her father to let her go out to play for just a few minutes before she went to bed. She had spent the morning shopping with her mother and had then watched some cartoons on a friend's television before going to a party in the afternoon. Her mother Annette had collected her afterwards and, when they got home, little Caroline had gone out to play while her mother prepared tea. When she called to Caroline to come in to eat, however, Caroline was nowhere to be found and the rest of the family sat down at the table without her. They had finished eating by the time Caroline returned, saying that she wasn't hungry, and asking whether her father would take her out for a while. But John Hogg was by then engrossed in a game of electronic chess, and it was Annette who set off with Caroline to fetch a video, racing her fun-loving daughter down the road as she rushed to buy an ice cream with the 50p her father had given her.

When they returned, little Caroline was still full of energy, and again wanted to go out to play, but Annette decided that now it really was too late. Undeterred, Caroline went to her father and pleaded with him to allow her to go out for just a little bit longer. He gave in eventually, as fathers do – but only on condition that it was just for five minutes and that she didn't go further than the garden gate. He also insisted that Caroline change out of her party shoes before she left the house.

It was just after seven when Caroline went out again, still wearing her lilac and white gingham party dress with its capped sleeves, but she had changed into pink trainers, and her blonde hair was tied in bunches on which she wore lilac bobbles. It was to be the last that her family would see of her. When Annette Hogg decided it was time for Caroline to go to bed, she called for her to come in. Caroline was nowhere to be found.

Her eleven-year-old brother Stuart had been playing outside too. But he hadn't seen his little sister either. So while Annette and Stuart searched neighbouring gardens, John Hogg set out for the promenade to see if Caroline had made her way there. Later, Annette and John headed for a nearby playing field, where a group of youngsters had been playing rounders, and then went on to search around the funfair and on the beach; but all to no avail. Finally, they called the police.

It didn't take local officers long to trace Caroline's movements that fateful night. Plenty of people had been out enjoying the warm evening, and many of them remembered seeing her. First Caroline had gone to the playground on the promenade, at the end of the street in which the family lived. Minutes later she was seen at the

Fun City amusement park, where a scruffy, unshaven man bought her a roundabout ride. Her eight-year-old neighbour Lee Demarco saw them walking hand in hand, and noted that Caroline was more subdued than usual, but no one tried to stop the pair as they headed away from the park together.

In the days that followed, thousands of volunteers joined some 150 police officers to search parks, golf courses, woodland and wasteland in and around Edinburgh in the increasingly forlorn hope of finding the missing child. Police also issued a description of the man seen walking with her in the amusement park. He was thought to be aged between thirty and forty, 5'8" tall and well built, with wavy hair reaching his collar. Unshaven, with horn-rimmed spectacles, he had been wearing a blue jerkin over his faded blue jeans.

It was ten days after Caroline disappeared that sales executive Gary Roberts pulled in to a lay-by on the A444 at Twycross in Leicestershire, 300 miles from Edinburgh. He noticed the smell as soon as he got out of the car – Gary Roberts had stumbled upon the naked body of a small child, face up in a ditch. Once again, the body was too badly decomposed to determine either the cause of death or whether the child had been sexually assaulted. But she was identified from dental records as the missing five-year-old from Portobello.

The body had been dumped just twenty-four miles from the place where Susan Maxwell had been found, and it was not long before police began to suspect that both murders had been committed by the same man. A few days after Caroline's body was discovered, Hector Clark, Assistant Chief Constable of Northumbria, was given overall command of the investigations into the murder of both girls. In press conferences Mr Clark confirmed that there were both similarities and differences between the two cases, but that information on the

Susan Maxwell investigation – then held on a card index system in Staffordshire – might be fed into the computer of the Lothian and Borders police. By this time, four regional police forces had become involved in the investigation, and it was announced that the Home Office would be advising them on how to make the best use of computers in such a joint investigation. In due course, the inquiry would grow into the country's largest computerised manhunt to date.

Each new piece of information, however insignificant, was diligently followed up in the months and years which followed. Police set out to trace every single person who had been in the playground or the amusement park on the evening that Caroline Hogg disappeared. They asked parents who had photographed their own children in the amusement park to hand over their holiday pictures to the police in case by chance one of them had captured Caroline in the company of her abductor. There were appeals for a woman seen filming on the promenade to come forward and let police see the pictures she had shot, and there was a massive hunt for a light blue Ford Cortina after another driver reported a near-collision with it, and that he had spotted a frightened-looking little girl answering Caroline's description in the back. Although the Ford's driver was offered an amnesty for any driving offences he may have committed that night, nobody ever came forward, and a check of thousands of possible cars proved fruitless.

Caroline's parents made a video recording pleading for information that might lead to the capture of their daughter's killer. A BBC TV programme about her murder uncovered information that another kidnap attempt had been foiled that same week by an unknown woman who had guessed that something was amiss. But still the identity of the abductor remained a total mystery. Within two years of Caroline's disappearance, police had linked a third death with those of Susan Maxwell and Caroline Hogg.

It was raining on the evening of Wednesday 26 March 1986 when ten-year-old Sarah Harper left her terraced home in Morley near Leeds to walk the 200 yards to the corner shop. Usually, her nine-year-old sister Claire would accompany her on such an errand, but she hadn't finished her tea and Sarah set out alone carrying a £1 coin to pay for her purchases. Minutes later, she left the shop with a loaf of bread and two packets of crisps in a white plastic bag, and with 11p in change. She never arrived home.

Her mother Jackie knew that Sarah had a tendency to dawdle when she was on her own, and twice sent little Claire out to look for her sister. When she came back alone, pregnant Jackie drove round with her boyfriend and her two other children to look for Sarah. Their search proved fruitless, and within hours the police had been brought in.

Twenty-three days later, a man walking his dog by the River Trent at Wilford, Nottingham, found Sarah's partially clothed body. She had been beaten and sexually assaulted before being dumped in the river. Jackie's estranged husband Terry was given the grim task of identifying his daughter, whose pink corduroy skirt and blue anorak had both disappeared, along with her shoes.

An important element of the inquiry, led by Detective Superintendent John Stainthorpe of the West Yorkshire force, was to establish the exact location where Sarah had been put into the water, since the river and its tributaries covered hundreds of miles and snaked their way through five different counties. It was eventually established that she had been thrown into the water on the night of her abduction, close to junction 24 of the M1.

It was not long before the police were also studying many other cases involving murdered or missing children, to see if they could establish any links; not surprisingly the deaths of Caroline Hogg and Susan Maxwell were among them. By August 1988, inquiries into the three murders had stretched across the globe as far as Australia, Japan and Italy, as officers from the murder team continued to follow the tiniest of leads in their attempt to track down what they now believed to be a single killer. They had travelled to Holland and Germany, too, and paperwork for the Maxwell investigation alone had mounted to a staggering 7.5 tons before the information was transferred to computer.

A fourth attack had, by then, also been reported. But on this occasion the outcome was a happier one.

Slightly built and just 4'10" tall, Teresa Thornhill looked a good deal younger than her fifteen years in her pink skirt and blouse and her white socks. She had been walking with her friends in the park, but was alone when she saw the blue van parked with its bonnet up near her home in Radford, Nottingham.

'Can you fix van engines?' the driver asked as she drew level with him. Then, before she knew what was happening, he had grabbed her from behind in a bear hug and was trying to force her into his van. Teresa, however, proved stronger than he bargained for, biting him on the arm as she tried frantically to struggle free from his grasp. Andrew Beeston, one of the friends she had just left, heard her cries and he, too, yelled at the abductor as he rushed to Teresa's aid. Only then did the man give up, leaping into his van and speeding away from his terrified victim. Later she would describe him to police: aged between thirty and forty, balding, heavily built, with stubble on his chin and spectacles. And he smelled strongly of sweat and oil.

Still the man's identity remained a mystery, and it would be a further two years before another attempted abduction finally gave Hector Clark and his team the break they so desperately needed.

It was another hot day, 14 July 1990, when Robert Black drove his blue van into the village of Stow on the Scottish border, and stopped to ask a twelve-year-old girl for directions to the nearest cafe. There he ordered a hefty brunch of bacon, sausage, egg and chips, and sauntered out to buy a newspaper while his meal was cooking.

Retired shopkeeper David Herkes was taking advantage of the fine weather to mow his lawn when he saw the blue van. He watched as its scruffy driver jumped out with a rag in his hand, and presumed that he had stopped to clean the windscreen. But at that moment, a little girl emerged from one of the gardens and disappeared behind the vehicle. Herkes saw the child's feet appear beside those of the balding, bearded van driver. But when the stranger leapt into his van, reversed into the drive from which the little girl had emerged, and headed off towards Edinburgh, the child was no longer anywhere to be seen.

Alarmed, Herkes noted the van's number and promptly alerted the little girl's mother, who immediately informed the police. But Black was already pulling into a lay-by to sexually assault his helpless captive before tying her hands behind her back, sticking adhesive plaster over her mouth, pulling a cushion cover over her head and pushing her roughly into a sleeping bag. He tossed the bundle carelessly into the back of his van and then, unaware that he had been spotted and that the alarm had already been raised, he doubled back through the village on his way southwards.

David Herkes could not believe his eyes when he saw the van, driven by the now bare-chested Black, hurtling back towards him as he stood talking to a policeman about the abduction. 'That's him,' he yelled, as the policeman ran into the road to flag the van down.

While the policeman handcuffed the van's driver, the

six-year-old girl's father rushed to the back of the van, calling his daughter's name. He saw the sleeping bag move, and within seconds the terrified child was safely in his arms. Doctors would later estimate that she would have suffocated within the hour had she not been rescued so promptly.

The following month Robert Black, who had admitted abducting, assaulting and endangering the life of the little girl, was sentenced to life imprisonment for the crime after a psychiatrist reported that he was a 'serious danger' to children and was likely to remain so. Black's defence counsel argued that his client had meant no harm to the child beyond the sexual assault, and had spoken of Black's own 'sorry background' and of the abuse he himself had suffered in a children's home. Judge Lord Ross was unmoved by such arguments. 'There are hardly words adequate to describe the disgust with which one listens to the details of this offence,' he told Black as he passed sentence on him.

Within weeks, Black was also being questioned about the murders of Susan Maxwell, Caroline Hogg and Sarah Harper, as well as the attempted abduction of Teresa Thornhill. Police from six different forces were now involved in the hunt for what was believed to be a single killer, and by August 1991 the details of no fewer than 185,651 people had been fed into the HOLMES (Home Office Large Major Enquiry System) computer. So, too, had 54,470 statements and details of 53,024 follow-up inquiries. A total of thirty-eight police officers and twenty-four civilian typists, using fifty computer screens, had taken eighteen months to input all the information gathered. But in the end, it all played a relatively minor role in bringing Robert Black to justice.

Instead, it was a painstaking search through Black's petrol receipts, credit card records, food bills and withdrawals from bank cash machines which finally enabled the police to piece together a case against him. Hector Clark had been convinced from his first meeting with Black that this was his man; but it would be July 1993 before Newcastle magistrates finally committed him for trial at the Crown Court. By then, the evidence totalled more than a million documents, weighing over twenty tons, and a good deal of information about Black himself had been collected.

Born in Falkirk Royal Infirmary on 21 April 1947, he was the illegitimate son of factory worker Jessica Hunter Black, who never revealed the name of her baby's father. Her own parents were strict, and had been appalled to learn that their unmarried daughter was expecting a child. So Jessica was farmed out to various relatives until her baby was born. She named him Robert after her father, a train driver, in the hope that it would reconcile her family to her child's existence; but it did not. Jessica was forced to give up her baby, and a year later she married factory worker Francis Hall. She went on to have four more children – Joan, another Robert, Frances and Frankie. Joan emigrated to Australia at the age of sixteen, and the rest of the family followed her. Jessica died there in 1982.

Her first son, meanwhile, had been sent to a foster home in Kinlochleven when he was six months old, and later attended a local primary school. When he was fourteen, however, his widowed foster mother, Isabel 'Betty' Tulip, became ill. Black was put back into care, and soon afterwards Betty Tulip died. Already Robert Black was beginning to show signs of the violence which would later bring about such tragedy, and former classmates recall him picking on a fellow pupil because he had an artificial leg. After his foster mother died Black found himself in a care home in Musselburgh, and it was there that he is believed to have himself been a victim of sexual assault at the hands of a member of staff.

When he left the home, Black found a job in a butcher's shop. But soon afterwards, at the age of fifteen, he appeared in court for the first time, charged with 'lewd and libidinous behaviour' after abducting and assaulting a seven-year-old girl. Even though he had left the girl unconscious in an air raid shelter, not knowing whether she was dead or alive, he received nothing more than an admonishment from Greenock Sheriff Court. A psychiatrist's report had concluded that his behaviour was simply an 'aberration', and unlikely to be repeated.

Later, Black would boast that over the next few years he assaulted more than thirty or forty children while working as a delivery driver. But it was 1967 before he again found himself in court, this time charged with three counts of indecent assault on his landlord's six-year-old daughter. Black, who was working back in Kinlochleven by this time, admitted all three charges and was sent to borstal.

Six months after his release, he left Scotland and moved south to an attic bedsit in the home of fellow Scots Eddie and Kathy Rayson in Stamford Hill, north London. He would remain there for the next twenty years, sharing the house with the Raysons, their five sons and two daughters. They saw him as the ideal tenant – quiet, respectable, and always on time with his rent. Admittedly, drinkers at his local pub knew him as 'smelly Bob', and colleagues at work also remembered his body odour problem, but his room was said to be neat and tidy, and the Raysons were quite content to have him as a lodger.

Unknown to them, however, Black had discovered a source of child pornography soon after his arrival in London and over the years he had amassed a considerable collection of books, magazines, films and videos, which were hidden away in his room. Later he would travel to Holland and Denmark to add to his collection. He was known to love playing darts and listening to country and western music. But in the privacy of his room, he would also spend many hours watching pornographic films. One of the Raysons' sons remembers discovering a suitcase filled with pornographic material in the lodger's room, *along with some children's clothing*.

The police, however, would need far more convincing evidence than this if they were to prove that Robert Black was a murderer as well as a paedophile. Even after years of diligent investigation, there was still considerable doubt as to whether a conviction would be possible from the evidence they had gathered.

Rulings at a pre-trial review in Chelmsford Crown Court (which could not be reported in the press at the time) strengthened the prosecution's case considerably. For Mr Justice Macpherson agreed that the jury could hear about Black's known attack on the six-year-old girl (although they were not to be told that he was now serving a life sentence for the offence). In general, and it is by and large a just rule, a defendant's past offences cannot be revealed to the jury. But if a judge decides that the earlier crimes are so similar in certain respects to those now being tried that the weight of evidence provided by those similarities actually exceeds their prejudicial effect, then the prosecution may be permitted to tell a jury about the earlier crimes.

At the same pre-trial review, the judge also ruled that there should be one trial for all four cases – the three murders and the attempted abduction of Teresa Thornhill. The police investigation team had amassed a considerable weight of circumstantial evidence against Black, but being able to present the evidence for all four cases at once would give them a considerable advantage. Black's presence in a single given area at a given time could be construed as mere chance. But that he was in the right place at the right time on a number of different occasions was much less easy to explain away.

Unable now to deny the fact that he was a child molester, Black's defence attorney could only try to prove that that didn't make him a murderer, and that all the evidence gathered against Black really was circumstantial.

Ten charges were read out when the trial opened on 13 April 1994. Three concerned the murders of Susan Maxwell, Caroline Hogg and Sarah Harper. Three concerned the kidnapping, imprisonment or unlawful carrying away of these three victims, and three more the prevention of their proper burial. Finally, there was the charge of kidnapping Teresa Thornhill. Black answered with a clear 'Not guilty' to all ten charges.

Mr John Milford QC outlined the Crown's case to the jury of six men and six women. Black, now almost completely bald with a neatly trimmed beard, listened impassively as Milford noted the similarity between the cases, such as the snatching in broad daylight (generally on hot days), the victims' bare legs and white socks, and the fact that none had broken bones. Only in Sarah's case was the cause of death known. She had drowned. But in each case a sexual motive was assumed. Susan's pants had been removed. Caroline was naked. Sarah had genital injuries. Milford also told the jury of Black's admitted sexual assault on the six-year-old girl, and how that abduction was foiled by an observant neighbour.

The jury heard how Black had been a lodger with the Rayson family, and how one of their sons had moved to the village of Donisthorpe, right in the middle of the area that had become known to police as the Midlands Triangle – the area in which all three murder victims had been found. Black was a regular visitor to the village. They were also told how his work as a delivery driver for Poster Dispatch and Storage Ltd took him all over England and Scotland, and how he would often sleep overnight in his van rather than pay for hotels. And they heard that police had placed him at the scene of all three kidnappings, through records of credit card transactions made when he was buying petrol, and from logs of his deliveries.

On 30 July 1982, for instance – the day Susan Maxwell disappeared – he filled his tank near Morpeth. From there, his most direct route north to his destination in Edinburgh would have taken him along the A697, right past the spot where Susan had been walking. On the day that Caroline was snatched, he had deliveries to make in Edinburgh, and would have travelled along Portobello High Street, just 300 yards from the funfair where Caroline was last seen. When Sarah disappeared near Leeds, Black had been making deliveries just 150 yards away.

Milford mentioned Susan's walk past the group of young people bathing in the river. 'It was a place that would be attractive to a man with an unhealthy interest in young girls,' he noted. 'A place likely to excite or arouse such a person.'

The prosecutor went on to claim that Black had actually continued with his deliveries in Edinburgh and Dundee after the abduction. The next day he had moved on to Glasgow and Carlisle, and it was believed that Susan had still been alive all this time – eventually being killed at or near the lay-by where she was found. It was thought that Caroline, on the other hand, had died soon after her abduction, and it was known that Sarah had still been alive (although perhaps unconscious) when she was dumped in the river. In all these cases, witnesses had reported seeing white vans in the area, and none of these had ever been eliminated from the enquiries. It was believed that all involved the same vehicle – that driven by Robert Black.

The court also heard about the attempted abduction of Teresa Thornhill by a man in a blue Transit van. Black had just such a van at that time. It was also known that he was back in the area three days after the attempt, and bought a local paper that contained a report of the attack. Part of it was later found in his London room, with traces of semen on it. 'Here we have brought together the attack on Teresa Thornhill and some private sexual activity on the part of the defendant,' John Milford pointed out.

On the other hand, there was no forensic evidence linking Black with any of the murdered schoolgirls; though James Fraser, from the Lothian and Borders police forensic laboratory, testified that he would not have expected to find a link when an arrest had been made so long after the crimes had been committed.

Other witnesses testified to Black's 'body odour problem'. (Teresa Thornhill had noted the strong smell of her attacker.) There was Teresa's own account of the attack on her, and the mothers of the murdered girls recalled the days on which their daughters had disappeared.

Mr Ronald Thwaites QC, defending Black, argued that police had latched on to Black as 'a murderer for all seasons'. He told the jury that his client had been used as a scapegoat after the continued failure of police to solve the murders. He acknowledged that Black was, as he put it, 'foul and wicked,' but insisted that that did not make him a murderer.

Thomas Ball was called to give evidence of how he saw a girl with a tennis racket hitting out at a mauve car, believed to be a Triumph, on the day of Susan's disappearance. Other witnesses had also seen the car in the same general location. The implication being that as Black could not be connected with a vehicle of this type he could not be linked with the murder of Susan Maxwell. Mr Thwaites also pointed out that a van seen in Nottinghamshire seventy minutes after Sarah Harper's abduction could not possibly have been that in which the youngster was carried away, since it could not conceivably have covered the eighty miles in heavy rain in that little time.

And so, when the jury finally retired to consider the evidence, the outcome of the trial was by no means a foregone conclusion. In fact, it took some thirteen hours of deliberations before the jury eventually reached a decision. On 19 May 1994 they finally returned verdicts of guilty to all ten charges. In the cases of Susan Maxwell and Teresa Thornhill, the decisions were unanimous. In the case of Caroline Hogg, the jury were split 10-2 in favour of a guilty verdict, while only one juror decided that Black was innocent of Sarah Harper's abduction and murder.

Mr Justice Macpherson responded by meting out one of the longest prison sentences in modern legal history. Referring to Black as 'an extremely dangerous man', he sentenced him to life imprisonment for each of the ten offences. He recommended that Black should serve at least thirty-five years in jail for each of the three murders, ensuing that he would be eighty-two before he would even become eligible for parole.

Only when he was finally taken down to the cells did Robert Black break the silence that he had maintained throughout the trial, sneering 'Well done lads' to the police officers gathered in the court to hear the verdict.

Afterwards, police forces in various parts of Britain and in France were said to be re-examining unsolved murders and disappearances to see if they, too, could be linked to Black. But, in view of his steadfast refusal to talk about any of the murders, even after his arrest, few held out any hope of proving a connection with other unsolved cases. Black's only published admission to police followed his arrest in Stow, when he claimed that the abduction of the six-year-old was 'a rush of blood'. 'I have always liked young girls since I was a kid,' he is reported to have said.

A chilling postscript came with the transmission of excerpts from thirty hours of prison interviews with

Robert Black carried out by a top expert on sex offenders, Ray Wyre. Several newspapers also published transcripts of some of the tapes, recorded over a period of two years, during which Wyre tried to discover not only why Black committed the offences but also how he managed to get away with his crimes for so long. Wyre himself said of Black, 'This man destroys childhood wherever he sees it. He's the murderer of childhood in reality and fantasy.' He added that perhaps it was the childhood that Black himself never had. On the tapes, Black could be heard describing that very first abduction in Greenock when he was just fifteen years old, and he talked of the thirty or forty other children abused by him after he obtained work as a delivery driver. According to Black, however, his interest in young girls had started even earlier. When he was just seven or eight, he would lie on the floor at his Scottish dance classes so that he could look up the girls' skirts, and he talks of interfering with a baby when he himself was only eight or nine.

Asked for his feelings about the girls who had died, Black grudgingly agreed that it was 'bad, actually – a waste'. But he also reasoned that the death of a child would spare them pain. He loved children and didn't want to hurt them, and if he didn't want to hurt them, they'd have to be dead. Wyre pointed out how strange it was that 'You don't want to hurt children, but they die.'

'Sometimes, you know, I think about them being unconscious – or drunk or drugged or something like that,' Black told him. He also told Wyre that children's parents were in no way to blame. 'I suppose the only way a parent could prevent something like that happening is keep the child tied to their apron strings all the time,' he said. 'Virtually putting them on a lead, never letting them out of their sight. It wasn't their fault, like.

They couldn't have done nothing about it.'

One question that still remains, however, is whether the police could have done more to uncover Black's identity and put an end to the attacks. And, even more important, what is being done to prevent the same thing happening again?

When Black committed his crimes, there was no national computerised database holding details of all known sex offenders. Instead, individual police forces were asked to comb their records to search for likely suspects. In 1992, two years after Black's arrest for the abduction of the six-year-old, the Home Office did set up the National Criminal Intelligence Service to keep track of the locations of known offenders. But, two years later, it was confirmed that Black's name could still not be found on it. With limited resources at their disposal, and a computer incompatible with that of any police system, NCIS were dependent on individual police forces sending information to them. Scotland and Ulster are not covered by the service, however, and no one had provided details of Robert Black. Fortunately, Mr Justice Macpherson's sentence should ensure that Black, at least, is prevented from inflicting harm on any more young girls. But just how many have already suffered at his hands is one more question that may never be answered.

And so it proved. On 1 July 1994 Robert Black lodged an appeal against his ten convictions. It could hardly be called a surprise – most killers make use of the appeal system to try to secure a reduction in their sentences or an overturned conviction. However, Black's move is said to have annoyed police who had applied to question him over seventeen unsolved murders. One senior detective was quoted as saying: 'By lodging these appeals he knows he can keep us away from him for a considerable time.'

A CRAVING FOR FAME
The Trial of Colin Ireland

Although he did not make the most auspicious entrance into this world, there were no immediate signs of the monster which was to emerge from the mind of the adult Colin Ireland. He was born the illegitimate son of a newsagent's assistant in Dartford, Kent, in 1954. Despite never knowing his natural father, Colin seemed to have had a secure childhood, living with his mother and grandparents in a council house in Myrtle Road. If anything gave an indication of things to come, it was that young Colin always seemed to be dressed in uniform – in his case either the Sea Cadets or the Army Cadets. Until the age of twelve he attended a local school, but then the family moved to the Isle of Sheppey and Mrs Ireland remarried. As is often the case, relations between the stepfather and his new child were strained, and Colin seems to have been beaten regularly and on the slightest pretext.

At about this time his personality began to change. He had always been something of a loner, but now Colin became 'difficult' and was removed to a school for maladjusted children. It is at this stage that we begin to be able to trace characteristics that are common to many serial killers (see the introduction in 'Serial Murder Update', page 265). For example, Colin Ireland was expelled from the special school for arson. This, combined with his self-imposed isolation and love of uniforms, begin to build into a very worrying profile indeed.

Colin also took to petty crime, and, following an appearance at Sheerness Juvenile Court on a charge of theft, he was put into the care of the local authority. Eventually stealing landed him first in borstal and then in prison. If that was meant to be a short sharp shock to drag Ireland back from the underclass of crime and reinstate him as a good citizen, then it failed dismally. No sooner had he been released than Colin Ireland moved on to plague the good people of Wiltshire, soon finding himself before Swindon magistrates on his way back into prison. In 1979, Ireland was in London again and soon facing charges of theft and possession of an offensive weapon; two more years inside.

Gradually, another piece of that jigsaw which makes up the serial killer profile was being slotted in to place. Colin Ireland began to develop an interest in survival tactics and military activity in general. He even went as far as to travel to France to enlist in the Foreign Legion – they did not want him.

By the age of thirty-five, in 1989, Ireland found himself down in south-west England, at Buckfastleigh, on the edge of Dartmoor. Here he courted and eventually married the landlady of the local pub, The Globe Inn. The lady was some years his senior, but despite the fact that Ireland had nothing to offer but his rather coarse self, they began their relationship happily enough. After the wedding ceremony at the Newton Abbot Register Office on 2 January 1990, the couple left on their honeymoon. It seemed odd to the regulars at The Globe who had so recently seen the couple off, that Ireland should return alone. Had they known something of his past perhaps it would not have come as too much of a surprise. Having plundered the pub of what cash there was, and loaded various portable items such as the video-recorder into the back of his wife's car, Colin Ireland took to his heels and was never seen in Devon again. Although the recent Mrs Ireland called the police on her return, he had faded into anonymity.

We next encounter Colin Ireland working at a night shelter for the homeless in Southend. And it is here that we find a clue to his future victim trait. Ireland had already made it plain to friends that he 'hated queers', but now came proof positive to his unbalanced mind that his prejudice was justified. It was in the days immediately before Christmas 1992 when Colin Ireland fell into a violent disagreement with a homosexual man at the night shelter. As a result, Ireland was dismissed from his job.

Soon he would be taking revenge.

'Something had been triggering me. I felt that if I was approached there was a likelihood I would kill. A man – he'd obviously been drinking – brushed past me, spilt some water down my clothes. I pulled him up about this. He asked me to beat him; it may seem strange, but that's what he wanted. I said to him: "Don't worry, I'll take care of that . . ."'

That is the way Colin Ireland recalled the meeting with his first victim, Peter Walker, on 8 March 1993 at the Coleherne, a pub in Earls Court frequented by homosexual men into sadism and masochism. And take care of it Colin did. He and Walker left the Coleherne and went back by taxi to Walker's apartment in Vicarage Crescent, Battersea. The forty-five-year-old theatre director submitted willingly to being tied to the bed, and awaited a good time – in his terms at least. What he could never have known was that his companion for the evening had far more than a little ritualised S&M in mind. As Ireland himself observed: 'Once I had tied him up I knew my intentions were different from his. I'm not sure if I really set out to kill him, but it went from there.' The apprentice serial killer headed for the kitchen, returned with a plastic bag and pulled it over Peter Walker's head, taking it off only just in time before he suffocated. Whether he knew it or not – and there is every reason to suppose that he did – Colin Ireland was simply engaging in one of the more risky games played out by S&M followers, either in company or alone. There have been more than a few tragic accidents where attempts at partial asphyxia, either with a ligature around the neck or with a plastic bag, to enhance orgasm, have resulted in death. But by now both Peter Walker and Colin Ireland knew how high the stakes were: 'It was a fate thing, and he said to me: "I'm going to die." And I said "Yes, you are . . ." He was quite controlled about it. In the end I killed him with the plastic bag. I put it over his head.' Just for good measure Ireland stole £200, and in a final act of gratuitous malevolence singed the dead man's pubic hairs – 'just to see what it smelt like'. After spending a few hours mooching about the house and watching television, Colin Ireland left.

But he had not finished yet. In common with a great many killers, Ireland was desperate to let people know how clever he was. (Wasn't it Oscar Wilde who despised murder because 'you should never do anything you can't talk about over dinner?') So Colin telephoned the *Sun* newspaper and announced: 'I did it. It was my New Year's resolution to murder a human being.' Having described the killing, Ireland asked: 'Is that of any interest to you – he was a homosexual and into kinky sex?' Although the call was made six hours after Peter Walker's body had been found, Ireland did not know this. In fact, it was colleagues at the Prince of Wales theatre in London's West End who alerted the police when their assistant director failed to turn up for rehearsals of the new musical *City of Angels*. Ireland also made two telephone calls to the Samaritans, again not knowing that the body had been found, to alert them to the fact that Peter Walker's two dogs, labrador Bess and German shepherd Sam, needed feeding and exercising.

Colin Ireland did not strike again until 28 May, when he returned to the Coleherne and got into conversation with thirty-seven-year-old Christopher Dunn, a librarian. 'I realised he was the type – he was masochistic. We talked about the Walker case but he wasn't aware of my part in it. In fact I reassured him: "Now that guy was some killer who done it and went off." So we went back to his place. I was quite prepared to kill this man, in fact I put him through some considerable pain . . .'

Like Peter Walker, Chris Dunn was a passive S&M homosexual – perfect for Ireland's warped purposes. The pair left the pub and went back to Dunn's flat in Wealdstone in north-west London. After having a few drinks and watching some of Chris Dunn's collection of sado-masochist videos, they got down to business. Christopher Dunn submitted to his new friend handcuffing him to the bed. Ireland then riffled through his victim's wallet, removed the money and a bank card, and demanded to know Dunn's PIN number. Dunn refused to give it. So Ireland began to burn his testicles with the flame from a cigarette lighter until he did. Having noted down the number, Colin Ireland strangled his helpless captive with a length of nylon cord. He searched the flat and decided not to take anything else, but he later used Christopher Dunn's bank card to withdraw £200 from his account. At first there was no suspicion that Dunn's death had been anything but one of those unhappy consequences of 'auto-erotic asphyxia.'

Perry Bradley III was a thirty-five-year-old sales director from Sulphur Springs, Texas. He was also gay and an *habitué* of the Çolherne. Which was very unfortunate for him, because that is where, on 4 June, he met Colin Ireland. Although they went back to Bradley's Kensington apartment together, it was only as a result of considerable persuasion on Ireland's part that Bradley subjected himself to being tied up – indeed, it was only because Ireland had claimed that he was an S&M man that Bradley agreed. Having rendered his victim helpless, Colin Ireland then confessed to Bradley that he was really only a thief and, having plundered his wallet, demanded to know the PIN number of his bank card. Perry Bradley seemed relieved to learn that he was in the hands of a mere thief and even offered to accompany Ireland to the local bankomat machine to withdraw some instant cash.

It must be said that Colin Ireland was becoming increasingly concerned about being caught – though he would probably have preferred to call it getting more professional. One thing that worried him more than anything else was looking so conspicuous walking the streets alone in the early hours of the morning that the police would pick him up. So, starting with Christopher Dunn, he decided to spend the night in the company of his victim's corpse, and then simply melt into the crowds of early morning commuters. It says something for Colin Ireland's appearance of sincerity that when he told Perry Bradley: 'It's going to be a long night, I suggest you get some sleep,' that is exactly what Bradley did. Ireland strangled him as he lay trussed up slumbering on the bed. Then he settled down to listen to the radio until the time came to clear up and leave.

Andrew Collier was also a regular at the Coleherne. He was thirty-three years old, the warden of a block of sheltered accommodation in Dalston, east London, and heavily into the S&M scene. On the evening of 7 June he was picked up by Colin Ireland and took him back to his Dalston flat.

Ireland was about to make his first big mistake. As the two men sat drinking there was some kind of commotion outside in the street and Collier went to the window to look; Ireland followed, and in leaning out of the window accidentally left a fingerprint on the concealed face of a window grille. Afterwards the ritual was much the same as usual – Andrew Collier was tied up and strangled with a noose. Then Ireland rummaged around in his wallet and found to his utter horror a document informing Collier that he was HIV positive. In his later confession, Colin Ireland remembered this about his reaction: 'Collier was the only one I was angry with. I was going through his documentation and I became aware he had Aids. He didn't tell me about this, he didn't warn me – could have been me in five years . . . I went fucking crazy. Well obviously you know that from the way the body was found. I burned certain areas of his body. He loved his cat, that was his life, so I did the cat with a noose, draped it over the body. It was building up like a roller coaster; it was exciting. I remember standing by the bed and saying: "Well what do you think of all this?"' In fact, 'draped over the body' was a rather coy description. What Ireland actually did was arrange the poor creature with the end of its tail in Collier's mouth and its mouth around his penis, both tail and penis sheathed in a condom. As usual, Ireland spent the night with the body and slunk away into the morning crowds.

Clearly peeved by the attention the murders were receiving in the media, but not so far linked to a single suspect, and the frustration of not being able to tell the world he was on his way to becoming a fully fledged serial killer, Colin Ireland did the next best thing. He telephoned Kensington police station to confess to all four killings. Then he called Battersea police, complaining: 'Are you still interested in the death of Peter Walker, why have you stopped the investigation? Doesn't the death of a homosexual man mean anything to you?'

Colin Ireland's fifth and last victim was forty-one-year-old Maltese-born chef Emanuel Spiteri. Ireland recalled: 'I'd seen him a couple of times at the Coleherne; he was obviously the leather type. We went back to his flat, I bound him – he was becoming very suspicious, because of the murders. I told him who I was. A very brave man, but I couldn't afford to let him stick around and recognise me, so I killed him with a noose.'

But Spiteri lived at Hither Green, in south London; and Hither Green is not on the underground network. So when they left the Coleherne on 12 June they travelled to Charing Cross Southern Region station and thence by overland rail to Hither Green. What Ireland did not know – to his cost – was that at Charing Cross station security video cameras were in operation and had filmed the two men's arrival. It is a curious thing that despite the fact that the image was widely splashed across the front pages of the papers and on television the following month the only person to recognise the image of Colin Ireland was Colin Ireland.

Meanwhile, on 13 June, Ireland telephoned the police again. At the time they had not yet become aware of the Spiteri murder. A section of that tape, dealing with his motives and methods gives a unique insight into the way one serial killer was prepared to take five lives just to become 'famous'.

> Ireland: . . . I get details of their bank cards, because I get them to give me the PIN numbers. I mean ones which I've done, well like Chris Dunn. I put a lighter to his balls for the number.
> *Detective: How did you kill him*? Ireland: With a noose.
> *Is that the same with all of these*? Right. Except the first one, that was with a plastic bag over his head.
> *Why are you doing this*? Because I set out to see . . . because I'd read a lot of books on serial killers; and indeed, you know, I wondered if it could possibly be done and actually get away with it.
> *But why in particular homosexuals*? Because they're a class of, er, keep their mouths shut and don't tell the police things . . . they're respectable . . . and that I don't like them.
> *Will you ring us again*? I don't know. Maybe. Maybe not.

We can have a chat any time if you want to ring. Yeah, I mean I actually don't think there's a likelihood of me offending again, because I've done five now and the actual FBI definition is four and above a serial would be . . .
I don't know. Yes you do. It's five. I know I've done five. That's why I can't be sure about the one . . . in Lewisham. You know, good grief, I could be wrong but I doubt if I'll offend again.
But what was your aim in all that? Just to see if it could be done. All right. So I'll leave you to get on with it. Bye bye.

On 16 June the police announced that a serial killer was at large and preying on the gay community. However, newspaper interpretations were rather more dramatic than the truth. The *Evening Standard* led with 'Revenge Killer Strangles Five', and suggested that the murderer was 'wreaking revenge at random after contracting the Aids virus from a homosexual encounter'. Which, given that the police had issued no details but simply a warning, was an intelligent guess.

But the warning given by Detective Chief Superintendent Kenneth John, who was co-ordinating the separate murder inquiries, was clear and forceful: 'We owe it to the gay community to go out and warn individual practising homosexuals, who are frequenting various pubs, restaurants and bars in London, to be aware that somebody who is prepared to attack their community is about in London.'

By the following morning the press had a new snippet to shout across their front pages – 'Gay Strangler Mocks Police'. Just hours after 'Mannie' Spiteri's landlady had found his body, Ireland was on the phone again: 'Have you found the body in south London yet? And the fire?' (He had tried to set fire to Spiteri's room to make it seem like a different *modus operandi.*)

Another weapon introduced into the armoury of an increasingly determined Scotland Yard was Dr Mike Berry, who has worked on behalf of a number of murder squads putting together psychological profiles of unknown killers. It is remarkable with hindsight just how accurate Dr Berry's outline was: 'This is a well organised serial killing and he takes great pleasure in it. I think it is unlikely that this man is HIV positive and is taking revenge on homosexuals. That is not the underlying motive. This guy has been fantasising about violence for a long time and has at last started.'

Another expert trained in psychological offender profiling is Dr Jonas Rappeport, medical director of the American Academy of Psychiatry and the Law. Dr Rappeport endorsed Dr Berry's opinions, adding of the killer: 'He may pretend to be homosexual until he had bound men who want to be restrained, and then of course he can do anything he wants to do. I would imagine police should be looking for a large or physically very strong man. He is clearly confident in committing crimes, and I would suggest they should look for someone with other features of criminality in his personality.' All true as it turned out.

Another tactic tried by the police was trying to get the killer to give himself up voluntarily. In the wake of the Spiteri murder, Detective Chief Superintendent John said at a press conference: 'Enough is enough. Enough pain, enough anxiety, enough tragedy. Give yourself up on whatever terms, whatever you dictate, whatever time, to me or my colleagues.' As he said it, Ken John could never in his wildest dreams have believed that that is almost what would happen.

In the meantime the gay community had to be protected, and most newspaper and news broadcasts were running advice lines from organisations such as GALOP

(Gay London Policing) and OutRage. The huge Lesbian and Gay Pride festival scheduled to take place in Brixton on 19 June went ahead, but with an increase in the number of plainclothes policemen and detectives mingling with the crowd. In fact as many as 100,000 homosexual men and women participated in the annual Gay Pride parade, but no incident that could possibly be linked with the killings took place; indeed it was seen by many as a defiant march *against* the murders.

On 24 June a description of a man police wanted to interview in connection with the killings was issued to the media. It was claimed to be based on several brief sightings by people who had seen the killer with Emanuel Spiteri on one or other part of their journey from Charing Cross to Hither Green. At this stage the police did not mention the station security video. However, with the benefit once again of hindsight, both the description and the video-fit based on it published on 27 June were remarkably accurate: 'White, aged between thirty and forty, heavily built and six feet or more in height. Clean shaven with a full to fattish face, short dark brown hair, and dirty, discoloured teeth. He was casually dressed in a dark jacket and jeans.'

At the same time leading forensic pathologist Dr Iain West had been invited to perform a second post-mortem on each of the victims in the hope of finding the one major clue that would link the killings to each other and to a single murderer. Echoing the entire Scotland Yard murder squad's feelings, Dr West is reported as saying: 'Bloody difficult one, this.'

At last the British Transport Police security camera images were released to the press; it was 2 July. On 20 July a man walked into Twitchen Musters and Kelly solicitors' office in Southend, Essex, and after three-quarters of an hour of discussions the solicitor advised him to make a statement to the police. The story that the man (using the alias Colin Williams) told Scotland Yard detectives was that he recognised himself on the security video and wanted to explain that he had parted company with Emanuel Spiteri just after the pictures were taken. He concluded: 'He was alive and well when I left him, and I am not responsible for his death or for the death of any of the other people who have been killed in London.'

The following morning the news was that the man being questioned by police at Kensington police station was thirty-nine-year-old Colin John Ireland. He appeared at Horseferry Road magistrates court the same day charged with the murder of Andrew Collier. Although it was not announced at the time, it was the fingerprint left carelessly at Collier's flat which had led to the charge. On the evening of 23 July, Ireland was charged with a second murder – that of Emanuel Spiteri. However, by 14 October Colin Ireland was reported being remanded by the Horseferry Road magistrates for trial at the Old Bailey on all five counts of murder.

Given the high profile of the crimes and the subsequent police investigation, the trial of Colin Ireland was something of an anti-climax. The reason was that Ireland had pleaded guilty to all five counts of murder, thus removing the need for a lengthy legal process to determine his guilt or innocence. All that was required was for Crown prosecutor Mr John Nutting to outline the case, and for Colin Ireland's defence attorney to make a brief representation on his client's behalf. He agreed that there could be no mitigation, but pointed out that Ireland had eventually confessed to all the murders.

The judge, Mr Justice Sachs, was less generous and, sentencing Colin Ireland to five life sentences, told him: 'By any standards you are an exceptionally frightening and dangerous man. In cold blood and with great deliberation you killed five of your fellow human beings in grotesque and cruel circumstances. The fear, brutality and indignity to which you subjected your victims are almost unspeakable. To take one human life is outrageous. To take five is carnage. You expressed your desire to be regarded as a serial killer – that must be matched by your detention for life. In my view it is absolutely clear you should never be released.'

'AS APPALLING A MURDER AS IT IS POSSIBLE TO IMAGINE'

The Trial of Glyn James Powell *et al.*

(Guest contributor: John Bevis)

Two major murder trials came before the courts in November 1993. By far the greater media attention was focused on the trial of the murderers of James Bulger (see page 157), and it would be no exaggeration to say that the nation was stunned by the betrayal of innocence which the case represented. But in many ways the murder of Suzanne Capper was more horrific, more cruel, more evil. Indeed, the case could almost be held up as a metaphor for a society gone wrong. Drug abuse, video 'nasties', unemployment, squalor, promiscuity, violence and cruelty . . . all contributed to 'as appalling a murder as it is possible to imagine'.

The ordeal of Suzanne Capper first came to light at 6.10 a.m. on 15 December 1992. Three workmen were driving to work along Cowshaw Road, Compstall, near Stockport, when they saw a naked girl at the roadside, screaming and waving for them to stop. She was badly burned, and told the men: 'Over there in the fields – they burned me, they burned me. They put petrol on me.' She claimed she had been kept in a bedroom for ten days, and had been injected with drugs. The workmen put a jacket around Suzanne and took her to a large detached house on nearby Compstall Road, which was occupied by

Stockport company director Michael Coop and his wife. While they helped the girl into the dining room, Mr Coop called the emergency services, and his wife, Margaret, fetched a navy towelling dressing gown to wrap around the girl.

'I instinctively went to put my arms round her but she pulled away because she could not bear to be touched,' Mrs Coop said in her statement. 'Her head was shaved and there were recent, not new, cuts to her head. Her face was almost featureless. Her hands were red raw and black at the fingertips. Her legs were red from top to bottom. She couldn't bear anything near her legs. She looked like the victim of an attack in the Vietnam war.' Michael Coop added that 'both her hands appeared like ash. Her legs were just like raw meat and her feet appeared to be badly charred. I was struck by how polite the victim was. She was constantly thanking my wife for her assistance.'

Suzanne drank six glasses of water and two cups of tea, assisted by Margaret Coop as she could hold nothing. When the ambulance came she cried out in pain as she was lifted on to the trolley, but managed to drink another two glasses of water on the way to Stockport Hospital. Medical staff transferred the injured girl to a burns unit at Withington Hospital in Manchester, where she lapsed into a coma and died three days later, on 18 December. She was just sixteen years old.

Despite her terrible injuries, Suzanne had been able to help Manchester police with their inquiries before she died. She named those responsible, and gave an address in Langworthy Road, Moston, Manchester. A police raid found the house a complete and utter mess. Car seats were arranged round the walls of the front room downstairs. 'It was just like a doctor's waiting room,' commented Detective Inspector Peter Wall, somewhat cryptically. Upstairs officers discovered rope, chains and flex in a room with an upturned bed. An audio cassette was found with a single phrase from the notorious video *Child's Play III* repeated hundreds of times. The words were: 'I'm Chucky – wanna play?' A shelf next to the Christmas tree held such books as *Blood Games*, *The Silence of the Lambs* and *Misery* – and the grotesque ornament of two broken front teeth. Six occupants of the house, including two women and a boy aged sixteen, were charged with kidnap and murder.

An inquest was held in Manchester in January 1993. Pathologist Dr William Lawler had performed a post-mortem examination, and he told the coroner that he had found cuts, scratches and bruising all over Suzanne's body. The abrasive injuries 'could have been produced by vigorous scrubbing with a brush with stiff bristles'. All of the head and body hair had been shaved or burned. The upper incisors had been 'forcibly extracted', and there was a burn on the bridge of the nose which had probably been inflicted by a cigarette.

Suzanne had suffered 75–80 per cent burns, consistent with having petrol thrown over her and set alight. The cause of death was 'multi-organ failure'. The coroner, Mr Leonard Gorodkin, concluded: 'Suzanne must have endured a great deal of pain and a lot of suffering and she had no chance of survival.' He offered Elizabeth Capper, Suzanne's mother, 'not just on my behalf but on behalf of the whole nation, my very deepest sympathy and condolences at this tragic happening'.

It was not until 16 November 1993 that the trial of those arrested at Langworthy Road opened at Manchester Crown Court. A charge of false imprisonment was admitted by Bernadette McNeilly and Jean Powell, and by Powell's younger brother Clifford Pook who also pleaded guilty to conspiracy to cause grievous bodily harm. The charges were denied by Jean Powell's estranged husband Glyn James Powell and the other two defendants, Jeffrey Leigh and Anthony Dudson. All six pleaded not guilty to murder.

Mr Peter Openshaw QC opened the case for the prosecution with a resumé of the all-too-brief life of the victim. Suzanne Capper had been a 'high-spirited but well mannered' girl, but after her mother had walked out on her stepfather she had begun truanting from Moston Brook high school and staying out late at night. This led to rows with the stepfather, with whom she lived at 6 Bewley Walk, Moston. Suzanne, a girl of below average intelligence whose only wish was to be a hairdresser, had fallen in with a group of people who lived a much more exciting life. They dealt in drugs, stole cars and shoplifted, held all-night parties, and shared an interest in the occult.

The group was centred on a house in Langworthy Road, the home of twenty-six-year-old Jean Powell, a mother of three, who organised the crime racket. Suzanne took to staying with her, and on one occasion was held captive at the house, beaten and forced to do housework, and to take Powell's children to school. After three days she broke loose and went back to her stepfather. But the lure of the group was too much for the simple girl to resist, and before long she was back at 97 Langworthy Road. In the autumn of 1992 they were joined by twenty-four-year-old Bernadette McNeilly, who moved in with her three children.

Mr Openshaw told the jury that there were a number of 'insubstantial, even trivial' incidents which might have turned the defendants against Suzanne. There was the time when Suzanne and her then boyfriend took Jean Powell to the home of a supposedly rich Arab. 'While at the house Suzanne, encouraged by her boyfriend, made a number of indecent proposals to Jean Powell, to which she took exception,' the court was told. Jean Powell thought Suzanne and her boyfriend were setting her up to have sex with the Arab for money, and felt justifiably insulted.

Another grievance was aired by Bernadette McNeilly and her seventeen-year-old boyfriend, Anthony Dudson. After Suzanne had spent a night in their bed they found themselves infected with pubic lice, and were obliged to shave off their pubic hair. Mr Dudson later admitted that he had had additional sexual relationships with Suzanne Capper in October 1992, and with Jean Powell from July until December 1992.

The last straw was that Bernadette McNeilly believed Suzanne had stolen her pink duffle coat, for which she had paid £50. McNeilly and Jean Powell visited Bewley Walk on 7 December 1992 and had an argument on Suzanne's doorstep about the missing coat. In her step-father's words: 'The discussion ended with my allowing Suzanne to go to see them, telling her she had to be back in the morning. I said it was time she made up her mind where she was living. Off she went, and that was the last I saw of her.'

Over at Langworthy Road, Anthony Dudson and twenty-nine-year-old Glyn Powell were waiting for the women. 'When Miss Capper arrived she was assaulted. They cut off her hair. They shaved her head and her eyebrows and made her shave her pubic hair. It was as if,' Mr Openshaw suggested, 'they intended to subject her to some kind of ritual humiliation in revenge for her having caused Dudson and McNeilly themselves to be shaved.'

But the humiliation did not stop there. Suzanne was punched, and hit with a belt and massive ornamental wooden spoon and fork. She spent the night locked in a cupboard, and the following day in a wardrobe in an upstairs bedroom. To get her out of the way of the children in the house, her captors took Suzanne by night a few doors down the road to number 91, which had been Bernadette McNeilly's home. There they tied her with electric flex to the slats of an overturned bed in the back room downstairs. Later in the week she was moved to an upstairs room. Blindfolded, and gagged with a sock, she was left to lie in her own urine and excrement. She was given a mug of soup which she did not drink, a plate of chips and peas which she did not eat, and the occasional glass of water.

Eighteen-year-old David Hill visited the house at this time and saw Suzanne tied to a bed. 'She asked me if I could help but I told her I couldn't. I thought they would batter me. If I'd said owt, they'd all have got me, wouldn't they?' Hill was most afraid of Jeffrey Leigh, who had formerly lived with his sister.

The cruelty continued when the six decided to give Suzanne a bath. 'A quite excessive amount of concentrated disinfectant was poured into the bath and she was scrubbed with a broom and a scrubbing brush,' Mr Openshaw told a horrified court. She was burned on the nose with a cigarette, injected with amphetamines, and forced to listen to repetitious rave music played at high volume through headphones. Finally, one of the group ripped out two of the girl's front teeth with a pair of pliers. One of those teeth snapped, exposing a dental nerve.

By this time Suzanne Capper was doomed. There was only one way to prevent her informing against the group, and that was to kill her, and so the Powells stole a white Fiat Panda car, which they fitted with false number plates. They forced Suzanne to put on knickers, leggings and a fawn raincoat, and walked her out to the car, stuffing her into the boot. The Powells, together with McNeilly and Dudson, drove to Werneth Low, near Stockport. There the victim was dragged from the car into the undergrowth of Benfield Clough and doused in petrol before being set alight. 'She went straight up in flames and was screaming . . . The flames lit up the whole forest,' Anthony Dudson later recalled. Suzanne was left for dead.

The murderers must have been incredulous that she could have survived at all, let alone long enough to inform against them. Their statements were confused, vindictive, implausible. Jean Powell claimed she 'loved Suzanne as a sister. I don't like violence. I don't even smack my own children.' She accused Bernadette McNeilly of taking the character of Chucky, the *Child's Play III* doll, repeating 'Chucky's coming to play' as she tortured Suzanne and injected her with amphetamines. It was McNeilly who had poured disinfectant into the bath, had ordered Suzanne's teeth to be extracted, had set fire to the girl.

In Anthony Dudson's statement it was Glyn Powell who had lit the fire, holding a cigarette lighter to Suzanne's back. Later he had sung *I Have Got a Burning Sensation in My Heart* and *Burn Baby Burn*. Dudson also claimed eighteen-year-old Clifford Pook had pulled the teeth. 'He started hitting her teeth with the pliers. He got the pliers on one, but it just snapped and chipped. He put the pliers on again and really, really pulled. He dragged Suzanne's head forward until there was a snap and he had the tooth in the pliers. He did the same again, and he was laughing.'

The other defendants played down their own roles in the murder. McNeilly claimed she had injected Suzanne with amphetamines to 'protect her from being dosed with heroin'. Jeffrey Leigh, asked why he had done nothing to help, replied with a tasteless attempt at candour: 'I acted like a coward and because I acted like a coward the poor girl is dead, God rest her soul.' Glyn Powell claimed he knew nothing about the capture until 13 December, and only agreed to dump the girl somewhere 'where she would find her own way home' because he loved his wife and would do anything for her.

It may seem that the murder was avoidable and that any member of the group could have prevented it by being just a little less feeble in their resistance to the pressure of the group. But according to Dr Nigel Eastman, consultant forensic psychologist at St George's, London, 'Group pressures can be enormously powerful – even if one member is dominant, it may be difficult for him or her to stand up against what is happening and reverse it. The stronger the sense of group identity, the weaker an individual becomes in opposing what is happening.' The extremes of violence were able to occur because 'if there is enough sadism in one or two of the group to start the process going, the rest will get caught up with it'. Several of the group presented acts of cruelty as gestures of compassion, which 'may suggest that the person has no idea of what it means to be a victim – or it may be a very puny attempt to avoid going along with the group.'

Jean and Glyn Powell and Bernadette McNeilly were found guilty of murder, and were each imprisoned for life. They each received concurrent twenty-year sentences for unlawful imprisonment and conspiracy to cause grievous bodily harm. Mr Justice Potts told them: 'I am satisfied that the three of you were the dominant personalities here.' Anthony Dudson was also found guilty, but because of his youth was sentenced to be detained at Her Majesty's pleasure. He received a fifteen-year concurrent sentence for unlawful imprisonment, after he had changed his plea to guilty. Jeffrey Leigh had also admitted unlawful imprisonment, but was cleared of murder and conspiracy, and was sent down for twelve years. Clifford Pook was jailed for fifteen years for conspiracy and seven years for unlawful imprisonment. He had been cleared of the murder charge early in the trial on the judge's direction.

Much space was devoted in the press to the connection

with the *Child's Play* series of films, which had so recently featured in the James Bulger case. 'How much more horror before we sweep this filth off the shelves of our video shops?' the *Sun* inquired. While it is true that Bernadette McNeilly used catch-phrases from the films in association with torture sessions, the influence of videos was discounted by DI Peter Wall. There was no video player in either house in Langworthy Road, and 'no suggestion that they sat around watching horror films'. While there were tenuous links – Chucky gets destroyed by fire – DI Wall concluded that 'throughout interviews with the accused there was no suggestion that the reason Suzanne was killed had anything to do with *Child's Play*'.

FOXES IN THE WOODS
The Trial of Sandra Wignall *et al.*

The headings seemed to say it all: 'Fox-lover Sees Thugs Kill Hubby for Kicks', 'Murder Widow Saved by Hero Husband'. The tragedy that was visited on Sandra Wignall and her husband in the summer of 1992 was the more awful because they had shared so short a time together.

Rogert Wignall's first wife, Rose, had died of cancer in 1990, and not surprisingly he was not in the best of spirits when he met a forty-seven-year-old widow named Sandra Quartermaine as they both walked their dogs in Sayes Wood near their homes at Addlestone, in the stockbroker belt of Surrey. Although he was troubled by chronic asthma, the fifty-five-year-old painter and decorator began to relax, and let romance back into his life. Bob moved in to Sandra's home at Rowhurst Avenue in August 1991 and they married that Christmas Eve. They had been married less than nine months when, on 5 September 1992, Sandra suggested that they go on one of their nocturnal visits to the local woods to feed the fox cubs. It had become one of those quiet intimate sort of activities which many busy couples develop as an excuse to spend time together.

Then, as Bob was about to arrange the small spotlight to attract the foxes, Sandra launched into one of their less frequent customs. She knelt in front of her husband, gently unzipped his trousers and performed oral sex on him. Then, as they were recovering from that compromising display, three men stepped out from the undergrowth and asked the couple if they had seen a boxer puppy go past. Bob said no, sorry, they hadn't, and all of a sudden all three strangers began to attack him, one stabbing him fatally. As he tried valiantly to defend himself, Bob Wignall shouted to his wife to run and hide somewhere. She did. After a while there was silence, and Sandra made her way cautiously back to the scene of the attack. As she did so she met with another three youths and asked them – heaven knows why – if they had just attacked her husband. After reassuring Mrs Wignall that they had done no such thing, they offered to escort the obviously distressed woman back to the village where she telephoned the police from a neighbour's house.

It was an odd story, but one which at the time the police had no reason to suspect. In fact, with the co-operation of the LWT programme 'Crime Monthly', Detective Superintendent Pat Crossan, in charge of the murder investigation, and Sandra Wignall appeared on screen asking for the public's assistance in tracking down the killer of a man described as 'easy-going, good-humoured and likeable'. A certain amount of information was available for use in the television reconstruction of the crime because, unlikely as it may have sounded, Sandra Wignall really had come across three innocent men and asked them if they had killed her husband. What's more, this trio was found and told the police that they had seen not three, but two other men in the area that night, and they had run off in a very suspicious manner. Scene-of-crime officers had also made their contribution; lying close to Robert Wignall's dead body was a gold bracelet bearing the initial H. As it belonged neither to Bob nor to Sandra, it was reasonable to suppose that it had become detached from one of the assailants during the struggle.

The 'Crime Monthly' public appeal could hardly have been a greater success. Among the telephone calls received after the show was one from a man with a very obviously false foreign accent. He confirmed that the police should be looking for two men, and hinted that Sandra Wignall was also involved. The caller arranged to meet Superintendent Crossan, but failed to turn up at the pub. However, he did phone again; his name was Martin Hughes, and his girlfriend Jane was the daughter of a man called Terence Bewley. As a result Bewley was put under immediate surveillance which linked him with Sandra Wignall and also with a thief he had met in prison called Harry Mount, until recently the proud wearer of a gold wrist chain bearing his initial H.

It was clear to Pat Crossan and his team that Sandra and Terence Bewley were the ones to watch, and by the time they came to trial in October 1993 the whole sordid story had been pieced together. Sandra met Bewley just after the death of her first husband in 1989, when Bewley was working as a chauffeur and having an affair with a woman living in the same street as Sandra. As the months went by, it seemed almost as though Bewley had cast a spell over this woman – not by being companionable or pleasant, far from it, he never took her out and it was a long time before he even disclosed his address – but by what can only be described as animal magnetism. Nor was it that he was particularly attractive; a bald, plump, bespectacled man of forty-five with an ingrained streak of violence, Bewley had already served one stretch for murder. It had been in November 1971, when he asphyxiated Lillian Shapiro, a fifty-four-year-old debt collector for a mail-order clothing company; Bewley owed her £50. The life sentence he received was clearly no warning to Terry Bewley; released in 1982, he was soon up to his old tricks.

When he and Sandra got together it was a perfect match. She had become obsessed with sex, and sex with Terry in particular – anywhere, anytime, anyhow. She even had sex with other men so that Bewley could watch. Terry was obsessed as well – with other people's money. And so, until Sandra looked like running out of cash the relationship ran as smoothly as such a relationship ever can. Then, almost on a whim, Bewley ditched Sandra. It was shortly after this traumatic experience that she married Robert Wignall. At the time Sandra was working as a cleaner and doubling behind the bar at a pub in Virginia Water. She had already confided to a fellow barmaid that she was still crazy about Terry Bewley, and when her friend asked: 'But what about Bob?', Sandra is reported to have replied: 'I still love Terry, but Bob is too good to lose.' Actually, Terry was a bit miffed about Sandra's marriage, and barely a fortnight after the wedding the old liaison was going as strong as ever. Only this time Sandra had access to more money – Bob's.

Truth to tell, Terence Bewley was in dire straits – up to his neck, as they say. For a start there were the mortgage arrears of £5,000, then £10,000 owed to his former employers, and another £4,000 to Mercantile Credit – and they were just the big ones. Bob Wignall's life insurance of £21,000 would cover that handsomely; and along with the £100,000 price on the house, which was under compulsory purchase, perhaps Sandra might even get a look in. She thought she might like to start a new life in Norfolk or Lincolnshire. Maybe she would buy a horse. But now there was a germ of a problem. Sandra had begun to see Bewley for sex every day, and coming home in time for Bob afterwards. The difficulty was that easy-going, good-humoured and likeable Robert Wignall was not blind or silly. He had become, in a word, suspicious. He had begun to check his wife's car's milometer and found it vastly at variance with her 'occasional trip to the shops'. Had he known the address at the time, Bob would have found that the figures fitted perfectly with a daily round-trip to Ruislip. Given all this, there seemed nothing else for it – Bob had to go; soon.

It was on 4 September that the man named Harry Mount came to visit his old prison pal Terry Bewley at the home he shared with his daughter and her boyfriend Martin Hughes (ironically, Hughes was a debt collector, just like Bewley's first murder victim). It was Jane's twenty-first birthday party, and as drink loosened tongues, talk began to be exchanged about 'sorting out' Robert Wignall. It was on that same evening that a knife was taken from the Bewley kitchen. Later, when he was in custody, Mount told the police exactly what had happened to that knife.

The night after the party, 5 September, Sandra and Bob Wignall set off on one of their nocturnal visits to feed the fox cubs . . .

But it was not quite as Sandra had described it to the police that same night. The sexual approach, that was real enough; but hardly as a gesture of affection, more to lull him into a false sense of security. As he stood there, his wife at his feet, Bob Wignall would have felt the crushing blow to his head first. If he cried out, which he must have done, it was stifled as Bewley and Mount jumped on their victim's chest. Although he later blamed Bewley for organising the attack, the mealy-mouthed Mount agreed that it was 'probably' he who stabbed Robert Wignall.

The whole sickening saga was exposed to a jury of six men and six women at the Old Bailey in the latter part of

October 1993. It was no surprise when they returned a unanimous verdict of guilty of murder on all three defendants – Sandra Wignall, Terence Bewley and Harold Mount, none of whom spoke during the nineteen days of the trial. The Common Serjeant of London, Judge Neil Denison, made no comment as he handed down three life sentences.

France

'OMAR M'A TUER'
The Trial of Omar Raddad

It had all the makings of a classic French *policier*, though, as it was to turn out, owing more to Inspector Clouseau than to Commissaire Maigret.

The Nice gendarmerie received the call on the afternoon of 24 June 1991. A resident on the exclusive Chemin Saint Barthélemy had become concerned at not seeing her neighbour for a couple of days and thought something might be wrong. Something certainly was. When officers arrived at La Chamade, a villa towards the top of the steep road which rose over Val de Mougins on the edge of Cannes, they found the house deserted. Of its inhabitant, Madame Marchal, there was no sign. Until they searched the cellar. The door had been locked from the outside and, a curious discovery indeed, it had been barricaded on the inside with old furniture and timber. In the boiler-room adjoining the cellar lay the body of Madame Marchal; she had been stabbed more than a dozen times and bludgeoned about the head. The blade appeared to have been removed from the scene of the crime, though a blood-stained length of wood lay beside the corpse. And there was something else, something which would lift this sordid killing almost into the realm of fiction. On the grubby white door of the cellar, a message had been written in the victim's blood – '*Omar m'a tuer*.' To anybody with the merest smattering of French the accusation was plain – 'Omar killed me.' Those three words would become the foundation of a trial which, in the words of one of France's most celebrated lawyers, compared with the notorious Dreyfus affair.

But that is to move too quickly into the plot. What of the characters involved in this drama? Madame Ghislaine Marchal was, at the time of her death, a wealthy widow of sixty-five. The Marchal fortunes derived from the manufacture of automobile accessories – spark-plugs and that sort of thing; not terribly lyrical, but handsomely profitable. Madame was what might most charitably be described as 'close' as regards her financial affairs, though it is reported that she had a number of 'business interests' in Switzerland. In fact, the late Madame Marchal seems to have spent some time each year in that country. She had lived for some years at the top of the Chemin Saint Barthélemy in a sprawling villa which bristled with security.

And Omar? Omar was thirty-two-year-old Omar Raddad, a Moroccan who had been in France for about four years. He lived quietly in a modest two-room apartment in Cannes with his wife Latifa; Latifa had given birth to their second child only days before the murder of Madame Marchal. Although he spoke hardly any French, Omar was seen as a polite, quiet man, some locals even referred to him as being 'timid', and he had built up a reputation for hard work and honesty that resulted in his performing a range of odd jobs around the district, most notably gardening. He was Ghislaine Marchal's gardener; and he also tended the garden of Madame Pascal, Marchal's neighbour who had alerted the police. This will in its turn become a significant fact.

Then there were the gendarmes; quite a lot of them

and, if reports coming out of the Côte d'Azure were true, not very efficient. It is always easy to criticise public servants with as high a profile as the police, and these are frequently unfair reflections on a group of men and women whose job is at best difficult and at worst downright impossible. That said, the task force in charge of the Marchal murder were guilty of some very 'Clouseau-esque' errors and omissions. For example, although the likely instrument of Madame Marchal's battery lay beside her, the scene-of-crime team failed to test that length of timber for fingerprints, nor did they check the door, furniture or fittings of the cellar for prints. And according to one report of the case (by Robert Chalmers in the *Observer Magazine*, 27 March 1994), a sample of the victim's blood dispatched for analysis arrived so badly contaminated that it was all but impossible to establish even what group it was. The reason for this carelessness is understandable, if unforgivable – what is the point of wasting time when the victim herself, with her own life-blood, fingered her killed: '*Omar m'a tuer*'?

'Omar killed me.' The problem is that this is English schoolboy French, and Madame was not only a well educated and cultured individual, but one known for her skill in solving crossword puzzles – truth to tell she was something of a pedant where *la langue Française* was concerned. What she *should* have written was '*Omar m'a tuée*' – she should have used the feminine past principle, *not* the infinitive. The police, however, are not paid to be pedantic with their language, they are paid to catch criminals. Which is why Omar Raddad was in custody charged with murder.

The French are not famed for the speed of their legal process, and so it was not until the end of January 1994 that Omar Raddad stood his trial at the Nice *Cour d'Assises*. By this time the evidence against him was embarrassingly slim; indeed, it was almost non-existent.

Let us look at his alibi for a start. It was calculated by the pathologist that Madame Marchal had been killed between midday and 2 p.m. on the afternoon of 23 June, a Sunday. It happened that on that day Omar Raddad had been working in the garden of Madame Pascal, Ghislaine Marchal's neighbour. At noon Raddad had climbed on to his motor-scooter and driven to his apartment at Mougins. On the way he stopped off to buy bread. He arrived at about 12.20, had his lunch of bread and cheese and rode back to Chemin Saint Barthélemy, pausing at a telephone box to call his wife who was holidaying with her family at Toulon. Despite this full and partly corroborated account of his movements the prosecution still insisted that there were twenty minutes unaccounted for – more than enough time to brutally stab to death one of his employers. But that raised another problem. There were witnesses aplenty (including the redoubtable Madame Pascal) to testify that Omar Raddad was wearing exactly the same clothes when he returned to work as he was when he left for lunch. These were the garments presented by the police to the forensic laboratory; the laboratory was unable to find one single blood spot on Raddad's clothing despite the accusation that he had stabbed Madame Marchal three times in the head, once in the neck, three times in the throat and six in the stomach – not to forget the bludgeoning. Indeed there was not one single piece of 'trace' evidence found on Raddad or his clothing linking him with the Marchal affair.

And what about motive – surely there must have been a reason? Oh yes, said the prosecution, money. Madame Marchal was renowned for carrying large amounts of cash about with her in her handbag. It was thought that on the day she was murdered Ghislaine Marchal had about 3,000 francs in her bag, and that money was missing. But wouldn't a thief, determined enough to murder, have plundered her other valuables – the large amount of expensive jewellery for example? Obviously not. However, clutching now at straws, the police and public prosecutor had been investigating Omar Raddad's background. Yes, he was generally regarded as a genuinely pleasant man, a good neighbour, husband and father; he had no criminal record of any kind and was respected as an enthusiastic employee. There was just one blip. In his small amount of spare time, Omar liked to play the one-arm bandits, the casino fruit machines which lurk in every corner along the Côte d'Azure. But a motive for murder?

The trial of Omar Raddad opened in January 1994. Raddad looked worn-out but quietly defiant; he also looked quite a lot thinner having lost a lot of kilos during a hunger-strike to protest his innocence. One thing was very noticeable – despite his unconscionable long time on remand, Raddad was the only person in court to look . . . well, dusky. And they are a bit suspicious of that in Nice. One Portuguese journalist covering the trial was reported as saying: 'I went down there on a motor-bike. When I stopped to ask the way, people ignored me. It's not easy to get directions if you've got too good a suntan.'

Which made it in many respects the more bizarre that Omar Raddad accepted the offer made by Maître Jacques Vergès to represent him free of charge. A flamboyant advocate, Vergès has never been far from controversy. For example, he voluntarily defended Klaus Barbie, the so-called 'Butcher of Lyon', and, during that lady's trawl through French lawyers, the notorious Madame Simone Weber, convicted of the crime of murdering her lover and dismembering the corpse with a circular-saw designed to cut concrete. For good measure, Vergès is on record as declaring that 'all my sympathies are with Saddam Hussein'. And so it was not easy to understand why Maître Vergès should espouse the cause of Omar Raddad. Not so surprising was that the trial judge, President Armand Dijan, exercised his right to pass comment on the proceedings. Making reference to the Islamic method of ritual slaughter of beasts, judge Dijan commented on being told that Omar would not hurt a fly: 'Yes, but he cuts the throat of sheep.'

Things were not going well for Omar Raddad. Despite the fact that there was almost no forensic evidence against him, it seemed that Raddad, clearly irritating the judge by his need to work through an interpreter, was quite incidental to a pre-judged verdict. French legal process operates in a different manner to that which informs those systems that underpin the English system. Omar Raddad was judged, not by a jury of twelve of his peers, but by a jury of nine lay 'peers', the judge and two assessors. And it would appear that such a combination results in the prevalence of the opinion of the strongest members – that is to say the President. Not surprisingly to anybody following the trial, when the jury announced their verdict on 2 February 1994, it was that Raddad was found guilty of murder and sentenced to eighteen years.

In the wake of what can only be regarded as a most unsatisfactory trial – and quite probably an unjust verdict – the world is beginning to see Omar Raddad as a convenient scapegoat. There remain a number of unanswered questions – many of which had been forcibly put during the trial by Maître Vergès on behalf of his client.

For example: when Omar advanced a convincing alibi for the alleged time of the murder, the prosecution thought again. Perhaps Madame Marchal had not died between noon and two on the 23rd; after all, the autopsy report claimed that it was the 24th – the day that Omar Raddad had been nowhere near Cannes (he had been visiting his wife in Toulon); was it a coincidence that the date was changed? And what of the sighting of a mysterious saloon car with Swiss registration plates that was seen by more than one witness parked outside La Chamade? And the young blond man who was seen ringing the bell at the heavily secured front gate?

Perhaps the biggest red herring of all has been the message allegedly scrawled in her own blood by Madame Marchal in the cellar of her home. The scenario raises a number of puzzling questions – such as why should a badly wounded victim barricade a door so that she could not get out and help would find it difficult to get in? Why, given her pernickety way with language, should she deliberately use the wrong construction in her dying message – it is not as though *tuée* is more difficult to write than *tuer*. As one might expect, there is no shortage of possible explanations. At simplest, perhaps a person, dreadfully injured and close to death might not be too concerned with the niceties of syntax. Or is it conceivable that Ghislaine Marchal was *forced* to write the message by her killer, a killer other than Omar Raddad, a killer whom she hoped to distinguish *because* she made the *deliberate* error? This is the faulty and contested evidence which keeps Omar Raddad inside Grasse prison; unlike in the British and American legal systems, there is no automatic or formalised procedure for appeal. Perhaps Raddad is guilty, but he was never proved to be; not by that bastion phrase of British law: 'beyond all reasonable doubt', but by a much shorter measure: the French '*conviction intime*' – sort of 'sincere belief'.

Few people have shared my own unease about the conviction of Omar Raddad; most, particularly in France, seem happy that another serious crime is 'solved'. But what happens when we allow fiction to triumph over process of law, when the 'hand of the dead' reaches out from the grave? I am sure that Robert Chalmers would not, in this context, begrudge me another quote from his article 'Murder on the Riviera' – it may well hold the key to the whole case: 'In the Museum of Modern Art in

Nice, they recently unveiled a new exhibit; a door inscribed with the words "Omar has kill me". Underneath is its title: "Justice has been do".'

USA

THE TRIALS OF THE 'LITTLE CAPTAIN'
The Trials of Byron de la Beckwith

Although the racist assassination of Medgar Evers was a fundamental landmark in the overall struggle against segregation in the Deep South of America, it should be seen in the wider political perspective. On 9 November 1960 John F. Kennedy was elected President of the United States by a narrow margin over Richard Nixon, and early indications were that he intended to implement a sweeping range of reforms aimed at giving the south's long-oppressed black population a measure of equality of opportunity. By May of the following year black activists had already begun to exercise their own strength when the so-called 'freedom riders', white and black, deliberately challenged the segregation laws relating to state and interstate buses in Montgomery, Alabama. Crowds of angry whites, many of them members of the Ku Klux Klan, attacked the freedom riders with fists and clubs, and Governor John Patterson was obliged to impose martial law in an attempt to halt the rioting. Meanwhile, the leader of the mainly peaceful black demonstrators, the Reverend Dr Martin Luther King had to be protected from a white mob as he held a church service. By 1962 Dr King was the undisputed leader of the 'integration movement', and in July he was arrested for leading an illegal march in Georgia, and the following month for holding a prayer meeting on the steps of Albany's city hall; arrested with him was the Reverend Ralph Abernathy, another leading anti-segregationist. On 30 September James Meredith became the first black student to attempt to enrol at the University of Mississippi, provoking an angry white backlash which led to rioting in which three people were killed and more than fifty injured, despite a force of 750 federal marshals led by the Deputy District Attorney. By the spring of 1963 dissent was spreading across the south, and in Alabama Governor George Wallace threatened to defy federal authorities by refusing to implement desegregation. When the civil rights leader Medgar Evers was ambushed and shot dead on 12 June it sparked off riots across the southern states.

The following account of the murder of Medgar Evers and the thirty-year battle to convict Byron de la Beckwith of the crime is told through contemporary news-media accounts, supplemented (in italics) by additional new information.

NAACP Leader Slain in Jackson; Protests Mount
Jackson, Mississippi – 12 June 1963

The victim of the shooting was thirty-seven-year-old Medgar W. Evers, field secretary of the National Association for the Advancement of Coloured People. Mr Evers, a native of Decatur, Mississippi, and an Army veteran of World War II, had been one of the key leaders in the Negroes' drive here to win a promise from the city to hire some Negro policemen and to appoint a bi-racial committee.

He left a mass meeting at a church last night, stopped at the residence of a Negro lawyer and then drove to his home on the city's northern edge. He arrived at his neat green-panelled and buff-brick ranch-style home on Guynes Street at 1.14 a.m. He parked his 1962 light blue sedan in the driveway, and as he turned to walk into the side entrance opening into a carport, a sniper's bullet struck him just below the right shoulder blade. The slug crashed through the front window of the house, penetrated an interior wall, ricocheted off a refrigerator and struck a coffee pot. The battered bullet was found beneath a watermelon on a kitchen cabinet. Mr Evers staggered to the doorway, his keys in his hand, and collapsed near the steps. His wife Myrlie, and three children rushed to the door. The screaming of the children awoke the neighbours. One said he had looked out of his bedroom window and saw Mr Evers' crumpled body in the carport. He had rushed out and crouched behind a clump of shrubbery, fired a shot in the air to scare off the gunman and shouted for help. Police who arrived a short time later helped place the still-living victim into a neighbour's station wagon. As the vehicle sped towards University Hospital, those who accompanied the dying man said he had murmured weakly: 'Sit me up,' and 'Turn me loose.'

When news spread through town of Medgar Evers' death, a spontaneous demonstration collected in the late morning, when approximately 200 Negro teenagers marched from the Masonic Building on Lynch Street, where Mr Evers had his office. About 100 city policemen and deputies armed with riot guns and automatic rifles stopped them a block away. A total of 145 demonstrators, including seventy-four aged seventeen and under were arrested. One girl was struck in the face with a club, and deputies wrestled a middle-aged woman to the sidewalk.

Evers knew that his position with the NAACP was a dangerous one, but since an early age he had been confronting racist violence. Only shortly before his death he had recounted how, when he was just fourteen years old, a friend of his father's was lynched for allegedly insulting a white woman – he had never forgotten the sight of the murdered man. Ten days before he was shot, Mr Evers said in an interview: 'If I die it will be in a good cause. I've been fighting for America just as much as the soldiers in Vietnam.'

As early as 4.00 a.m. President Kennedy was informed of the murder, and was reported to be 'appalled by the barbarity of the act', while his brother, Attorney General Robert F. Kennedy, said he was 'saddened and shocked by the crime'. However, many southern senators, including their leader Richard B. Russell of Georgia made it clear that the untimely death of Medgar Evers would in no way affect their implacable opposition to civil rights legislation. One somewhat eccentric reaction to the tragedy was the offer made by Ghana for an 'African Peace Corps' to be sent to the United States on what was described as a 'civilising mission'. Meanwhile, the NAACP had announced a reward of $10,000 for the arrest and conviction of Medgar Evers' killer; this supplemented the $5,000 reward already offered by the mayor and city commissioners of Jackson.

In its editorial comment, the *New York Times* invoked President Kennedy's plea for a 'vast moral awakening': 'But beyond the bulwarks Congress writes into law is the necessity for the reassessment of individual attitudes and behaviour, for which the President called so eloquently. The justification for fuller implementation of constitutional guarantees does not rest primarily in the damage discrimination does to our world image, or the danger that it will touch off mass disorders, or the vast waste it entails in our economic and social resources. Important as all these are, real as all of them are, they are less costly than the hurt we do ourselves by the systematic humiliation of one-tenth of our people solely on the basis of colour. Every family, every home, every community is in the front lines of the crusade for decency to which Mr Kennedy has summoned America. We can all be bucket-carriers, helping to quench "the fires of frustration and discord" that rage in every city, North and South.'

Jackson Negroes Clubbed as Police Quell Marchers
Jackson, Mississippi – 13 June 1963

Police attacked adults and teenagers as they congregated, chanting: 'We want freedom', and battered them into submission. Six demonstrators were struck or choked by police nightsticks drawn across their throats, others were snatched or pushed from a Negro home; a white sociology professor, John Salter, was felled by a blow to the head before being arrested and put in custody. This was the second major confrontation with the city police since the murder of Medgar Evers the previous night.

Evers Lying in State
Jackson, Mississippi – 14 June 1963

Despite a tense atmosphere among the city's Negro population, not helped by the sweltering 101 degrees temperature, officials issued permits for a march following funeral services offered as a final tribute to slain integration leader Medgar Evers. This could, of course, be seen as a simple exercise in damage limitation on the part of the city council, as widespread sentiment had been expressed for a mass march whether officials granted a permit or not, and without sanction it could more easily have degenerated into a violent confrontation.

By now considerable solidarity was being shown by other high-profile Negro individuals and groups. Dr Martin Luther King had sent messages of support from his Atlanta-based Southern Christian Leadership Conference; and James H. Meredith, who became the first of his race to enrol in a white educational establishment – the University of Mississippi – and whose cause Medgar Evers had championed, called for an end to mass protest marches and the implementation of a general strike of Negro workers.

All this time Medgar Evers lay in state dressed in a

modest dark grey suit and white shirt, his blue-trimmed Masonic apron around his waist and an Elk emblem hanging round his neck. Hundreds of mourners had filed past his grey metal casket at the Collins Funeral Home.

Washington – 17 June 1963

Hundreds of Negroes turned out to honour the memory of Medgar Evers; about 500 marched behind the hearse carrying his body from Union Station to the funeral parlour. Leaflets bearing a picture of Mr Evers and the slogan: 'He sacrificed his life for you' were handed to members of the huge crowd lining the streets. As a war veteran, Medgar Evers was provided with a plot in the military section of Arlington cemetery in recognition of his three years' service with the Allied armies in northern France during 1943–6.

Evers Interred at Arlington
Washington – 19 June 1963

Medgar Evers was buried with full military honours under the tall oaks at Arlington National Cemetery while soldiers held a United States flag over the coffin and fellow civil rights workers sang what has become the movement's anthem – *We Shall Overcome*. As smoke from a volley of rifle fire hovered in the air, Bishop Stephen Gill Spottswood of Washington, chairman of the NAACP, reminded mourners that: 'He is not dead, the soldier fallen here. His spirit walks through the world today . . . I hope Medgar Evers will be the last black American to give his life in the struggle to make the Constitution come alive. He laid down his life for Negroes that they might be free from segregation and discrimination, that we might share in the full fruits of democracy. Now, he rests from his labours.'

Mississippi Man Seized by FBI in Evers Slaying
Washington – 23 June 1963

The FBI announced the arrest of forty-two-year-old Byron de la Beckwith in connection with the murder of Medgar Evers. Beckwith was taken into custody at 11.00 p.m. yesterday and was being detained on a holding charge of violating the 1957 Civil Rights Act; in precise terms the complaint charged Beckwith 'and others unknown' with conspiring to injure, oppress and intimidate Medgar Evers in the free exercise and enjoyment of rights and privileges secured to him by the constitution of the United States. The FBI undertook to provide all the information they had gathered against Beckwith to the authorities in Jackson pursuing the killing of the civil rights leader. Meanwhile in Jackson, Hinds County District Attorney William L. Waller said he would be bringing a murder charge against Beckwith.

J. Edgar Hoover, director of the FBI, announced that his agents had linked Beckwith to the Evers case through a fingerprint found on a telescopic sight on the gun abandoned not far from where the victim was shot. A bureau expert explained that the Gold Hawk 'scope' had been traced by a process of elimination, first asking the manufacturer to list the serial numbers of all items sent to their local distributors, and then tracing each number to its individual purchaser. The sight that agents were interested in was sold to none other than Byron de la Beckwith. But there was an added bonus – a fingerprint had been deposited on the sight which, when compared with Beckwith's service record, proved a perfect match.

Byron de la Beckwith was described as a chronic letter-writer on the racial issue. He is said to have been a lifelong resident of Leflore County and a member of a prominent local family. He is a gun collector and a Marine veteran of World War II. It was later revealed that when he became aware of being under surveillance by FBI agents Beckwith communicated with his lawyer, Mr Hardy Lott, and arranged to turn himself in to the police.

[Some time later we were to learn much more of the eccentric life of Byron de la Beckwith – 'Deelay' to his friends. Beckwith was born in California, though when he was just five his father died and Byron and his mother returned to her home in Greenwood, Mississippi. The family, as might be expected, had adhered to the Confederate cause during the Civil War, and Beckwith's grandfather Lemuel Yerger had ridden with General Nathan Bedford Forrest's cavalry (Forrest, it is worth noting, later became the first Imperial Wizard of the Ku Klux Klan). Byron was eleven when his mother died, and his guardianship was taken over by the Yergers – Uncle William to be precise. It is recalled that when he was young, Byron was naturally surrounded by hundreds of black servants and plantation workers, and by some accounts got on well with them. Perhaps he was flattered by the name they called him – 'Little Captain'. Beckwith was sent to the Webb School at Belt Buckle, Tennessee, where he was a poor student, and then attended Mississippi State University, but did not graduate. At the age of twenty he joined the Marines and fought with them in the South Pacific during World War II; he was awarded the coveted Purple Heart at the Battle of Tarawa where he was wounded.

When he returned home to Mississippi, Byron de la Beckwith married the former Mary Louise Williams and took his new bride to live at the almost derelict plantation house where he had spent his childhood, and which was all that was left of the family fortune. Whether it was the pressure of living close to poverty, or whether it was the regular physical abuse which Beckwith was accused of giving his wife, she eventually left him in 1960. That said, whatever Mary Louise may have thought of him, Beckwith

– or Deelay to his ever increasing circle of friends – was by all accounts the very model of a Southern gentleman, known as a courteous man and well-liked around Greenwood. He found his niche as a salesman – first in tobacco products and later in fertilisers – one former employer described Deelay as a friendly man 'with the gift of the gab'. He was also a dyed-in-the-wool racist and segregationist. Beckwith's return to Mississippi from the conflict in Europe had confirmed him in his political views. He became, as one acquaintance put it, 'rabid'. He regularly attended meetings of the Sons of the American Revolution, lectured to the KKK, and joined the White Citizens' Council. It was said that his favourite 'purist' organisation was the Identity Group: 'They live by the Bible' – whatever that may mean. One thing that it meant to Deelay was that he took up position outside church on Sundays, a gun tucked in his pants, to 'see off niggers'. And when he wasn't protecting the church, he was at the bus station making sure the Nigra didn't get uppity and use the white waiting rooms. Depending on your view, Deelay was a good ol' boy or an out-and-out fascist. And possibly a murderer; but it would take Mississippi almost thirty years to prove it.]

Trial of Beckwith is opened
Jackson, Mississippi – 31 January 1964

[Many local residents, of both colours, saw little chance of Deelay being convicted; the defendant himself included. There was a story that District Attorney William Waller, prosecuting, had some difficulty selecting a jury. In order to find a panel of twelve, Waller had to find that number of people who could answer in the affirmative the question: 'Do you believe it's a crime for a white man to kill a nigger in Mississippi?' It took him four days to find his jury.]

'Our witnesses will show in ten ways that Byron de la Beckwith is guilty of this crime.' That is the way Mr William L. Waller opened the state's case. In the small courtroom packed mainly with Negroes, a Jackson detective, John Chamblee, told the jury how, by standing on the spot where Medgar Evers died and directing his flashlight in a straight line the light picked out a clump of small sweetgum trees and honeysuckle vines in a vacant lot opposite; he found the vines bruised and a branch snapped, as though somebody had been standing and lying there. Another officer then testified that he had found a .30-06 Enfield rifle hidden in the honeysuckle not far from the trees.

Vital evidence was presented by Mr I.T. McIntyre, a farmer from Greenwood, who testified that he had sold a .30-06 Enfield rifle, which he had bought through a Canadian mail-order outfit, to Mr Beckwith in January 1960. The manufacturer of the rifle and the date on which it was made were the same as the murder weapon.

Rifle is Linked to Beckwith

Jackson, Mississippi – 1 February 1964

Agents from the Federal Bureau of Investigation presented the court with evidence that the telescopic sight on the murder weapon had been sold to Mr Byron de la Beckwith, and furthermore a fingerprint on the scope no more than twelve hours old matched his.

Jackson, Mississippi – 3 February 1964

Two white taxi-cab drivers testified that Beckwith was in Jackson four days before the shooting inquiring for the address of Medgar Evers: 'He asked me if I knew where the Negro NAACP leader lived. I said I did not.' Beckwith then went back to the station and consulted the telephone directory and returned to the cab driver, Mr

Speight, to ask where Livingston Drive was: 'I said that couldn't be it because it was all white.'

If anybody thought such evidence would ruffle Deelay they were wrong. Throughout the trial he seemed to be thoroughly enjoying himself, sharing jokes and hand-shakes with Governor Ross Barnet, offering cigars to District Attorney Waller, smiling and waving genially to visitors in the court and to the jury. One report says that he is such a popular figure with the court police that he is allowed to keep his gun collection in his cell!

Beckwith's Car Near Scene of Slaying?
Jackson, Mississippi – 4 February 1964

Two witnesses testified today that they saw Byron de la Beckwith's car parked a few hundred feet from Medgar Evers' home on the night of his murder. The parking lot is only 150 feet from the shrubbery from which the assassin's bullet was fired. Three teenage boys also claimed to have seen a white Valiant such as Beckwith drives in the area on the same night.

As DA Waller announced that he was resting his case, Byron de la Beckwick rewarded him with a wide, friendly smile.

Beckwith Takes the Stand
Jackson, Mississippi – 5 February 1964

Although in his testimony today Byron de la Beckwith denied that he was implicated in any way in the murder of Medgar Evers, he was prepared to acknowledge a letter which he had written to the National Rifle Association on 26 January 1963, in which he said: 'For the next fifteen years we here in Mississippi are going to have to do a lot of shooting to protect our wives and children from bad niggers.' As for the evidence of the rifle which killed Mr Evers being his, Deelay's answer was simple – it was stolen the day before the murder. Handed the weapon and asked whether it belonged to him, Beckwith handled it fondly and pulled the bolt, aiming it above the jury's heads, before grumbling that: 'There's a little dust in the barrel.' Before putting his star witness on the stand defence attorney Lott had questioned two policemen who swore that on the night in question they had seen Beckwith in Greenwood.

Beckwith Case a Mistrial
Jackson, Mississippi – 7 February 1964

Although the jury were sent to a hotel overnight after failing to reach agreement after a retirement of more than seven hours yesterday, they were still unable to declare a verdict today. The vote taken on the twentieth ballot after eleven hours' deliberation was announced by the bailiff as being split 7–5 for acquittal. When the jury foreman told the court that it would be impossible for them to reach agreement, Judge Leon F. Hendrick announced a mistrial, and said he would set the date for a second trial.

[Byron de la Beckwith's second trial opened on 6 April 1964. The courtroom was the same, as were the judge and the attorneys. In fact the final verdict if not exactly the same was still a hung jury unable to agree; it was Judge Hendrick who dismissed them after ten hours' retirement, saying: 'I've never been in favour of wearing out a jury'; and then declaring a mistrial. After encountering even more difficulty in assembling a jury than the first time round the judge was obliged to order the court to sit at night in order to try to speed things up. One prospective juror was dismissed when he gave his opinion that the state had made a pretty poor job of presenting its case the first time. And it was much the same evidence at this second trial – there were no new revelations, no new witnesses,

and nothing new said by any of the former witnesses. The only thing that had changed in the Beckwith camp was the show of force put on by the local Ku Klux Klan who burned ten crosses in the Jackson area on the night before the trial opened, and sent a squad of their toughest and most intimidating members to hang around inside and outside the court. One victim was Mr H.R. Speight, the taxi driver who claimed at the first trial that Beckwith had asked the way to the Evers household; after being allegedly beaten up, he now only thought it might have been somebody who looked like Beckwith. And so on 17 April Byron de la Beckwith walked from court, part conquering hero, part martyr to the cause of white supremacy.]

No Third Trial for Beckwith

[Over the following years, the Little Colonel kept a comparatively low profile, earning his living as a fertiliser salesman. In 1967 he did put himself forward as a prospective lieutenant-governor of Mississippi, but without any great hope of success. And then he hit the headlines again. He had been arrested in New Orleans with a bomb in the back of his car and directions how to get to the home of one of the leaders of the Jewish Anti-Defamation League. Although he pleaded that he was framed for the job, he was a long way from the good ol' boys who rallied to his defence before. After a short trial Byron de la Beckwith was sent down for five years for possessing explosives. When he was released, Beckwith returned to Greenwood where he continued as a salesman and married Thelma Neff, leaving the ramshackle plantation house for the comforts of her Tennessee bungalow. By the mid-eighties age was beginning to take its toll of Deelay's health. In late 1989 it was announced that the district attorney's office had agreed to open the Beckwith case again with a view to putting him on trial. The problem was that all the tangible

evidence plus the trial transcripts and other documents had disappeared or been destroyed. Over the following months the issue of the trial rested not only on trying to assemble evidence (for example the murder rifle was handed over by the wife of a segregationist judge who, before his death, had just hung on to it as a souvenir) but also trying to prise Beckwith out of Tennessee and extradite him to Jackson, where with the benefit of three decades' development, there seemed to be a genuine new need for the city to cleanse itself of the uglier incidents of its past. On 19 December 1990, Byron de la Beckwith was charged again with the murder of Medgar Evers. Some idea of what was involved in getting the new trial underway can be judged from the newspaper headlines through 1991:]

January 15: Judge orders Beckwith to return to Mississippi to face trial for first-degree murder
Beckwith appeals extradition with Tennessee Court of Criminal Appeals
June 4: Tennessee Appeals Court orders return of Beckwith to Mississippi
June 6: Beckwith loses extradition fight
June 7: Original autopsy report on Evers found to be missing
June 8: Evers' body exhumed from Arlington Cemetery for new autopsy
October 1: Beckwith loses extradition appeal
October 4: Beckwith returned to Mississippi
October 30: Prosecutor seeking to block bail links Beckwith with obscure racist group the Phineas Priesthood – called 'God's Executioners'
November 14: Beckwith denied bail; must remain in Jackson jail

[At last, in the first month of 1994 the long-awaited trial opened.]

White Supremacist Faces Third Trial for Murder
New York – 17 January 1994

Byron de la Beckwith goes on trial today as Mississippi tries to lay one of the most troublesome ghosts in its troubled racial history. Beckwith, now seventy-three years old, seems to have lost none of his racist views [*Interviewed in jail he was reported as saying: 'If you lay down, toss your panties off and let a nigger have intercourse with you, you are going to produce mongrels for ever'*] and in his autobiography maintains the stand he took at the two 1964 trials as far as the evidence against him is concerned – that is, that his rifle was stolen and that he was a hundred miles away in Greenwood at the time of Medgar Evers' murder. However, the new trial was allowed because of subsequent information amounting to 'new evidence'. First, there are fears that the juries at Beckwith's original trials had been screened by a state agency called the Sovereignty Commission set up to maintain segregation in Mississippi. Secondly, Delmar Dennis, a former member of the Ku Klux Klan and an FBI informer, claims that Beckwith admitted to a Klan meeting that he had shot the civil rights leader; he is quoted as telling the meeting: 'Killing that nigger gave me no more discomfort than our wives endure when they give birth to our children.'

The trial will be held in the same courtroom that played host to Beckwith's other appearances, though in order to empanel the least biased jury possible, recruitment will take place in the more liberal northern districts of the state. Nevertheless, in the weeks leading up to the trial, racists have been leafleting the streets reminding prospective jurors that Byron de la Beckwith stands firm as: 'A Hero in War; a Hero in Peace'.

Stirring Memories of Hatred
Jackson, Mississippi – 28 January 1994

Once again the people of Jackson have been forced to remember the tragic assassination of Medgar Evers as his wife Myrlie stood in the witness box for the third time and recounted for the court the events of the night she saw her husband die. Bobby DeLaughter, the Hinds County prosecutor told a jury of eight blacks and four whites: 'What you are going to see from the evidence is a life snuffed out on 12 June 1963, by a bullet that tore through his body, a bullet aimed in prejudice, propelled by hatred and fired by a back-shooting coward . . . The person who pulled the trigger was an absolute, self-proclaimed rabid racist,' continued Mr DeLaughter as he pointed a finger at Beckwith in the dock.

Mississippi Killer Guilty After 31 Years
Jackson, Mississippi – 5 February 1994

By 5 February it was all over. The new information was tied in with the old and few could have doubted the outcome of this trial any more than previous commentators could doubt the outcome of Byron de la Beckwith's two previous trials. After a deliberation of just over six hours, the jury found Beckwith guilty and he was sentenced to life imprisonment. As he walked from the dock clutching his Bible his wife Thelma cried out: 'He's not guilty. He's never been guilty and they know.'

But all eyes, ears, and above all hearts, were focused on Myrlie Evers as she spoke the only possible epitaph: 'It's been a long journey, Medgar, I've gone the last mile.'

THE BEST SHOW IN TOWN*
The Trials of Lyle and Eric Menendez
(Guest contributor: Trisha Reed)

When the trial of Lyle and Eric Menendez opened in July 1993, there were few who had any doubts as to what its outcome would be. For more than three years, the brothers had been held without bail in Los Angeles County Jail, accused of the brutal slaying of their parents. For more than three years they had vehemently protested their innocence but most followers of the case had long since decided on the verdict. They saw the killings as the work of two spoilt rich kids, who couldn't wait to get their hands on the inheritance that would one day be theirs.

Then, just a week or so before the trial was due to begin, came a dramatic announcement. The brothers had changed their story. Yes, it was a sad fact that, on the evening of 20 August 1989, they had shot their parents dead; but their defence would be that the deed had been the direct consequence of years of physical, sexual and emotional abuse. The announcement did little to elicit any public sympathy for the pair. Their new story was merely seen as the last resort of two desperate men who could face the death penalty if convicted of first-degree murder.

Things were very different when, months later, the trial finally drew to its close. By then, it seemed that the entire lives of victims Jose and Kitty Menendez had been dissected by the media, and the case had attracted media and public interest not only in America but the world over. For this was no ordinary family, and the story that unfolded was every bit as riveting as any movie to emerge from the nearby Hollywood studios.

* 'The law is not about a search for truth, it's about who puts on the best show.' (Prosecutor in the Menendez trial)

Jose Menendez had come to America from his native Cuba where his father, a prosperous accountant, had lost everything as a result of political change following Fidel Castro's revolution. His mother, Maria, had been a champion swimmer, and the young Jose had clearly inherited much of his parents' competitive spirit and drive. When, at sixteen, he was sent to stay with relatives in Pennsylvania, he already knew he wanted the good things in life, and single-mindedly set out to grasp them.

It was at the University of Southern Illinois, when he was just nineteen years old, that Jose met Mary Louise Anderson, known as Kitty. Despite his father's opposition, Jose married Kitty only months later and, following his graduation, they moved to New York, where Jose enrolled in an accountancy course. In his spare time he washed dishes and worked as a door-to-door salesman to help pay his way.

Soon Jose Menendez was gradually working his way up the hierarchy of a small container company in Chicago, rising first to the post of Chief Finance Officer and then, in his early thirties, that of President. Just a few years later, he was appointed senior executive with Hertz, the vehicle rental company, and also with RCA records, where he was involved in the signing of such major acts as the Eurythmics. By 1989, Menendez was Chairman of the Board, President and Chief Executive Officer of the video distribution company, Live Entertainment. RCA's massive success with such titles as *Teenage Mutant Ninja Turtles* was reflected in Jose's own income, and at the time of his death it was estimated that the company was earning him some $2 million per year in the form of salary and bonuses. He was also on the board of directors of the film company Carolco, along with Sylvester Stallone.

Jose's personal lifestyle paralleled the progress in his working life. His first son, Lyle, had been born in 1968. Erik had arrived three years later, and Jose had moved his young family to a succession of ever more luxurious houses. The year before his death they settled in prestigious North Elm Drive in Beverly Hills. Admittedly, theirs was not among the most expensive dwellings in an area settled by film stars and movie moguls. But the six-bedroomed, $4-million, Italian-style mansion had once been home to such rock celebrities as Elton John, and went a long way to demonstrating that its owner was well and truly on his way to the top.

Thick shrubbery shielded the front of the house from the road, while behind the building a 200-foot garden accommodated the requisite swimming pool and an equally well-used tennis court. A gardener kept the grounds in pristine condition, and there was a maid too. It would be no exaggeration to say Jose's sons lived in a world of comfort and privilege. Both had attended expensive schools, and there had been a succession of little luxuries such as private tennis coaches. The boys were growing into attractive and apparently confident young men.

But, even before the murder, there were signs that all was not ticketyboo in the Menendez family. Lyle, at university in Princeton, had been suspended after being accused of plagiarism. Then, prior to the family's move to Beverly Hills, Erik had been accused of robbery from two nearby houses and, as a result, started regular (and expensive) therapy sessions with psychologist Dr Jerome Oziel. Lyle, too, would become one of Oziel's patients. Kitty and Jose also had their problems. Kitty had long suspected her husband of a whole string of affairs. Now she had become secretly addicted to alcohol and Valium, and there was little trace of the beauty queen she had once been as the drink and drugs took their toll on her face and figure.

Nevertheless, the evening of 20 August 1989 seems to have started pleasantly enough. It was the maid's day off, so Jose and Kitty had eaten their supper in the kitchen before settling down to watch a film in the family room. Later, Kitty had gone back to the kitchen to dish up two large bowls of blueberries and ice cream.

At 11.47 p.m. the Beverly Hills police received an hysterical phone call. It was from Lyle Menendez. Crying loudly, he reported that someone had killed his parents, that they had been shot. Meanwhile, according to neighbours, Erik could be seen outside the house, rolling around and sobbing uncontrollably. When patrol officers reached the scene, they found the brothers totally consumed by grief and, still in the family room, the bodies of forty-five-year-old Jose and his forty-seven-year-old wife. So devasting were their injuries that it would be days before it was known precisely how many shots had been fired, and how many had entered each of the victims.

The Medical Examiner's Office reported that Jose had been hit a total of five times, with the final shot blowing away the back of his skull. The pathologist's opinion was that he was still alive when the barrel of the gun was held to his head and the trigger pulled this last, fatal time. Kitty, too, had survived a whole volley of shots – nine in all. Then the gun was placed against her cheek and a final blast took away the side of her face.

The bowls of fruit and ice cream lay unfinished on the table.

Initially Homicide Squad detectives suspected that the killings had been a Mafia execution. There was, they discovered, no sign of forced entry into the mansion, nor of any subsequent struggle. The killing had been carried out with some speed, and afterwards all the spent cartridges had been systematically removed. And there were rumours of a somewhat dubious business deal, so security guards quickly surrounded the mansion to protect Lyle and Erik should the killers return for them. Ironically, the sources of those rumours were Erik and Lyle themselves.

It did not take long for the Mafia theory to be discounted, however. There had, for a start, been simply too much 'overkill'. The Mafia would not have used any more force than was absolutely necessary and, in addition, why would they have killed Jose's wife too? What's more, the police could find absolutely no evidence linking Jose to the mob.

Gradually, investigators began to turn their attention to the Menendez brothers themselves – their suspicions fuelled when the pair suddenly embarked on a massive spending spree. First Erik abandoned his plans to go to university. He had dreamt of becoming a professional tennis player and now he hired an expensive coach whom he hoped would help him to achieve world stardom. Lyle, on the other hand, spent tens of thousands of dollars on clothing, a Porsche and a Rolex watch. He acquired a condominium in Princeton, not to mention a restaurant. Even when Jose's own sister, Maria Cano, tried to explain that this was simply the brothers' way of grappling with their grief, it did little to lessen the speculation. It would still be some months, however, before any charges were brought.

The police case was not helped by an important omission in their preliminary gathering of evidence. On the night of the killings they had neglected to carry out standard forensic tests on Erik's or Lyle's hands and clothes, in order to determine whether or not they had recently fired any guns. (When a gun is fired some of the chemical discharge will blow back on to the hand holding it, and swabbing the hands of a person suspected of having fired a weapon should be carried out as soon as possible to secure the residues before they can be cleaned off.) At the time, officers had been totally taken in by the brothers' display of grief. Now it was too late.

As the months passed speculation continued. There were, for instance, press reports about a screenplay said to have been written by Erik together with one of his friends. In it a wealthy couple were murdered by their eighteen-year-old son, who was unwilling to wait for his multi-million dollar inheritance. Kitty, it was said, had typed out the tale for its authors.

Far more damning was the story told by Judalon Smyth, a one-time patient and former mistress of psychologist Jerome Oziel. She claimed to have overheard the brothers confessing to the murder during one of their sessions with Oziel. And like a gift from Nemesis, the confession had been taped. Although it was eventually proved that Smyth's eavesdropping could not possibly have happened in the way she claimed, that did not stop the police from seizing several tapes that they found in Oziel's offices. Nor from making an application for them to be admitted as evidence.

On 8 March 1990, Lyle was arrested. Erik was in Israel, taking part in a tennis tournament, but he did promptly return to America and he did give himself up to police. For the next three years, the brothers would remain in jail without trial while their lawyers fought to keep the Oziel tapes out of court. At a preliminary hearing, the judge had ruled that the recordings *could* be used in evidence. The defence had responded by immediately taking the matter before a higher court. And while the legal battle dragged on interminably, interest in the Menendez family was kept alive by a never-ending flow of new 'revelations' from the media. By the time a date for the trial was finally announced, most observers saw its outcome as a foregone conclusion. Neither did they see any reason to change their opinions when the defence revealed its strategy, and child abuse was mentioned for the first time.

Such an approach was nothing new for Erik's attorney

Leslie Abramson, a diminutive New Yorker who had become well known for her defence of so-called 'lost causes'. When Arnel Salvatierra killed his fifty-year-old father Oscar in 1986 with three shots fired at point-blank range, Leslie Abramson was the attorney he hired. She presented a picture of a bullying father who had taunted his son until he could stand it no more. In the end Arnel was charged only with manslaughter rather than first-degree murder, and his punishment was simply a probation order. Abramson had used similar defences on other occasions. It was, after all, at a time when it was fashionable to blame all manner of ills on parental abuse.

In contrast to the fiery, aggressive Abramson, Lyle's lawyer was a cool blonde, Jill Lansing. The prosecution was in the hands of Lester Kuriyama and Pamela Bozanich, and the testimony of therapist Jerome Oziel would form the lynch pin of the state's case.

For reasons of his own Judge Stanley Weisberg decided that the small San Nuys courtroom should be the setting for a trial that would attract media interest from all over the world. The court itself had space for just ten members of the press, but a single ceiling-mounted camera was also permitted by the judge, albeit reluctantly, and reporters from other newspapers and television stations watched the proceedings on TV in an adjoining room. The trial was also transmitted live by the Court TV network, providing a gripping alternative to the daytime soaps.

In fact there was not one trial but two, running simultaneously, and there were two juries, so that the case against each brother could be considered separately. Both juries would be present in the courtroom when evidence relating to both brothers was presented. Judge Weisberg saw over a thousand possible jurors before he was satisfied that he had two entirely neutral juries. It would be more than five months before they were discharged from their duties.

The trial finally opened in July 1993. By then twenty-five-year-old Lyle and twenty-two-year-old Erik had spent more than three and a half years in prison. Once tanned and fit, their pale faces now contrasted starkly with their dark sober suits as they listened to the prosecution's opening arguments. Lester Kuriyama detailed the horrific injuries sustained by the two victims, gruesome photographs of which would later be paraded before the juries. His colleague Pamela Bozanich spoke of conspiracy between the brothers to commit what she contended were 'unlawful, unjustified and wholly premeditated' killings. 'But for a few mistakes they made, this was almost the perfect murder,' she claimed.

The defence, in their turn, did not dispute that the brothers had, indeed, killed their parents. But, they said, the important question was not *who* had killed them, but *why* they had been killed. This presented the juries with a number of options to consider. If the killings were premeditated, as the prosecution asserted, then the crime was that of first-degree murder. If, on the other hand, they were unplanned, then it was a case of second-degree murder. *But,* if it could be shown that the brothers had acted in self defence, then the lesser verdicts of voluntary or involuntary manslaughter could be brought.

The opening arguments from Lyle's attorney graphically indicated the direction the defence would take. For over an hour Jill Lansing described in great detail what she insisted were years of physical and sexual abuse. Jose was presented as an overbearing father. Kitty was said to be violent and addicted to alcohol and drugs – and to have acquiesced in the abuse. Stories were recounted of Jose brutally killing a pet rabbit, and of Kitty cutting herself and smearing the blood over Lyle. And it was said that when the fourteen-year-old Lyle wet the bed, the soiled sheets were placed on the breakfast table for all to see. Then there was the sexual abuse. The abuse of Lyle,

Ms Lansing continued, had begun when he was six and had lasted the next two years. That of Erik had endured for a full twelve years.

Erik's attorney promised expert witnesses who would describe the gruesome crime scene as a 'classic example of the overkill one sees when frightened and powerless people kill those they fear and perceive as all powerful – the crime scene of abused children who kill their abusers out of fear'. Over a period of some weeks, the defence would call a succession of witnesses to support these claims. Relatives, teachers, friends and neighbours would tell of bullying suffered by the boys. One of their former tennis coaches, Charles Wadlington, described Jose as 'the harshest person I ever met', and even Jose's own sisters took the stand to testify in the brothers' defence.

Then, eight weeks into the trial came the moment everybody had been waiting for – Lyle himself was called to give evidence. First he was questioned by his own attorney, Jill Lansing. He told the court that his father believed the showing of any emotion was a sign of great weakness, and that he had forced Lyle to learn a special creed off by heart. 'Today I will be master of my emotions,' it began. 'If I feel depressed, I will sing. If I feel sad, I will laugh. If I feel ill, I will double my labour. If I feel fear, I will plunge ahead.' He said Jose had wanted him to excel at sports such as football and swimming, and would hold his head under the water in an attempt to increase the capacity of his lungs.

Gently, however, Lansing also probed him about other aspects of his relationship with his father. She introduced photos said to be of the boys' private parts, and Lyle responded that his father would take such pictures when his sons were in the bath or shower or changing their clothes. He said his father would also talk about soldiers having sex with each other before going into battle, as a way of bonding with each other, and had told Lyle of the special nature of the relationship between a first-born and his father. A hushed courtroom listened intently.

'Between the ages of six and eight, did your father have sexual contact with you?' asked Lansing.

'Yes,' came the reply.

Asked how it started, Lyle talked about being massaged and fondled after sports practices, and then of things becoming 'more involved'. He spoke of oral sex in the bathroom of his home and, when asked if he had ever wanted that, simply shook his head, crying. After several moments during which Lyle sobbed and hid his eyes behind his hand, Lansing continued.

'What else did he do to you?' she asked.

'He raped me,' responded Lyle. 'And he said that he didn't mean to hurt me. He loved me.' His father, Lyle said, had told him it was their secret, and that bad things would happen if he told anyone.

Yet when, at one stage in the questioning, he was asked if he loved his mother and father, he still answered 'Yes.'

Ms Lansing then moved on to the fateful night in August 1989. 'On August 20th 1989, did you and your brother kill your mother and father?' she asked.

The answer was a single word. 'Yes.'

'Did you kill them for money?'

'No.'

'Did you kill them because you wanted to pay them back for the way they had treated you?'

'No.'

'Why did you kill your parents?'

'Because we were afraid.'

Lyle said that Erik had confided to him just days before the killing that the abuse was still going on and after Lyle had gone to his mother with the information but received no support from her, he decided to confront his father and tell him that it had got to stop. His words fell on deaf ears. 'He just said, "You listen to me. What I do with my son is none of your business . . . I warn you, don't throw your life away, just stay out of it" '.

According to Lyle, he then yelled at his father that he would tell the police, and that he would tell the family what was going on. But his father had remained unmoved, telling Lyle that 'We all make choices in life . . . Erik made his, you've made yours.' Then, said Lyle, 'He just looked at me and he got up to leave.'

'What did you think was going to happen?' asked Lansing.

'I thought we were in danger,' replied Lyle. 'I thought . . . he felt he had no choice.'

'But to what?' his attorney wanted to know.

'Kill us,' came the response.

It was, Lyle said, two days later that the final confrontation with his father occurred. Jose and Kitty had disappeared into the den, and he had believed that now they were going ahead with their plans to kill their sons. Lyle ran upstairs to warn Erik of the danger, and together they had loaded their guns and burst into the room, firing as they went. He spoke of noise and smoke and chaos, and of going out and reloading their guns before the final shots at close range. With so much noise they had, he said, expected the police to arrive at any minute. But when nothing happened, they started to think of constructing an alibi. They went out and bought cinema tickets, threw their blood-stained clothing in a skip, and disposed of the guns outside the city. Then, with Erik by this time hysterical, they had returned to the house to make that 911 call to the emergency services.

It was powerful and emotive testimony and public opinion, initially so strongly against the two brothers, gradually began to shift as Lyle Menendez' version of events was told. Now opinions were divided between those who saw his evidence as a fine piece of acting, and those who saw it as proof that child abuse was as rife in wealthy families as it was amongst the poor.

One problem facing the defence was that there was little independent evidence to corroborate Lyle's story. Worse than that, his former fiancée Jamie Pisarcik testified that, while he was awaiting trial, Lyle had asked her to look up some cases for him in the law library and to photocopy them. She noticed that all were instances of children killing their parents, but being acquitted because of previous molestation by their parents.

In addition, state prosecutor Pamela Bozanich played the court a tape recording of the hysterical 911 call in order to illustrate Lyle's ability to lie convincingly. She also questioned his claim to love his mother. 'When you put the shotgun up against her left cheek and you pulled the trigger, did you love your mother?' she wanted to know.

'Yes,' came the answer.

'And was that an act of love, Mr Menendez?' she persisted.

'It was confusion and fear,' he insisted.

Asked why he hadn't simply left home, Lyle argued that with a father like his you just didn't do that sort of thing. And in any case, he still loved him, whatever had happened in the past. In all, Lyle Menendez' testimony lasted nine days. A further two weeks were taken up with Erik's evidence.

He, too, spoke of abuse by his father – abuse that, so he said, had started when he was a young child and had persisted right through his teens, up until the time of his father's death. He testified that it had increased in severity over the years, and spoke of his father sticking tacks into his thighs while giving him oral sex. Again, however, there was little evidence to support Erik's testimony, although a cousin, Andy Cano, did recall a conversation he had had with Erik when Erik was thirteen. 'He asked me if my dad ever gave me massages,' Cano said and, on further questioning, agreed that the massages in question were genital massages. Erik, he said, wanted to know whether such massages were normal between fathers and sons.

Like his brother's, Erik's evidence was both powerful and convincing, but prosecutor Lester Kuriyama set out to damage his credibility by proving that even during the trial Erik had been telling untruths. Erik had claimed that he and Lyle had visited a certain store to buy handguns on the morning of 18 August, but had come away empty-handed. The store had, he maintained, informed them that there was a fifteen-day waiting period before they could collect the guns. According to Kuriyama, however, the store in question had not carried handguns in stock for more than three years at the time of the Menendez brothers' shopping expedition.

The prosecution also pointed out that Jose and Kitty Menendez were actually filling in Erik's university entrance papers at the time of the shootings – hardly the action of parents who were planning to kill that son; the defence never refuted that evidence.

Then there was the evidence of Jerome Oziel. In the seventeenth week of the trial, the judge finally permitted the tapes to be played in court. Oziel himself also testified that in his counselling sessions with the brothers at that time, there had been no intimation of any kind of abuse, and no mention of any threats to the brothers. Nor was there any suggestion that they had killed in self defence. For their part the defence team tried to discredit Oziel by exposing the fact that his licence was on probation at the time of the sessions, and that he had not informed the brothers. He was also questioned about his relationship with Judalon Smyth, and admitted that there had been a sexual element to it. But when Jerome Oziel testified that he firmly believed the Menendez brothers were planning to murder him, it dealt an observably damaging blow to the defence.

Even so, many followers of the case were by now convinced of the veracity of the brothers' story. Thousands of letters of support were pouring in to the defence lawyers, and Lyle himself was receiving anything up to forty a day, some of them even containing proposals of marriage. Trial 'groupies' were turning up at the court each day, hoping that they would be allotted one of just nine spaces reserves for the public. And car bumper stickers proclaiming 'I believe Lyle and Erik' had also sprung up.

Two television films were nearing completion. One, *Honour Thy Father and Mother: The True Story of the Menendez Murders*, was based on the book *Blood Brothers* by Ron Soble (an *LA Times* reporter) and John Johnson. Its stars included Cybill Shepherd as Kitty. The other was a four-hour mini-series under the title *Deadly Games*.

After twenty weeks, the time finally came for the closing arguments for Lyle, with Jill Lansing in tears as she asked for a verdict of involuntary manslaughter to be returned. Closing arguments for Erik followed. The plea of mitigation had, however, been rejected by the judge. There was, he said, no 'direct' need for self-protection – the brothers could simply have left the house.

While the juries retired to consider their verdicts, the controversy continued to rage in the press and in homes throughout the country. There were, for instance, those who believed that killing and maiming could be justified in certain cases, and the defence themselves had drawn parallels with the cases of battered wives who had killed their husbands even when the danger was not strictly imminent. The verdicts would therefore be seen as having implications far beyond this particular trial.

For nearly three weeks Erik's jury reviewed the

evidence; but a unanimous decision was required, so just one dissenting juror would mean that no verdict could be reached. After twenty days, Judge Weisberg finally announced that they were 'hopelessly deadlocked', and duly declared a mistrial. The jury for Lyle were also said to be split, and there can have been little surprise when there, too, a mistrial was declared after a record twenty-five days of deliberation. Los Angeles District Attorney Gil Garcetti, however, made it abundantly clear that he had no intention of letting the case rest there. He vowed that both brothers would be retried for first-degree murder, and the prosecution would be seeking the death penalty. What was more, at the end of February 1994, he promised that the new trial would begin within the next two months.

Now, though, a new factor had been thrown into the equation. That huge amounts of money had been used to line the lawyers' pockets was no surprise, but it was the sheer scale of the fees that staggered even America. Erik's lawyer alone accounted for, according to one report, $790,000; notwithstanding that, Leslie Abramson described the fee as 'inadequate' and estimated that if she were to represent Erik at a further trial it could bankrupt her. With this in mind, Ms Abramson sought to persuade the supervisor of Los Angeles County Criminal Court to pick up her $100 an hour tab out of taxpayers' money. Observing that the lawyers' fees were already 'anything but insubstantial' the judge flatly refused – prompting Ms Abramson to complain that she was being pushed into 'serfdom'. The problem seems to be that the Menendez estate, valued at around $14–$16 million, has already been swallowed up by vast debts, mortgages, taxes and the fees of the tax lawyers that accompany them, and, above all, legal fees. However, the resilient Leslie Abramson had another card up her sleeve. After her successful transformation of the brothers from greedy parricides to abused children deserving of sympathy, Ms Abramson received thousands of letters from people supporting her and the Menendez boys; she is now in the process of mailing those correspondents asking for financial contributions to the Menendez Legal Defence Fund. As one correspondent in *Newsweek* cynically observed: 'Don't let Erik down. Remember: he's an orphan.'

Killed on Duty

KILLED ON DUTY

(Guest contributor: John Bevis)

Whenever there is an apparent miscarriage of justice, the press heaps contempt on the heads of those in the firing line – the police. It is true there have always been a few serving officers who have been over zealous in their pursuit of suspects; true, too, that the 1970s and 80s saw a cancerous spread of corruption in certain forces, which thankfully has now been virtually eliminated. But amidst all this adverse publicity it is easy to forget that the overwhelming majority of police officers are decent, honest public servants doing an unenviable job under increasingly troubled conditions. Those officers often show bravery and heroism beyond the call of duty. No fewer than 20,000 of them are assaulted every year. And sometimes they are called upon to make the ultimate sacrifice – to be killed in the line of duty.

Looking through the files on police homicide, it is apparent the great majority falls within certain categories: drug-related offences, organized crime, terrorism, and what can only be described as 'police-phobia'.

Drug-related Offences

A high-risk crime in the hands of gangsters, drug trafficking is today's equivalent of the protection rackets of the 1950s and 60s. Well-armed criminals are prepared to kill indiscriminately in the battle for their 'pitch': in this case, sales of the lucrative cocaine derivative, crack. 'The combination of drugs, money, firearms and ruthless criminals is very dangerous,' Mr Paul Condon, the Metropolitan Police Commissioner, commented in a BBC

'Newsroom South-east' interview. 'Armed and desperate gangs are locked in a vicious war to control London's drug trade.' In this world life is cheap, and guns and knives are carried as a matter of habit. When, on top of this already volatile situation, the drug dealers may themselves be acting under the influence of drugs, it is no wonder that violence often erupts.

Drug-related crime is on the increase. Property crime in Britain costs the country about £2 billion a year, and half of those offences are drug-related. Whether it is armed gangs protecting their territory, or pathetic addicts stealing to finance their 'habit', the escalation of drug abuse goes hand in hand with remorseless, wasteful crime.

One tragic victim of the drugs war was forty-four-year-old Community PC Patrick Dunne, described by his superior officers as 'a good, honest, kind, gentle, local bobby'. He had had a successful career as a maths teacher and head of year at a comprehensive school in Bolton, Lancashire, before moving to London in 1986 to be closer to his elderly parents. Patrick Dunne took an Open University degree to enhance his chances of getting into the Metropolitan Police, and gave his reasons for wanting to join the force as: 'to help society and contribute to the community aspect of police work'. He was accepted at the age of forty-one, in 1990.

On the evening of 20 October 1993, PC Dunne volunteered to cycle to a house in Cato Road, Clapham, to investigate a burglary. Cato Road, a quiet stretch of red-brick terrace houses, is situated near to Landor Road, which one officer has described as the 'epicentre' of drug dealing in the capital – it is the base for the ruthless Yardie gangs from Jamaica. As PC Dunne entered the house he heard shots from across the road, and rushed out to see three men running towards him. He shouted at them to stop; one of the men turned, and fired a single bullet from a semi-automatic pistol into the constable's chest at point-blank range. Sickeningly, as the gang ran off they were heard to laugh. PC Dunne plunged through a glass door in his efforts to get help, but collapsed; although an ambulance crew succeeded in restarting his heart, the officer was found to be dead on arrival at St Thomas's Hospital.

The other victim of the shooting was Mr William Danso, a night-club and pop concert bouncer in his early thirties. He had been stabbed and shot three times in the stomach, but managed to crawl back into his house and dial 999. He collapsed and died soon after. Danso had recently been under surveillance in connection with a drugs enquiry.

Four men were arrested in the aftermath of the murders. Three of them appeared before South-west London magistrates' court on 29 November 1993, one accused of the two murders, and the others of conspiring to murder William Danso. The charges were dropped on 10 February 1994 through lack of evidence. But on 30 April 1994 it was announced that fresh evidence from an informant, allegedly a member of a Yardie gang, would enable detectives to charge three men with the murder.

Less than five months after the murder of PC Dunne another two police officers were shot in the same area of London. PCs Simon Carroll and Jim Seymour were carrying out a routine vehicle registration check in Rushcroft Road, Brixton, on the evening of 9 March 1994 when the attack occurred. They had spotted a motorcycle in Rushcroft Road, and a radio check revealed that the bike was unregistered. When the two officers left their Sierra patrol car and went to investigate, the pillion passenger tried to escape. PC Carroll moved to stop him, and the biker pulled out a gun from inside his jacket and shot the officer in the leg. Carroll shouted a warning to his colleague to back off, and as PC Seymour turned to radio for assistance he was shot in the back, the bullet passing straight through his body. The gunman fired a final triumphant shot into the air before he and the bike's driver sped off, leaving both officers seriously injured.

Armed Robbery

Statistics show that there has not been an increase in arms-related incidents in recent years. Indeed, the number of armed robberies in London in 1993 fell by 40 per cent compared with the previous year, and the number of shots fired in crime has fallen over the past ten years. But statistics tell only part of the story. There are now criminals 'renting out guns as though they were running a car-hire business', according to Police Commissioner Paul Condon. In February 1994 Merseyside police uncovered a huge cache of guns for hire including Armalite rifles, Czech machine-guns and eight Kalashnikov AK47s, and it is likely that other cities conceal similar arsenals. But the most alarming change in gun-related behaviour is that there appears to be a great willingness to pull the trigger, almost gratuitously. Guns are no longer merely for show.

A chilling testament to the brutality of armed robbers was the murder of Police Sergeant Derek Robertson. Based at South Norwood station, Robertson was 'a popular well-respected supervisor, a very active and enthusiastic policeman and also a very courageous one'. He had been in the force for twenty-one years, and had had a variety of postings, including with the CID. Scotland Yard reported that the sergeant had been injured once before, during racist disturbances at Welling in 1993, but he had carried on working. Derek Robertson had been married for just six weeks to Christine, the mother of his son and daughter.

Robertson responded to a 999 call at 8 a.m. on

9 February 1994, to a sub-post office at Calley Down Crescent, in the tranquil suburb of New Addington. The postmaster, John Brittain, had been surprised by raiders who had broken in and lain in wait for him, and had been able to convey to his wife when she had phoned him that morning that something was wrong. At the scene three officers covered the front of the building while Robertson alone went to the back, where he found three balaclava-clad robbers trying to escape. One of them had a knife and the sergeant was stabbed several times in the chest before collapsing.

A radio call quickly summoned the London Hospital helicopter, and Dr Sean Keogh gave the sergeant open-heart massage on the spot. This emergency procedure, known in medical terms as a phoracotany, involves cutting through the chest bone with a saw and prising the ribs apart. Damage to heart and blood vessels is repaired to stem the flow of blood, and the heart is massaged by hand to keep the blood circulating. Despite this surgery, and a transfusion of some thirty-six pints of blood, Sergeant Robertson died on the operating table at 10.37 that morning.

Three men were arrested at the scene of the crime, and on 11 February 1994 thirty-one-year-old Robin Eades appeared before Croydon magistrates' court charged with murder and the attempted robbery of £29,000. Brothers Christopher John Snelling and Terry David Snelling were also charged with attempted robbery.

Other Organised Crime

Besides drugs and robbery, there is another crime racket widespread enough to involve the use of weapons – illegal immigration. The extent of the problem was revealed in the investigation into the murder of Detective Constable Jim Morrison.

DC Morrison, who had recently been recommended for a bravery award, died after receiving three stab wounds at about 10.25 p.m. on Friday 13 December 1991. He had come off duty at Bow Street station at 6.00 p.m., and had gone for a drink with some colleagues at the Nell Gwynne pub in the Strand. While he was waiting for his wife, who worked at the Theatre Royal in Drury Lane, he spotted a thief and gave chase. At around 10.20 p.m. he was seen struggling with a man in a brown leather bomber jacket outside the London Transport Museum; he threw off his overcoat and chased after the man shouting: 'Stop! Police!' The pursuit continued up Aldwych, past the Waldorf Hotel, and across the road into Montreal Place, where the 'well-groomed' suspect turned and stabbed Morrison. He was rushed to St Bartholomew's Hospital, but died two hours later.

Jim Morrison had enrolled in the Metropolitan Police as a cadet at the age of eighteen; he had been married to his twenty-four-year-old wife Vicky for four years, and would have been twenty-seven just a week after his death. He was described as 'a popular and highly regarded and committed police officer' by one of his superiors, and as 'a fearless individual' by his parents.

Detectives investigating the stabbing uncovered a trail of illegal immigration from Algeria. They interviewed 300 suspects, and discovered half of them to be in the country with bogus papers; many had turned to pick-pocketing, bag-snatching and shoplifting. Jim Morrison had been attached to a squad formed to combat bag snatches, had been responsible for hundreds of arrests and was an expert in spotting the activities of the thieves. On 18 May 1993 a twenty-eight-year-old Algerian was arrested in connection with Morrison's murder.

Terrorism

Despite recent peace initiatives, there remains a very real threat of sectarian violence both in Ireland and on mainland Britain. The police in Ireland, of course, are constantly on alert, and are targets for terrorist attacks both on and off duty. Many are victims of reprisal bombings and shootings. And on mainland Britain the IRA have scored recent 'successes' with the spectacular and obscene bombings at Warrington and the City of London, as well as a showpiece rocket attack at London's Heathrow airport in March 1994. Consequently the Metropolitan Police have thrown a cordon around the City, with random road checks of suspect vehicles, and routine checks have uncovered a number of loads of high explosives carried by vans and lorries in the London area. Despite these successes, lives are still at risk – the lives of police officers in particular.

A reminder of that danger occurred in June 1992, on the A64 near Tadcaster, North Yorkshire. PC Alexander 'Sandy' Kelly and Special Constable Glenn Goodman had stopped a Sierra car for a routine check when their suspicions were aroused by the occupants of the vehicle, who both spoke with Irish accents. PC Kelly returned to his patrol car to make a radio check, and saw the Sierra's passenger get out and walk to the side of the road. 'I presumed he was going to urinate,' Kelly recalled. 'The next thing I saw, he was standing with both hands in what I can only describe as the combat position. He was pointing the gun straight at SC Goodman. I did not hear anything but I saw two flashes from the barrel of the gun and presumed he had shot Goodman twice. I saw two holes appear in the windscreen in front of me and felt pain in my chest.' PC Kelly slumped to the passenger seat, and looked up to see the gunman once more pointing his weapon at him. 'He shot me again in the right-hand side of my body. At that time I did not know how many shots – there seemed to be a lot.'

PC Kelly played dead until the Sierra roared away, then got on the radio. Using the code name Echo Tango 24, he shouted 'Ten-nine, ten-nine' – the police term for SOS. 'We've been shot, we've been shot, we've been shot!' Alexander Kelly had four bullets in his body. Glenn Goodman was already dead.

Two suspects were picked up after a car chase in which a constable and a woman police officer were fired at, and in March 1993 forty-six-year-old Paul Magee and thirty-three-year-old Michael O'Brien, both IRA terrorists from Belfast, appeared in the dock at the Old Bailey. Each was jailed for life, for murder and attempted murder.

Glenn Goodman's funeral service was held at Selby Abbey. Representatives of almost every police force in the country turned out to hear the Bishop of Selby, the Rt Rev. Humphrey Taylor, describe the officer as 'a fine man, loving husband, father and son, who was killed in the prime of life'. He left a widow, Fiona, and an eleven-month-old son, Tom.

A very sad footnote to this tragedy was that another police officer, village bobby Joe Hinchliff, was also scarred by the event. He was one of the first on the scene, and travelled to hospital in the ambulance with PC Kelly. Later he had the unenviable task of breaking the news of her husband's death to Fiona Goodman. Hinchliff was profoundly affected by the traumatic event and, with his marriage already collapsed and his life seemingly in ruins, he took to drink. Eventually he was caught driving near Eggborough, Selby, with almost double the legal blood-alcohol limit. He was fined £300, banned for a year, and summoned to appear before a disciplinary hearing of the North Yorkshire police.

'A magnet for hostility'

It is not only terrorists who make random attacks on police officers because of *what*, rather than *who*, they are. Police are also under threat from the disturbed, the psychopathic, the frenzied mob. In some people's minds, when there is no other body to take the blame, it is the police who become – by default – the scapegoats for their grievances. Be it a quite legitimate complaint about a genuine injustice, or the violent abuse of a deranged mentality, it is all too often the police who are 'the bastards'. As a Los Angeles police sergeant put it: 'Cops have become a magnet for hostility.'

A report commissioned after the murder of no fewer than fifty-six officers in the USA in 1992 drew a bleak conclusion: 'good cops' are more likely to be killed. From interviews with fifty convicted murderers, FBI psychologists have constructed a profile of the typical victim officer: friendly, hard-working, tending to use less force than his colleagues, and to look for good in others. Hardened criminals revealed to the psychologists how there was a tacit struggle for control at the initial moment of confrontation between officer and suspect. If the policeman did not immediately establish the upper hand, the criminal might feel entitled to set his own agenda. One deputy sheriff let a prisoner he was transporting back to jail sit in the front seat because he had promised to co-operate. When the deputy stopped the car to help a woman who had broken down, the prisoner snatched his revolver and shot him dead.

The most notorious instance in recent years was the killing of PC Keith Blakelock on 6 October 1985 at Broadwater Farm estate near Tottenham, north London, during riots which followed the death from a heart attack of Cynthia Jarrett after a police raid on her home. Blakelock, a friendly, easy-going community bobby, was escorting some firemen at the height of the riot when he was separated from them and surrounded by a screaming mob of up to 150 people. A central core of forty-odd aggressors lashed out at him with knives, swords and machetes. He fell, fatally wounded, with forty-two savage cuts to his body.

A massive police investigation was put under way, more than 3,000 officers taking part. They netted no fewer than 369 arrests, and made 167 charges. Forty-two separate trials were held at the Old Bailey. Three men were convicted of murder, and forty others served from one to six years on lesser charges.

But, on 25 November 1991, Winston Silcott was cleared of murdering PC Blakelock. Engin Raghip and Mark Braithwaite, the others convicted of the murder, were released two days later, Silcott remaining inside on a life sentence for killing Tony Smith, a professional boxer. Two key Crown witnesses, Detective Chief Superintendent Graham Melvin and Detective Inspector Maxwell Dingle, were committed for trial charged with perjury and conspiracy to pervert the course of justice.

Consequently Elizabeth Blakelock, the policeman's widow, appealed to Peter Imbert, the then Metropolitan Police Commissioner, to instigate an inquiry. It fell to Commander Perry Nove to head the investigation. He was well aware that community relations had been poisoned by the armed raids which had become a daily occurrence at Broadwater Farm after the murder. He had to handle the case with kid gloves, and it is to his credit that his team of fifteen detectives interviewed hundreds of people without there resulting a single complaint. It was Nove's vision to get the estate and the community back to normal. 'There is still a perception that Broadwater Farm is a place where people riot. This is deeply offensive to the normal, decent people who live on the estate.'

Commander Nove set about enabling 'quality' dialogue, 'so the person was not compromised, waiting until we could speak to them alone'. Witnesses were taken in unmarked cars to King's Cross police station, where they were shown police and television videos of the riot. Their evidence was itself recorded on video. All those who were not implicated in actually attacking Keith Blakelock with a bladed instrument were granted immunity from prosecution by the Crown Prosecution Service. Because of this amnesty, police were able to gather invaluable evidence from people who had assaulted PC Blakelock or other officers, who had looted shops or thrown petrol bombs.

In February 1994 the police inquiry closed, with the conclusion that the identities were known of about a dozen people who had struck Blakelock with sharp weapons, but not the individual who delivered the fatal blow to his neck. The report recommended that there was enough evidence to prosecute up to half a dozen suspects. The final decision on whether to charge anyone rests with the Director of Public Prosecutions, Barbara Mills QC, who when practising at the Bar had acted as Winston Silcott's defence counsel at the 1987 Old Bailey trial.

Another brutal and random attack on a police officer occurred on an estate in Gateshead, Tyne and Wear, on 20 March 1993. Twenty-six-year-old Paul Weddle and sixteen-year-old Philip English were among a group of young people who had spent the day gathered around a bonfire in a woodland clearing, drinking alcohol, taking sleeping pills and sniffing lighter fluid. In a 'wrecked' state the two youths went to the Sunniside home of Weddle's former girlfriend, fifteen-year-old Nicola Robinson, and smashed a window with a fence post. The girl's call for police assistance was answered by Sergeant Bill Forth and his patrol colleague, PC Bill Hay.

The officers separated at Sunniside, Sgt Forth going to

a grassed area at the back of the house where he encountered Weddle and English. He approached them coolly, trying to calm the belligerent youngsters by saying: 'Now lads, now boys, come on.'

But the response of the youths was far from calm. Shouting 'Kill him, kill him', they launched an attack so sudden and so ferocious that the officer had no time even to draw his truncheon, Weddle lashing out with a fence post and stabbing at the sergeant with a knife while English, standing behind him, rained blows on his head with a lump of wood. Forth's legs buckled under him and he slumped to the ground, screaming out in pain. As PC Hay arrived on the scene English ran off and was quickly arrested, but even then Weddle continued stabbing at Sgt Forth's legs and back, not giving up on the attack until a man with a rolling pin went to the policeman's aid. Bill Forth died soon afterwards.

At Teesside Crown Court on 17 February 1994, Paul Weddle and Philip English were found guilty of murder. Weddle was jailed for life, while English, as a juvenile, was sentenced to be detained at Her Majesty's pleasure. Mr Justice Owen told the accused: 'I regard offences against police officers as particularly heinous.' Northumbria Chief Constable John Stevens said after the verdict: 'His death emphasises just how dangerous everyday policing is for all officers.' And the policeman's widow, Mrs Gill Forth, said: 'I just thank God that justice has been done. I don't believe in capital punishment but I believe life should mean life, and they should stay behind bars for the rest of their lives.'

Ironically, Bill Forth had been planning to leave the force because he was disillusioned and angered by lenient sentences which he felt were letting down officers on the front line. It had been his ambition to take a psychology degree course at Sunderland University.

Officers as Citizens – the Other Side of the Coin

Police officers are expected to display exemplary behaviour at all times, but like the rest of us they are human and fallible.

Detective Constable James Bourke was a fifty-year-old divorcé attached to the West Midlands police force. It was his habit to play classical music, and occasionally pop music too, at a high volume, sometimes late at night. Usually he opened his windows, which made his unsocial behaviour all the worse. In the first week of September 1993 police were called twice to his flat in Quinton, Birmingham, after a neighbour complained about the noise; on the 10th day of that month they were called out to investigate a more serious disturbance. DC Bourke had been found in his blood-stained hallway, his head so badly bludgeoned he was barely recognisable. There was a hole on the right side of his skull which looked as if it could have been made by a bullet.

Maureen Ball, a neighbour who lived three doors away, was used to being disturbed by the loud music. On the night in question she heard 'a row and commotion and raised voices', and later saw 'the man from the top flat stuffing clothes into his car. He sped off so quickly his tyres were squealing at the top of the road.' Police later arrested the occupant of the flat above Bourke's, Jeffrey Gould, a fifty-two-year-old toolmaker. It was Gould who had borne the brunt of the excessive noise.

In contrast to the case of DC Bourke, who was merely unsociable in trying to relieve his loneliness, Police Sergeant Stephen Jones turned to murder in an attempt to solve his marital problems. The thirty-four-year-old sergeant wanted to leave his wife Madallin, a mother of two, because he was having a secret affair with teenage barmaid Julie Rutherford. Worried about how a divorce could harm his chances of promotion, and tempted by the prospect of £60,000 life insurance, 'Smudge' Jones used his police experience to try to commit the 'perfect murder'.

On Sunday 3 January 1993, he lured his wife into the garage at their home in Carlines Avenue, Ewloe, Clwyd, where he killed her with a single blow of his truncheon, and put a bin-liner over her upper body to prevent any tell-tale signs of blood. He then drove his wife's red Metro car along the A550 to Tinkers Dale Wood, a beauty spot two miles away, where he crashed the vehicle through a hedge and down a wooded bank into a tree, protecting himself from injury by wearing his police riot helmet. The sergeant then smashed the windscreen with a hammer, removed the bin-liner and dragged his wife's body into an icy stream close by. After that, it was a simple matter for Jones to jog back to his own car which previously he had parked nearby, return home and raise the alarm because his wife was late home.

At this point the scenario for the 'perfect murder' went awry. A young couple had spotted the Metro shortly after the 'accident', and made a 999 call. Inspector Gareth Jones insisted on spending the night with Stephen Jones and his two sons to console them. The murderer put on a show of crying with grief, but perhaps he was more upset because the presence of the inspector was preventing him from disposing of incriminating evidence.

The suspicions of forensic scientists were first aroused because the Metro's driver's seat had been pushed well back to accommodate Jones's six-foot frame, and it would have been impossible for his 4′11″ wife to have driven the car. Three impact points on the car were inconsistent with Mrs Jones's single head injury, and there had been no contact between her head and the windscreen, which had been broken from the outside. It was inconceivable that she could have been thrown yards from the car into the stream. A routine search uncovered the blood-stained bin-liner in the boot of Jones's Rover car, together with his truncheon, with fresh blood on it, and the riot helmet.

At Caernarvon Crown Court on 25 November 1993, Stephen Jones was jailed for life for the murder of his wife. After the sentence had been passed David Owen, the chief constable of North Wales, commented: 'The investigation was carried out with a degree of thoroughness and impartiality, and this reflected highly on the professionalism and integrity of the police officers involved.'

Protection

After her husband's murder, Mrs Gill Forth was at the forefront of a campaign for body armour for the police. In autumn 1993 she presented a 20,000-signature petition to Home Secretary Michael Howard. 'I don't believe all policemen should be armed,' she said, 'but I do want the campaign in Northumbria for protective vests for police officers to be spread to the rest of the country.' In view of Mrs Forth's enlightened and progressive campaigning for reform, it was particularly distressing to learn on 1 May 1994 that the widow and her eight-year-old daughter had been forced to move from their home in Sunderland after receiving a series of menacing and obscene telephone calls.

The Kevlar body armour is now being issued to front-line officers by the Derbyshire force. In Greater Manchester, police are committed to wearing their own body armour, and in the notorious Moss Side area even the ambulance service is testing the feasibility of wearing flak jackets. This seems an eminently sensible move in the face of the increasingly defensive nature of modern policing. The question of arming police officers is a more controversial one, and one which is resisted by the Association of Chief Police Officers. About 5 per cent of officers in each force have been trained to use firearms; the number in the Met is 1,800, most of them involved in diplomatic protection duties with some attached to the Flying Squad, Anti-Terrorist Squad and Special Branch.

Rather than arming policemen on the beat, current practice is to deploy armed response vehicles (ARVs) to protect unarmed officers as well as to contain the criminals. The ARV Rover 827s are equipped to carry two Heckler & Koch single-shot carbines, ballistic shields and powerful searchlights. The crew are armed with model 10 Smith & Wesson handguns. Body protection includes riot shields, ceramic helmets, gas masks and a body suit which is proof against petrol bombs and some chemicals.

Every police force in the country is now equipped with ARVs, although only in small numbers. In the capital there are just four or five ARVs on duty at any one time, manned from a pool of about 100 trained officers, but Metropolitan Commissioner Paul Condon announced in February 1994 that Scotland Yard would increase that manpower by 30–40 per cent. At the same time seven out of twelve chief constables throughout the country said they wanted more ARVs.

Sentencing

Police officers suffer crimes against the person as an occupational hazard, and because of this there has been for many years a body of opinion that believes such crimes should carry more punitive sentences. Ever since abolition a minority has called for the return of capital punishment for the murder of officers on duty. It has to be said that there is no evidence that this would act as a deterrent, and indeed crime figures from the USA indicate that the re-introduction of the death penalty has not prevented policemen from being killed. The value of capital punishment as a means of satisfying society's demand for retribution is highly questionable, as it would only tend to escalate a cycle of vengeance and counter-vengeance between the law and the criminal. The violence of outlawed sectarian 'justice' in Northern Ireland demonstrates the futility of the creed of 'an eye for an eye, a tooth for a tooth'.

Perhaps the strongest argument against capital punishment is its finality – in the event of a miscarriage of justice, it cannot be revoked. A salutary reminder of this was the prosecution of three men for the murder of PC Tony Salt outside an illegal drinking club in Birmingham in March 1989. In 1991 charges against the men – Tony Francis, Peter Gibb and Mark Samuels – were dropped, when pathologists found that PC Salt's death had been accidental resulting from the officer falling and striking his neck against a mechanical digger. Labour MP Chris Mullin claimed that members of West Midlands serious crimes squad had extracted 'fraudulent confessions' from the men under duress, had threatened to plant drugs at the home of one of them, and had 'connived in the disappearance of inconvenient evidence'.

In the absence of the capital option, there have been demands – not least from Mrs Gill Forth, herself the widow of a murdered officer – that 'life should mean life'. Under current legislation murder carries a mandatory life sentence, and the minimum term of imprisonment is at the discretion of the trial judge, the Lord Chief Justice, and ultimately the Home Secretary. It seems quite just and appropriate that the recommendations of those august authorities should be in favour of the maximum term for the murderers of police officers. In 1993 a Home Office spokeswoman said that 'There is no real policy on police killers, except that they should serve a minimum of twenty years, as laid down by Leon Brittan in 1983.'

Lest it should be thought that a life sentence does *not* mean a permanent restriction of freedom, the case of police killer Tony Jeffs demonstrates otherwise. Jeffs, driven by 'a pathological hatred of police', broke into a Coventry gun shop in July 1972, deliberately triggered the burglar alarm and laid in wait to kill an officer. That officer was PC Peter Guthrie, newly wed and just twenty-one years old, who was wasted by a shotgun wound to his chest. When, to the outrage of MPs, police federation chiefs and the dead officer's family, Jeffs was released in April 1993 after serving twenty years, he was only the second police murderer to be freed. (The first was John Witney who left jail in 1992, having been sentenced to thirty years for his part in the murder of three policemen in Shepherd's Bush in 1966.) Tony Jeffs was completely unrepentant and showed no remorse or regret as he celebrated his freedom and said: 'I might be sorry for shooting that copper – but I might not.' In February 1994 Jeffs was locked up again on the orders of Home Secretary Michael Howard. He had not re-offended, but his parole licence was revoked 'because of concerns over the risk he might have posed by remaining at liberty'. It is unlikely that Tony Jeffs will be allowed a second opportunity to celebrate freedom.

Epitaph

Perhaps the most dignified and courageous testament to an officer killed on duty was that delivered by Christine Robertson at the scene of her husband Derek's murder at New Addington. On 10 February 1994 she took their two children to the spot where he fell, in a brave attempt to explain to them how their father had died doing the job he loved. Standing before a blanket of floral tributes outside the sub-post office, she said: 'Derek was a dignified, gracious and thoroughly decent man. Our son Frazer, and our daughter Sasha and I want everyone to know we are very, very proud of him. We loved him very much and shall go on loving him. We shall miss him more than any words can ever express, and we know that his colleagues and friends feel the same way too.'

Postscript

On 16 May 1994, Metropolitan Police Commissioner Paul Condon announced that the streets of London were to be patrolled for the first time by policemen openly carrying guns. This was in response to a review following the murders of PC Patrick Dunne and Sgt Derek Robertson, and was designed to boost morale in the force. In fact the new regulation applies only to officers of the armed response vehicles, which have been doubled in number. There will in future be a minimum of *twelve* ARVs patrolling London at any time, each manned by three highly trained officers. They will carry Smith & Wesson revolvers in visible side holsters, and will be able to use them without authority from a senior officer. But they will still require high-level permission before drawing their Heckler & Koch machine guns.

At the same time Mr Condon announced that the 22-inch plastic baton was to be introduced as an alternative to the traditional wooden truncheon. The new batons were to go on trial at four stations for eight months; tests continue on the 24-inch and 26-inch models. Further evaluations are also to be made on bullet- and stab-proof vests, which are currently issued in Brixton and the Chapeltown district of Leeds. The final ingredient of Mr Condon's package was the testing of pepper sprays, aerosols containing oleoresin capsicum extracted from chilli peppers, which cause disorientation, breathing problems and burning sensations in the eyes. Fears have been expressed about the spray's effects if used against an asthmatic, and the possibility that it may be carcinogenic.

Although confused media coverage of the new measures led many to *believe* erroneously that large numbers of uniformed policemen patrolling the streets of London on foot would in future be routinely armed, on the whole the announcement received greater approval from the general public than from serving officers. One senior policeman at New Scotland Yard was alarmed at the potential for accidents and bad judgement, as well as the danger that officers would be overpowered and their weapons taken from them. 'Imagine a situation where two armed officers are set upon by a crowd in a sensitive inner-city estate,' he said. 'What are they going to do if the crowd does not back off? If they shoot someone, there could well be a horrendous public order situation. If they don't, they are in danger of being attacked and maybe even shot with their own weapons. *Routine arming raises the stakes*.'

Whatever the outcome of this debate, it will be too late to save the life of one young Scottish policeman. On 17 June 1994, PC Lewis Fulton and Sgt William Blair answered a routine call to assist colleagues involved in an incident in the Glasgow Gorbals. The two officers attempted to disarm an eighteen-year-old youth when PC Fulton was stabbed to death and Sgt Blair was wounded. A police officer for nine years, twenty-eight-year-old Lewis Fulton left a wife and a seven-month-old son.

Children Who Kill

INTRODUCTION

(Guest contributor: John Bevis)

The murder of James Bulger on 12 February 1993 was considered to be particularly disturbing because it was so 'unusual'. Only the case of Mary Bell, some twenty-five years earlier, seemed to offer a parallel. But statistics tell a rather different story. In England and Wales as many as ten to fifteen young people are convicted of murder every year. And between 1982 and 1991, on average one child aged under five was killed every week. The vast majority of these were killed by somebody known to them, usually their parents, and often in ways no less grotesque than the death of James Bulger. On average there was one killing of an infant by a stranger every year.

In the United States the problem of juvenile homicide has begun to reach epidemic proportions. One in every six murders in 1991 was committed by a teenager, with 2,465 minors being arrested for homicide. There is no doubt that the trend for carrying guns and knives, almost as fashion accessories, has contributed to the escalation of violent deaths.

Juveniles appearing before English courts charged with a serious crime such as murder, manslaughter, arson or rape, are dealt with under Section 53 of the 1933 Children and Young Persons Act. This provides a mandatory life sentence for those convicted of murder, while offences attracting an adult sentence of fourteen years or more, such as attempted murder or manslaughter, carry terms of detention up to the adult maximum.

The minimum age of criminal responsibility is a somewhat arbitrary demarcation. It is usually set somewhere between the ages of eight and fourteen, but varies from one jurisdiction to another, is often lower for more serious crimes, and may be liable to review from time to time. For example, the age at which boys may be prosecuted for rape in England and Wales was reduced from fourteen to ten on 20 September 1993. Ten years of age is the absolute minimum for criminal responsibility here, which means that if the murder of James Bulger had been committed only eight months earlier, Jon Venables and Robert Thompson would have been too young to stand trial. Indeed, no charges could be brought against two boys from Wolverhampton who admitted in 1978 to battering eighty-four-year-old Mrs Katherine Willits to death with a brick. Although police said it was murder no charges could be brought because of the boys' ages – six and four.

The minimum age was raised from eight to ten in the 1963 Children and Young Persons Act, after the acquittal of an eight-year-old boy charged with murdering his seventeen-month-old brother. Its crying kept disturbing him as he was trying to do his homework at their home on the Isle of Wight, so he hit the baby on the head with its feeding bottle. The prosecution felt it could not sustain an argument against the presumption of innocence, offered no evidence, and the case was dismissed.

Because of that strong presumption of innocence of intent in children between the ages of ten and fourteen, many who kill are convicted of manslaughter rather than murder. Recent cases include a twelve-year-old babysitter from Blyth, Northumberland, found guilty in March 1992 of the manslaughter of eighteen-month-old Sean Graham who would not stop crying; and a boy aged eleven, charged with the manslaughter of ninety-three-year-old widow Rosetta Fort of Dagenham, Essex, in June 1992.

Professor Dewey Cornell of the University of Virginia has made a study of over 200 child murderers, and found that children kill for petty reasons, often on impulse, with a bland cynicism and rarely any show of remorse. A classic case supporting this thesis was the murder of taxi driver Yves Quettant in West Palm Beach, Florida, in January 1994. His passenger, a thirteen-year-old girl, shot him in the back of the head – to avoid a $6 fare. Another instance occurred in the Shandong province of China in November 1992, when an eight-year-old boy laced his mother's porridge with rat poison after she refused to buy him a toy car. Hearing him confess to the murder, the boy's father threw him across the room, killing him instantly. The distraught man then drank liquid fertiliser and died.

Some murders seem to be without any obvious motive. One such case occurred on 29 October 1993, just three days before the James Bulger case came to court. In the Paris suburb of Vitry-sur-Seine three boys aged between eight and ten kicked and beat a tramp known as 'Pierrot' before throwing him to his death down a well. No charges could be brought as French law decrees an age of responsibility of thirteen. The previous month, in California, an apparently normal middle-class twelve-year-old boy walked into Sam's Bicycle Shop and cold-bloodedly shot dead the owner, Jung Sam Woo. He later bragged of the victim 'twitching in his own blood'. Convicted and sentenced to twenty-five years to life, the youth must be released when he turns twenty-five, under the provision of California state law. In cases such as these, the perpetration of a violent crime may be the first outward sign of some repressed mental disturbance or profound stress.

It is more usual for a murder to be committed for a purpose, and one of the commonest motives is the lust for revenge. A horrific instance occurred in Jefferson County, Madison, on the night of Friday 10 January 1992. Four teenage girls lured twelve-year-old Shanda Renee

Sharer into a car, bound and gagged her, slashed her legs, battered and sexually abused her with a tyre lever, doused her in petrol and burnt her alive. She had been accused of 'trying to steal' the affections of the girlfriend of Melinda Loveless, one of the accused. Dr Charles Ewing has pointed out that it is rare for girls to kill, but when they do 'they usually do it in a group, with accomplices. Many girls "overkill" their victims, using more force than is needed. A kind of one-upmanship among the group comes into play, which evolves into a brutal homicide.'

Boys, too, often kill together. A recent example was the shooting of thirty-nine-year-old Lonnie Dutton in Rush Springs, Oklahoma, on 12 July 1993. Dutton was a hard-drinking bully who submitted his family to appalling deprivation. He would thrash his wife Marie with hoses and pistols, and force the children to throw darts at her. His family deserted Dutton in 1989, but amazingly he won custody of the children who were forced to return to his wretched trailer. He treated them like slaves, beating the boys and sexually abusing their ten-year-old sister. It came as no surprise when the two eldest boys, twelve-year-old Druie and his elder brother Herman, put a deer-hunting rifle to their father's head while he slept. As one of them aimed the firearm the other pulled the trigger and shot him at point-blank range. The boys await trial at the time of writing, and are liable to face detention in a juvenile facility until the age of nineteen if found guilty.

Similar cases of the revenge killing of an adult, usually a parent, are not uncommon. Murder charges against an eleven-year-old boy from Mansfield, Nottinghamshire, in 1990 were dropped after the coroner recorded a verdict of lawful killing, finding that the boy had stabbed his father to protect his mother from attack. The same year a boy of the same age was found guilty of the manslaughter of his 'tyrannical' father, whom he shot at their remote farmhouse in Rossendale Valley, Lancashire.

Murder often occurs as a complication of some other felony, such as housebreaking or rape. A disturbing case occurred in Houston, Texas, in June 1993. Two teenage girls, Jennifer Ertman and Elizabeth Pena, were taking a short cut home from a party through some woods when they stumbled into the path of six members of the Black N White gang. The teenage gang was initiating two new members with a drinking and fighting induction ceremony. All six stripped and raped the girls repeatedly, finally strangling them with belts and shoelaces. After their arrest, the gang members showed no remorse, seeming even to revel in their moment of notoriety.

Finally there are those murders which seem to be committed as an experiment in cruelty. A twelve-year-old boy from Glasgow battered a three-year-old boy with a stone and drowned him in a stream in 1992. He has been detained indefinitely on a conviction of culpable homicide. The case of Mary Bell was, of course, the most notorious before the Bulger case. Mary, aged eleven, was accused with thirteen-year-old Norma Bell at the Court of Assizes in Newcastle of the manslaughter of four-year-old Martin Brown in May 1968, and of three-year-old Brian Howe two months later. It was alleged by the prosecution that the girls had murdered 'solely for the pleasure and excitement afforded by killing'. Norma was acquitted, but Mary was found guilty on two counts of manslaughter on grounds of diminished responsibility. She was released in January 1980 on 'life licence'. Now aged thirty-six, she has a new identity and a nine-year-old daughter.

The problem of what to do with young offenders has always provoked controversy. In February 1993, in the wake of the James Bulger case, the Home Secretary announced proposals to grant courts the power to lock up 'really persistent, nasty little juvenile offenders'. Sir Ivan Lawrence, chairman of the all-party Home Affairs Select Committee, recommended 'a return to the approved schools where they are punished, taught discipline and educated'. But it has been claimed that youngsters who attended approved schools, which were abolished in 1969, 'emerged 50 per cent more likely to commit further crimes'. Certainly a punitive regime imposed throughout the formative years of convicted juveniles, many of them immature, would not help them to integrate into society on their eventual release. If the killers of James Bulger are, like Mary Bell, one day to walk free, we must be sure they have first learned social responsibility.

Postscript

A grim tale of young serial killers emerged from Moscow in the spring of 1994. Ten-year-old Volodya Yakovlev and his thirteen-year-old brother Vitya claim to have killed six *bomzhi*, the down-and-outs who live around the capital's railway stations. They murdered one of their victims by smashing his head with paving stones after he had refused to give them a light for a cigarette, and another at Strogino station after he had refused to pay a fine for fare-dodging. They claim to have killed three men in the town of Oryol, although police say they invented the murders. But the boys, who live with their certified mentally ill mother Svetlana in a squalid, mould-encrusted high-rise flat, cannot be brought to justice. Under Russian law, crimes committed by children under fourteen years old are the responsibility of their mothers. Only fourteen-year-old Andrei, the eldest Yakovlev brother who was also present at the killings, has been detained and will be brought to trial.

THE TRAGIC DEATH OF JAMES BULGER

Susan Venables packed her ten-year-old son Jon off to St Mary's primary school as usual on Friday 12 February 1993. He was a bit late leaving, hurrying out of the door just before nine o'clock, saying he was looking forward to bringing home the school gerbils for half term. What made him change his mind we do not know. In any event, Jon hid his school bag in some shrubbery and walked to the nearby Liverpool suburb of Walton where, by accident or design, he bumped into his friend Robert Thompson.

The two boys were 'sagging' – slacking off school – and headed for Bootle, two miles distant. The shop assistant at Clinton Cards, in the new Strand shopping precinct, was the first of many locals to question them that day. Why were they not at school, she asked? And exactly which school did they attend? Bobby and Jon ran off. They were out for a lark, pinching stuff and as quickly discarding it: pens, sweets, toys, tins of food. The boys were noticed at 1.40 p.m. 'shouting and acting stupid', and later in the afternoon, at about 3.15 p.m., pestering an elderly lady, prodding and poking her until she had to swing at them with her shopping bag.

Another woman, sitting on a bench outside Boots, noticed the youths walking out of T.J. Hughes, followed by a small child. It seemed to her they were goading the infant into following them. When the little boy's mother appeared, calling for him, Jon and Bobby made themselves scarce.

Their next port of call was Tesco where the miscreants waited for an assistant to turn her back before making off with some tins of Humbrol enamel paint. It was while they were fooling around with the paint outside A.R. Timm's, the butchers, that they spotted a little boy in a blue anorak. Jon Venables had the idea of approaching him. 'Come on, baby,' he said. Jon and Bobby led the toddler away, out of the shopping centre. It was 3.43 p.m.

At almost exactly the same time Neil Venables arrived at St Mary's to collect his son, only to be told Jon had been absent from school all day. The concerned father reported the boy missing at Walton Lane police station, then alerted his wife. Although they were divorced the Venables were trying for a reconciliation, and doing their utmost to provide a caring environment for their three somewhat difficult children. Jon's brother and sister had to attend a special school for pupils with learning difficulties, while Jon himself had been suspended from his last school and was now in the year below his age. An affectionate boy, he was shy and timid, but easily led. In the words of his mother: 'If you told him to put his hand in the fire he would.' Perhaps he modelled himself too closely on his brother and sister, for his conduct at school was often wildly inappropriate. He was unruly and disruptive, and occasionally violent. Sometimes he would throw things at his classmates, or cut himself deliberately with scissors. His bizarre behaviour – whining and making strange noises, banging his head on the furniture, pulling displays off the classroom walls – greatly concerned his teachers. The school had been in touch with his mother, but she thought he was merely 'hyperactive'. She did not know that, since he had palled up with Robert Thompson, Jon had begun to play truant.

Susan Venables had to search the streets that Friday evening for several hours, shouting Jon's name in the dark. Finally, some time after 6.45 p.m., she tracked down the truants in a video store. They'd been absent all day, up to goodness knows what mischief, and here they were, their clothes dirty and muddy and stained with blue enamel paint, *watching cartoons*. Angry but relieved, Mrs Venables grabbed Jon by the hair, Bobby by the wrist, and dragged the urchins outside. Bobby Thompson collapsed sobbing on the pavement before making good his escape, while Jon was frog-marched to Walton Lane police station, where his mother insisted the duty officer give her son a good ticking off.

When Robert Thompson got home that evening he showed his mother a scratch on his face. Mrs Venables had done it, he accused. Down to the police station Ann Thompson stormed – the same one, Walton Lane. 'What are you going to do about this?', she demanded of the duty officer, parading the wounded Bobby in front of the counter. The policeman thought grounds for a complaint of assault against Sue Venables were probably insufficient.

Ann Thompson had something of a reputation, deserved or not, of being unable to look after her children. She was regarded by some as 'a moaner, a troublemaker and a fighter'. But fortune had shone sparingly on the thirty-nine years of her life. She had been beaten by her father, up until a week before her marriage at eighteen. The husband was a drinker who eventually walked out in October 1988, prompting Ann herself to take heavily to drink for eighteen months. She had lost control of her four eldest sons, who were taken into care by Liverpool social services. And then the house had burnt down. Now Ann had only Robert and his two younger brothers staying at home, in the terrace house they rented from Liverpool Housing Trust. By this time Robert was known as a sly, manipulative boy, a natural liar who frequently played truant. He had few friends. It was rumoured that he was cruel to animals, and bullied his younger siblings just as he himself had been bullied. And at school he had acquired a rather sinister nickname – Damien.

Over the coming weekend the main item of news was the disappearance of an infant aged just two years and ten months from the Strand shopping centre in Bootle. Photos in the press and on television showed a happy, fresh-faced little boy with a cheeky grin and a sparkle in his eyes. His name was James Bulger, and he had been taken to the precinct by his mother Denise and her sister-in-law, Nicola Bailey, who had wanted to change some clothes. Denise first noticed the little boy was not by her side at 3.38 p.m.; she had panicked and raced out of the shop. Jamie was nowhere to be seen. He had vanished.

Jon Venables read about the incident in the *Sun*, read every word of the report. 'Is there any more news on little James?', he kept asking his mother. 'Have they got them yet?'

Bobby Thompson, too, was taking an unusual interest in the tragedy. He watched the television news items, when Denise Bulger made a tearful and impassioned plea for the return of her son. Stills from a video security camera in the Strand shopping centre showed two boys apparently leading James away by the hand. 'That doesn't half look like you,' said his mother. 'Where were you on Friday?'

On Sunday 14 February, at 7.30 in the morning, a freight train was travelling from Edge Hill to Bootle. The driver saw something on the line – he wasn't sure quite what it was, but it stuck in his mind, and he reported it at the depot later in the afternoon. But by then the police already knew what the driver had seen. At 3.15 p.m. four teenagers had raced in to Walton Lane police station crying: 'Quick, quick, someone is dead out there.' An action squad of officers on the case tore out of the station and followed fourteen-year-old Terence Riley to the nearby railway embankment.

James Bulger had been beaten to death. He had suffered multiple fractures of the skull, caused by a series of twenty-two blows with heavy blunt objects. A patterned bruise on the right cheek suggested a severe blow from a shoe. His lower lip was partly torn away. There were a further twenty bruises and cuts to the body, on the shoulders, elbows, ribs, thighs, knees and feet. There was blue-grey enamel paint on the left side of the face, and large amounts of brick dust and pieces of brick on the clothing and around the head, partly covering the face. The body had been severed by the wheels of a train, the torso coming to rest some six railway sleepers distant from the lower body. The lower body was naked. The boy's trousers were found between the tracks, while his socks and shoes were scattered along the line. Further down the track was a tin of blue paint, a box of chocolates and some sweets.

A shock wave of grief, anger, revulsion and above all sheer incomprehension stunned the nation. Rewards totalling more than £40,000 were offered for information leading to the arrest and conviction of the killers. Police warned: 'For goodness' sake keep tight hold of your children.' Shops sold out of children's safety harnesses. Technicians from IBM and the BBC wrestled with the fuzzy video stills, trying to read between the pixels to create an enhanced image of Jamie's abductors. And in Bootle friends and neighbours and total strangers showered floral tributes outside the butchers where James had been snatched, and near the embankment where his body was found. Among those tributes was one single red rose, placed there, in an act of chilling hypocrisy, by the hand of Robert Thompson.

Detective Superintendent Albert Kirby led the massive police operation, beginning with house-to-house inquiries, a poster campaign, and the scanning of the truancy records from local schools. Officers compiled lists of known troublemakers from their own patches. Friends and neighbours phoned in their suspicions. As a *Sunday Times* reporter put it: 'It was surprising, and worrying, that so many boys could be thought capable of such a crime.'

In all, 150 boys were interviewed by the police in connection with the murder. They included a twelve-year-old who was arrested after a tip-off at his home in Snowdrop Street, Kirkdale because he was thought to resemble one of the boys caught by the video camera. The police operation, which involved eight vans and three cars, attracted a 200-strong mob in an ugly mood, jeering and shouting abuse and there were two arrests for breach of the peace. The boy spent twenty-three hours in police custody before he was found to have an alibi. The boy's family had to be rehoused, at a secret address in the Manchester area.

The Bulger case was highlighted in a police appeal on BBC1's 'Crimewatch UK' on Wednesday 17 February, attracting a record audience of 14.2 million. Shortly after the broadcast, at about 10.30 p.m., the incident room took a call from a woman whose mother's friend had a son who had been truanting from school on that Friday with another boy. One of the figures on the enhanced video-still resembled the boy. His name was Jon Venables. At 7.30 the following morning, Venables and Thompson were arrested on suspicion of being involved in the murder of James Bulger.

The boys were led through their interviews with commendable circumspection by two Detective Sergeants, Phil Roberts at Walton Lane where Thompson was held, and Mark Dale over at Lower Lane police station where Venables had been taken. The officers scrupulously followed copybook procedure, keeping the sessions brief and ensuring the presence of a solicitor and parent or other non-partisan adult at all times. But their task was not an enviable one. The detectives could put the young boys under no pressure, and must back off when the questioning got too hard. On the other hand they knew, too, that the suspects would be cloaking their answers with lies and fantasy. The truth would have to be prised out, gently but firmly, one fact at a time.

Bobby first. Yes, they had been to the Strand. Yes, he knew about James Bulger. He remembered seeing him there – he had been with his mum, and was wearing a blue coat.

Jon Venables was much less assured as DS Mark Dale led him through his first interview. Bobby was the one who had wanted to 'sag'. Bobby had said: 'You had better come with me or I'll set some lads on you.' They had walked across Walton Park to Liverpool football ground, that was all. No mention of the Strand.

Back to Bobby. Why was Jon being so coy about the shopping centre? Had something happened there? 'Like the baby got took?', volunteered Thompson. 'Yes,' said Roberts. 'Did you leave with baby James, and with Jon Venables?' 'No. I never left with him. It shows in the paper that Jon had hold of his hand. I never touched him.' They had walked James round the Strand and let him go at the church, Bobby remembered. He began to cry. It was a false cry, Roberts noted. A cry without tears.

So what did Jon have to say about that? 'Yeah, we was in Bootle Strand, but we never got a kid.' The tears were streaming down Jon's face. 'We never, we never, we never got a kid.'

On the Friday morning Bobby Thompson was changing his story again. They had taken James up to the reservoir, and on to the railway line. They had some paint, which Jon had stolen from Toymaster. 'Jon threw it in baby James's eye.' Did anybody hit baby James? 'Jon might have in sly – because Jon is sly.'

'Bobby's a liar,' was Jon's retort. 'Bobby's getting me into trouble.' He was beginning to get distressed and hysterical. Susan Venables did her best to console him. 'We never touched a boy, I never killed him, we took him and left him at the canal, mum, that's all.'

By this time forensic reports were starting to come in. The police had taken everything from the Venables and Thompson households, even the washing from the line, and had found paint stains and blood stains on clothing and shoes.

Back in the interview room Ann Thompson told Bobby: 'It will all be over if you just tell them the truth.' The 'truth' which DS Roberts elicited from the boy was more, much more, than Ann Thompson was prepared for: 'Jon threw a brick in his face. Jon threw another brick. Then he hit him again with a big metal thing. He was not moving. His eyes were open.' Why did Jon do all this? 'I don't know. That is what I don't know.' Ann Thompson could not believe what she was hearing.

Over, once more, to Jon Venables. This proved to be the crucial interview, the one when he confessed. Both his parents were with him, one on each side, their arms round him, reassuring, telling him they loved him, they would always be there for him. They simply wanted him to tell the truth, no matter what it was. 'I did kill him,' Jon sobbed, at last. 'What about his mum, will you tell her I'm sorry?'

At 6.40 p.m. on Sunday 21 February Robert Thompson and Jon Venables were charged with the abduction and murder of James Bulger. They were also charged with the attempted abduction of another boy, aged two.

The boys appeared in Court Five at South Sefton Magistrates Court at 10.06 a.m. on 22 February, when they were remanded in the care of Sefton social services until 3 March. As they were escorted from the court a crowd of 300 surged forward, beating their fists on the sides on the police vans, hurling missiles and yelling 'Kill the little bastards' and 'A life for a life'. There were seven arrests for public disorder.

An extended warrant of detention was granted on

3 March. After the hearing Jon Venables was sitting in a police car when Thompson walked past towards another vehicle. 'Thompson looked at Venables and smiled,' DS Roberts recalled. 'It was a terrible, chilling smile. It was a cold smile – an evil smile.'

Before the case came to court, James Bulger was buried. Father Michael O'Connell led the service at the Church of the Sacred Heart, where the lessons were read by James's uncle and Superintendent Albert Kirby. A tape was played of *Heal the World* by James's favourite, Michael Jackson. Outside, a crowd of 1,000 mourners shivered in silence. The service closed with Eric Clapton's tribute to his own dead son, *Tears in Heaven*. And then James resumed his final journey, a three-mile drive to Fazakerley, where he was to be interred in Kirkdale cemetery. Ralph and Denise Bulger placed a wreath on their son's grave bearing the message 'Goodnight and God bless, baby James Patrick'.

Over the coming months DS Kirby compiled the case for the prosecution. Hundreds of people were interviewed, and from their evidence a picture of the final three hours of James Bulger's life was pieced together like a jigsaw puzzle. The first sighting placed him just outside the shopping centre, where a taxi driver, David Keay, had seen one of the two boys 'yank the child up to his chest and carry him off down Stanley Road'. The toddler was 'bawling his head off', according to an environmental health officer. A woman had noticed a child a short distance down the road, on the banks of the Leeds and Liverpool Canal, looking 'extremely distressed', while another witness, Lorna Brown, remembered two boys carrying a small child up from the canal and back across Stanley Road. The child had a mark on his forehead which seemed to have been caused by a blow from some solid object.

Twenty-five-year-old Mark Pimblett had been driving

past in his delivery van when he noticed two boys dragging a younger lad by the arms. One of the boys had kicked the toddler in the ribs with his left foot. Mr Pimblett noticed that the 'child's face was all bright red and he was crying. I thought they were older brothers taking him home.' It was the natural assumption – an assumption made by witness after witness. As Mr David Turner QC was to put it later to one of those bystanders: 'Although you felt a little uneasy, you were not sufficiently uneasy to intervene.'

Mrs Kathleen Richardson had felt very uneasy indeed when she saw, from the top deck of the 67a bus in Oxford Road, two boys 'standing each side of the baby. Each had hold of him by one arm and they were swinging him up quite high. I shouted: "What the hell are those kids doing to that poor child? What kind of frigging parents let him out with kids like that?".' At Breeze Hill reservoir Irene Hitman, out walking her dog, had confronted the children. The toddler was sobbing and had 'a lump on his forehead and a terrible lump on the top of his head'. One of the boys said they had found the child at the bottom of the embankment and would take him to the police.

The fatal exodus continued, out of Bootle and into Walton. Mrs Elizabeth McCarrick had just collected her seven-year-old daughter from school when she came across the children in a subway in County Road. 'They both had hold of the little boy's hand. I managed to make the chubbier boy [Thompson] let go of his hand. I was going to the police myself. But the taller boy said: "It's all right, Missus, we'll take the boy to the police station." The chubbier one grabbed the little boy again.'

Staff from a DIY shop and a pet shop both remembered two boys keeping a firm hold on a 'distressed-looking' child. In Church Street a twelve-year-old boy had met Robert Thompson, whom he knew, with Venables and a child who Bobby said was Jon's brother. When the toddler started to cry, the twelve-year-old threatened Thompson: 'If you don't take him home I'll batter you.'

Finally, three individuals came forward to report having seen the boys taking James on to the railway line near Walton Lane, at about 5.30 p.m. When William Howes had tried to intervene, Robert Thompson said: 'I am fed up having the little brother. I'm going to tell Mum I'm not having him any more.' A fifteen-year-old girl recollected the boys running up the embankment to the railway line. Asked if she could hear what state the baby was in, she replied: 'No, I could only hear laughter.'

The trial of Robert Thompson and Jon Venables opened at Preston Crown Court No. 1 on Monday 1 November 1993, before Mr Justice Morland. Richard Henriques QC led the prosecution, while Thompson was represented by David Turner QC, and Venables by Brian Walsh QC.

At 10.40 a.m. the two youngest murder trial defendants this century were led in to the court room by their social workers. An audible gasp ran round the court as these chubby little eleven-year-olds in school uniform took their place on a specially raised platform in the dock. Too young, too small, too *ordinary*, surely, to have committed such an atrocity? Child A, as Robert Thompson was to be identified on the order of the judge, looked dazed, his face white and expressionless, staring straight ahead, fiddling with a signet ring. Venables – Child B – was hunched and bewildered looking, twisting and shredding a paper tissue and, as the charges were read out, sobbing and burying his face in the arm of his social worker.

The case which the Crown intended to prove was that both boys had committed the abduction and murder together. 'Notwithstanding their age,' Mr Henriques addressed the jury, 'it is alleged that they both intended either to kill James or at least to cause him really serious injury, and they both knew their behaviour was seriously wrong.' According to the law children aged between ten and fourteen are presumed not to know the difference between right and wrong and are therefore deemed to be incapable of committing an offence. When a child of such an age is brought before the courts, the onus is on the prosecution to prove he knew that what he was doing was seriously wrong, and not merely naughty or mischievous.

A total of twenty-six witnesses to the kidnapping was called. Many of them were clearly distressed, and full of remorse that they had somehow 'failed' to save the toddler. But it would be very hard to suggest they had in any way neglected their duties as responsible citizens. The proposal made in the light of this case, that adults should be expected and encouraged to interfere in the affairs of children unknown to them on the slightest pretext, 'just to be on the safe side', would surely have unacceptable, potentially dangerous, implications.

The defendants themselves were not called to give evidence, but the appalling truth of the injuries and murder – those events to which there were no witnesses – was revealed in transcripts from the nineteen police interviews. The interviews, Mr Henriques told the court, indicated that each defendant had a 'fluent capacity to tell lies. They demonstrate the progression from total ignorance of James Bulger and events surrounding his death, to partial knowledge, through to each of them placing as much of the blame as possible on the co-accused.'

Jon Venables' final version of the events went some way to shouldering the blame. He admitted it had been his own idea to abduct the child. He claimed that Thompson had said: 'Let's get him lost outside, so when he goes into the road he will be knocked over.' They had taken the frightened little boy to the canal, where Bobby had suggested throwing him in. James had been 'slammed down' by Thompson, causing a bump on his head. Both boys had then half dragged, half carried the toddler a further two and a half miles, reaching the embankment at dusk. There they had pelted James with bricks. Jon claimed he had thrown only smaller stones, 'but he kept on getting back up and would not stay down'. He admitted kicking James and punching him, 'but only lightly'. 'Bobby threw paint in his face, then a brick. He said: "Pick it up and throw it," and I just threw it on the floor.' Jon had demonstrated to his interviewing officers the two-handed technique by which Thompson had brought down a heavy iron bar on to James's head. 'I thought Bobby was probably doing it for fun or something, because he was laughing his head off.' After Bobby had removed the child's lower clothing, both boys had put bricks over the child's face 'to stop the bleeding', and left him lying across the track. Why did Venables think they had done those things? 'I don't know, just mad, I went, I just went like that. Just something to do. I wasn't angry, I was upset.'

In Robert Thompson's account it was Jon who had abducted the child; Jon who had stoned him with bricks; Jon who had hit him with the iron bar. Bobby had tried unsuccessfully to stop him. He told police officers: 'I would not hit the babe. I would not touch him.' Asked why he had not pushed James away from the railway line, he replied: 'Blood stains, doesn't it, and then my mother would have to pay.' He went on: 'I never touched him except to see if he was breathing. So I've nothing to bother about.'

Forensic evidence, however, indicated that both boys had participated in the murder. On James's right cheek was a shoe pattern matching Thompson's blood-stained footwear. The blood was of the same group as James's, and a hair on the lace of one of the shoes was microscopically matched to a sample from the baby's head. More blood had been found on both of Venables' shoes, enough to enable a genetic fingerprinting test. The DNA match performed by Mr Graham Jackson indicated that the blood was 'extremely unlikely' to have come from anyone other than James Bulger. Blue paint found on James's face matched that from a small tin of Humbrol enamel found on the railway line, and similar paint was found on both defendants' shoes and clothing.

Dr Alan Williams, a pathologist at Macclesfield district hospital, described the injuries suffered by the two-year-old. He told the court James probably survived only a few minutes after the attack, and concluded: 'In my opinion, the cause of death was multiple head injuries. There are so many, you could not single out one particular blow to the head and say that was the one that was fatal.' An array of the weapons alleged to have inflicted the injuries was exhibited in court, including twenty-seven blood-stained bricks and a number of stones. Exhibit 34 was a thirty-inch-long cast-iron fish plate, of a type used to bolt together lengths of railway track. When it was passed across to the jury for consideration, one of the jurors refused to touch the murder weapon; another gasped as she tried lifting the dead weight.

Evidence that both defendants were in it together may have seemed conclusive, but it had still to be proved that they knew right from wrong, were sane, and fit to stand trial. Dr Eileen Vizard, a consultant child psychiatrist, interviewed Robert Thompson and found he suffered from both academic disorder and conduct disorder. He was also suffering post-traumatic stress. But he was a boy of 'good, at least average, intelligence, able to answer questions perfectly well'; in her opinion 'he did know the difference between right and wrong'. Dr Susan Bailey came to similar conclusions from her interviews with Jon Venables, but on each occasion he 'burst into tears and cried inconsolably', and was 'not able to talk about the subject of this indictment in any useful way'.

The defence lawyers had to be content with laying the blame on each other's clients. Mr Brian Walsh QC told the court that Robert Thompson 'is a cocky, confident, devious, arrogant little liar', who had 'kicked James, beaten him and battered him;. David Turner QC, for Thompson, made a counter-accusation, claiming that 'for whatever reason – petulance or a sudden swing of mood – Jon Venables unhappily and tragically carried out a sudden but sustained attack on little James'.

In summing up, on 24 November, Mr Justice Morland reminded the jury that there was no dispute that the injuries which killed James Bulger were inflicted by the defendants. But in order to find both boys guilty of murder, the jury would have to be sure they were in it together, and certain of 'the intention of each defendant on the railway line when the injuries were inflicted'. He reminded the jury that James was stripped of his shoes, socks, trousers and underpants: 'Was that to suggest that the child had been subject to some form of assault, possibly by an adult, and then run over by a train?' Recalling the 'untruths' the boys told the police, the judge asked: 'Did they lie because of the fear of being charged, or because they knew what they had done was really seriously wrong?' He warned the jury not to let their emotions affect them when considering their verdicts.

It is 5.15 p.m. on Wednesday 25 November, when the jury files back into a hushed court. They have been deliberating for five and a half hours. During the absence Denise Bulger, expecting another baby soon, has taken her place in court for the first time. She is beside her husband Ralph, who has attended the entire trial, sitting quietly and looking straight ahead. The foreman of the jury rises to his feet. He pronounces that on the charge of the murder of James Bulger, it is the opinion of the jury that both defendants are guilty.

First to react is the man at the centre of the prosecution, DS Albert Kirby. He steps across to where the Bulgers are sitting in the public gallery, and gives Denise a kiss on the cheek. She looks relieved, evidently satisfied with the verdict. From the back of the public gallery her brother yells: 'How do you feel now, you little bastards?' In another part of court Susan Venables bursts into tears, while husband Neil buries his face in his hands. Robert Thompson sits as lumpenly and impassively as ever, not even turning to look for his mother, who as it happens is not in court. Jon Venables simply stares wide-eyed at the jury. Then he breaks down, saying: 'Would you please tell them I'm sorry.'

Mr Justice Morland described the abduction and murder as a cunning and wicked act of 'unparalleled evil and barbarity'. He sentenced Thompson and Venables to be detained at Her Majesty's pleasure, and told them they should expect to be kept locked up for at least eight years. He ordered that the further charge of the attempted abduction of another child at Bootle's Strand shopping centre, on which the jury had been unable to reach a verdict, should be allowed to lie on file.

There was outrage when it was announced on 26 January 1994 that the trial judge had recommended to the Home Secretary minimum sentences of just eight years. At the same time the Lord Chief Justice, Lord Taylor, made his own recommendation of ten years. Although this seemed excessively lenient to many people, it has to be remembered that the minimum term, or 'tariff', fixed by the Home Secretary is often longer than the judges' recommendation. It represents the length of time required to satisfy the demand for retribution and deterrence; prisoners may be detained longer, even indefinitely, if at the end of that period they are considered to be still a danger to the public. And in July 1993 Home Secretary Michael Howard stressed that he would also take into account the 'public acceptability' of early release. As Robert Thompson, at least, has never admitted any responsibility for what happened, it seems very unlikely that he would be sufficiently rehabilitated to make an early return to society. Nevertheless, in a controversial decision, Michael Howard set a minimum limit of fifteen years' detention.

Since the trial it has been revealed that a certain amount of evidence was suppressed, after a deal struck between the prosecution and defence. Both sides agreed there was 'no point in dragging the horror for the Bulgers out any further'. The evidence related to certain questions which the police had asked the boys concerning some batteries found at the scene of the crime, and the reason why James had been partly undressed. Both of the accused were particularly reluctant to answer those questions. It is sufficient to comment that, despite official protestations to the contrary, the boy had been sexually interfered with, and the batteries had apparently been forced into his mouth. Since these matters were passed over at the trial, we can only speculate on whether or not they imply a possible motive for the crime.

The motive, of course, is the one thing missing. Why did it happen? At home and abroad journalists, politicians, criminologists and opinion-formers struggled for an answer. Society was compelled to scour its conscience, like the cast at the denouement of a J.B. Priestley play when it is revealed that *everybody*, in his or her own way, is culpable. One of the first opinions to be given an airing was that of the trial judge who, after the boys had been taken down, made a statement attacking the influence of 'video nasties' on children: 'It is not for me to pass judgement on their upbringing, but I suspect exposure to violent video films may in part be an explanation.' He was referring specifically to a film called *Child's Play III*, which purportedly included scenes suggestive of some details of the murder. The video had been rented by Neil Venables three weeks before the murder. Did Jon see the film? He and his father both deny the possibility. But he was known to be very susceptible – if he had seen it, might it not have pushed him over the edge? Parents, police and defence lawyers all rejected the suggestion. At the very least, it would be banal to say that *Child's Play III* turned Jon Venables into a murderer. None the less, the judge's comments provoked a witch-hunt in which many copies of the video were destroyed.

Many other causes were found to explain away the crime. DS Albert Kirby, a committed Christian, had no doubt that the boys were 'evil to the extreme'. The idea that every child is capable of reverting to a kind of animal or psychopathic condition was put forward in some quarters, with *Lord of the Flies*, William Golding's seminal novel, being invoked. DS Phil Roberts' conclusion that 'these two were freaks who just found each other', left much unanswered. PC George Scott may have been closer to the truth when he commented: 'I believe the two boys were fixated with causing a disaster which only they would know about – which to the general public would look like an ordinary accident.' At the other extreme some observers saw the tragedy as a parable for our times. 'Are our children spinning off, out of control, towards some kind of spiritual abyss?', thundered the *Sunday Times*. 'Has the age of video nasties, drugs, one-parent families, football hooliganism, yuppiedom, lousy education' – here the writer brandished the ultimate symbol of degeneracy – '*trainers*, the whole rotten lot, finally given us what we so richly deserve?'

Robert Thompson and Jon Venables are detained indefinitely in secure units, where they play with their computer games and Airfix kits. Susan and Neil Venables, brought back together by the trial, now live at a secret address outside Merseyside. Ann Thompson, too, has moved away. And the Bulgers, helped by funds raised by public appeal, have moved from their one-bedroomed tower block flat into a new house in Liverpool. On 8 December 1993, the couple were blessed with the arrival of a baby boy, Michael James.

Postscript

Ralph Bulger's name hit the headlines again in May 1994, when he appeared at Manchester Crown Court on a wounding charge. Ralph and his brother Philip were accused of a revenge attack on brothers Gary and Mark Loftus following a two-year grudge; it was alleged that the Bulgers had slashed their victims with bottles and a glass in a night club at Kirkby, Merseyside, in September 1993. But the jury found that Philip Bulger had acted in self-defence after Gary Loftus had attacked him, and that Ralph was in a different part of the night club and took no part in the incident. As they walked free on 19 May, Denise Bulger commented: 'I am not angry. We just want to get on with our lives.'

On 22 May 1994 it was announced that an appeal had been lodged in the name of Robert Thompson at the European Court of Human Rights in Strasbourg. The court will be asked to rule that Thompson and Jon Venables were denied a fair trial and suffered inhuman or degrading treatment when they were tried in public as if they were adults. The North Carolina attorney behind the challenge, Thomas Loflin III, claimed that 'many Americans were aghast that England would lock up children so young for murder. They are eleven-year-old children who need the best of treatment, not punishment.' An avowed liberal with a passion for fighting the cause of the underdog, Loflin has spent six months preparing a fourteen-page document outlining the basis of the appeal. Wealthy Americans are reported to have pledged to underwrite the estimated £200,000 cost of the appeal.

The appeal will claim that the sentence, an indefinite period in custody, breaches articles 5(4), 6(1) and 14 of the European Convention on Human Rights, which the British government ratified in 1953. It will also challenge the prerogative of the Home Secretary to decide when the two should be released since the Convention on Human Rights states that the ultimate power to determine the conditions of detention and length of sentence should rest with the judicial system, and not with a politician. The appeal will also contend that the two could not fully conduct their defence; that they were too young to waive their right to remain silent in a knowing and understanding way; that they possibly showed signs of psychiatric disorders which made a murder trial unfair; that the interviews should have been ruled inadmissible evidence; and not least, that the boys' identities should not have been revealed on the judge's orders at the end of the trial.

Media reaction to the announcement was predictably hyperbolic. Typical was the *Star*'s comment: 'The British people won't stand for the early release of these dangerous savages. Rather than free them a day too soon we should quit Europe.' In an unusual move Prime Minister John Major said he would 'vigorously contest' the appeal. And James Bulger's uncle, Ray Matthews, stormed: 'We are totally shocked and surprised by this. This should be a matter for British justice, not for the European courts and certainly not for the Americans.' On Wednesday 25 May 1994 Denise and Ralph Bulger delivered a 207,000-signature petition to Home Secretary Michael Howard in an attempt to persuade him to impose a 'life means life' sentence when he sets the retributory tariff. 'I am going to do everything I can, if it takes me the rest of my life, to keep those two behind bars,' Denise said.

But lawyers acting for the two convicted boys have denied that they are seeking to have their clients' life sentences reduced or quashed. Dominic Lloyd, the solicitor for Robert Thompson, said that the intention of the appeal was 'not against the sentence passed, it is an application to change the *way* it has been passed'.

One law highlighted by the James Bulger case has already been reformed. On 29 March 1994 Lord Justice Mann, sitting with Mr Justice Laws, threw out the 'utterly outrageous and outdated' rule that the prosecution must prove that offenders aged between ten and fourteen know their actions are morally or legally wrong. Lord Justice Mann said the rule was 'perverse' because it tended to absolve 'the very children most likely to commit criminal acts' – those who are morally irresponsible. But his historic decision will probably be contested in the House of Lords. Allan Levy QC, an expert in the law on children, has pointed out that the new ruling reverses the trend of most western countries to raise the age of criminal responsibility.

Released to Kill

RELEASED TO KILL

(Guest contributor: John Bevis)

There has been considerable alarm at the growing number of serious crimes, including murder, committed by offenders who have been 'released to kill'. It is thought, naturally enough, that an important purpose of custodial sentencing is to prevent re-offending. To this end it is essential that prisons and psychiatric units should be secure; that prisoners on life sentences should not be released until they are considered to be adequately rehabilitated; that bail should not be granted if there is a danger that further attempts at violent crime will be made. In the case of offenders in psychiatric care, it is reasonable to expect that they will be closely escorted on day release or transfer, and that they will not be granted liberty until they have been properly diagnosed as being of no further threat to society. But overcrowded prisons, inadequate funding, poor medical diagnoses, ignorance of mental illness, and the very questionable policy of 'care in the community' have all resulted in one unfortunate outcome: the presence at large of those from whom society has a right to be protected.

Released From Psychiatric Care

In November 1991, forty-year-old **James Rudman** stabbed his wife Sue more than forty times in a frenzied attack following a row over a missing video-recorder. He pleaded guilty to manslaughter on grounds of diminished responsibility, and was sent to a secure unit at Leicester Towers Hospital. But on 1 August 1993, after a mental health review tribunal rejected his application to be released from the hospital, Rudman walked out; he knew that, if he could lie low for four weeks, he would become a free man. This was because Section 37 of the Mental Health Act incorporates a loophole: the order of detention lapses if the patient is absent 'without leave' for twenty-eight days, unless there is fresh evidence of mental illness. Fortunately Rudman was tracked down before he had an opportunity to demonstrate any such 'fresh evidence'. He was found in a house in Kerry, southwest Ireland, and arrested just sixty-two minutes before the order expired.

The government promised to close the Mental Health Act loophole after the Rudman case, but to date no action has been taken. Consequently Steve Newson became a free man on 13 May 1994, after he had escaped from a mental hospital and evaded capture for the statutory period. Newson, who had been locked up after threatening shop staff with a knife, was said to be so dangerous that police warned the public not to approach him.

In December of the previous year, two convicted killers escaped from Broadmoor within twenty-four hours of each other. Kenneth Erskine, known as the Stockwell Strangler, who had murdered seven pensioners in south London, was at large for only thirty minutes, after escaping while being taken out for medical treatment at Heatherwood Hospital in Ascot. He was recaptured on Ascot racecourse. But another escapee, who had spent eight years planning his escape, was a little more successful. Forty-seven-year-old **Anthony Pilditch**, a twenty-stone former market trader, had been jailed for life at St Albans Crown Court in 1984 after admitting the murder of Agnes Duff, a seventeen-year-old waitress from Scotland, whose decomposed body was found in a bedsit in Luton, Bedfordshire, in 1978. He was suspected of the murders of four other women, including three London prostitutes, and the abduction of a woman on the M4 motorway.

Pilditch was transferred from Parkhurst Prison to Broadmoor in February 1986 when his mental condition deteriorated. His chance to escape came on 15 December 1993, when he was taken on a Christmas shopping trip. He had £1,000 in his shoes, and £6,000-worth of watches and jewellery belonging to other patients strapped to his arms. After lunch in the George Hotel in Reading he gave his two escorts the slip when he was allowed to visit the lavatory unaccompanied. Pilditch caught a train to London where he set out a 'table of missions', which included testing his ability to drink alcohol, picking up a prostitute, and visiting Battersea Dogs' Home. He was planning his final 'mission', to go to Morocco where his wife lived, when he collapsed at a bus stop and was taken to the Royal Free Hospital. Tony Pilditch was arrested, having been on the run for seven days, after he was recognised by a hospital nurse.

An inquiry made thirty-four recommendations to tighten security, including metal detectors to search patients and the monitoring of telephone calls. But Frank Mone, chairman of the Broadmoor branch of the Prison Officers Association, claimed that four members of staff were suspended as scapegoats for the more liberal regime introduced at Broadmoor in 1989, when it came under the full control of the Special Hospitals Service Authority. 'Between 1981 and 1991, there were three escapes,' he commented. 'In 1993, we have had eight or nine. Patients have access to phones, to banking systems, their mail is not looked at. A number of patients are manipulating the prison system to their benefit. The nursing staff walk a fine line between defending themselves against patients and being prosecuted by their own management.'

The government's controversial 'care in the community' scheme for the rehabilitation of the mentally ill has provoked much criticism. Indeed a government review of the scheme in 1992 produced no fewer than 276 recommendations, of which just two had been implemented by July 1993. Of Britain's quarter of a million schizophrenics, 4,000 are violent, and there is a need for 1,500 medium-secure hospital beds. At present only 700 such beds are available. Since the programme of closing long-stay psychiatric beds began in 1991, there have been forty murders and one hundred suicides committed by the mentally ill. One schizophrenic, Ben Silcock, was badly mauled when he climbed into the lion enclosure at London Zoo to feed the animals. In December 1991 Carol Barratt, a schizophrenic with a history of violence, stabbed to death eleven-year-old Emma Brodie with a twelve-inch carving knife, in a Doncaster shopping precinct, just two days after being released. Barratt was subsequently committed indefinitely to Rampton Hospital, and considered suing the psychiatrist who had diagnosed her as safe to be released into society. It is to be hoped that the government's policy will be drastically overhauled to prevent the occurrence of more tragedies of this nature.

But already there have been too many preventable deaths. One case which illustrates the pitfalls of the scheme was the killing of an old-age pensioner by schizophrenic **Paul Gordon**. Gordon watched eighty-three-year-old William Hoarsley draw his £50 pension from a post office in New Cross, south London, on 9 September 1992. When the old man sat on a wall to feed the pigeons, twenty-six-year-old Gordon seized his opportunity: he pushed the old man off the wall, grabbed the money and fled. But Mr Hoarsley hit his head as he fell and suffered a heart attack, from which he died.

Paul Gordon, who had previous convictions for violence, appeared at the Old Bailey before Mr Justice Henry Pownall QC in July 1993. After a hearing of a mere twenty minutes, the judge told Gordon: 'What you did in bringing this old man's life to an end was a pretty horrid thing to do. But the circumstances are such that I can take a pretty unusual course.' The judge was as good as his word. He made *no* order under the Mental Health Act, and sentenced the killer to three years' probation, with a condition that Gordon should accept treatment at Bexley Hospital in Kent. DC Leslie Oke, who led the investigation, expressed the view of many in court that day when he said: 'The sentence is an outrage and completely out of step with the crime Gordon committed.'

The case which provoked the closest scrutiny of government mental health policy was that of **Christopher Clunis**. Clunis was first diagnosed as schizophrenic in 1986, and had been involved in a number of 'serious incidents involving knives and his apparent fascination with them', including the attempted stabbing of a policeman in 1988. In May 1992 he was arrested after knifing a hostel inmate, but the case was dropped when the victim failed to give evidence. Clunis was released in September 1992 from York Clinic, a special unit at Guy's Hospital, when doctors agreed he was fit to return to the community.

On 9 December 1992 Christopher Clunis was reported threatening children and adults with a breadknife and screwdriver, but no action was taken. Eight days later he attacked Mr Jonathan Zito, an Italian musician, as he was waiting with his brother for a train at Finsbury Park underground station in north London. Eighteen-stone Clunis stabbed Zito three times, one of the blows piercing his eye and brain, then stepped on to a train and sat down to await arrest. He showed no concern to officers, telling them: 'I have murdered someone, haven't I?' Jonathan Zito died in hospital two and a half hours after the attack.

At the Old Bailey Clunis, of Marlborough Road, Wood Green, admitted manslaughter on grounds of diminished responsibility. On 28 June 1993, Mr Justice Blofeld said that it was only 'with some hesitation' that he ordered that Clunis be held at Rampton Hospital instead of being sent to prison. 'There will be no question of you being released while there is the remotest chance that you might be unwell,' he told the defendant. Dr Nigel Eastman, a consultant forensic psychiatrist, had told the court that Clunis responded well to treatment in a controlled environment, but as soon as he was released his condition would deteriorate again. 'In my opinion, if he had got a place at Rampton Hospital it is very much less likely that this offence would have occurred. The reason he did not go there is that no bed was available at the time.'

Ironically the victim's widow, Jayne Zito, had been an assistant manager in a rehabilitation centre for the mentally ill. She had given up her job out of exasperation with having to send 'frightened' people like Clunis back into society. After her husband's death Jayne Zito led a successful demand for a public inquiry, and has since been a figurehead in the campaign for a revision of the government's care in the community policy. In December 1993 she was appointed to a post with the mental health charity MIND. After Clunis's trial Jayne Zito commented: 'I would like the government to understand that the changes they are making led to destruction and fear and extreme loss, not only for me and my family but for Christopher Clunis and his family. I am holding Virginia Bottomley accountable for the murder of Jonathan Zito.' She believes her role is to 'expose the inhumanity of the system of community care that has been set up by this government. Community care is not working well. It has never worked well. It is in crisis. The service needs resources, it needs beds, it needs accountability.'

The *Report into the Care and Treatment of Christopher Clunis* was published on 24 February 1994. Its author, Jean Ritchie QC, concluded that care in the community was desirable and preferable to the degrading conditions of the Victorian-style 'lunatic asylum', but recommended a number of drastic courses of action to improve the practical application of the policy. There should be 'havens' for patients unable to cope in the community; professional 'keyworkers' and volunteer 'befrienders' to ensure the care of their charges; planned after-care; special supervision for the most vulnerable; minimum standards for community psychiatric services; police to be trained in understanding mental illness. Most overdue, perhaps, were the recommendations that the Home Office should issue guidelines on prosecuting mentally ill offenders, the Crown Prosecution Service should receive medical recommendations, and a psychiatrist should determine whether a defendant needs detaining, irrespective of the outcome of the case.

Until at least some of those recommendations are implemented, the killings will continue. Just a week after the manslaughter of Jonathan Zito by Christopher Clunis, a former policeman was killed by twenty-three-year-old **Michael Buchanan**. A martial arts expert, Buchanan had a history of convictions for violence and dishonesty, leading to his detention at Shenley Hospital, near Borehamwood, Hertfordshire. In August 1992, a panel of doctors at the hospital signed the papers for his release into the community, on provision that he was supervised and took medication. But he failed to comply with conditions at a hostel in north London and was ordered to leave.

Buchanan enjoyed the 'care' of the community as a free man for just seventeen days. During that time he was arrested in connection with alleged offences of robbery and burglary, and was put on police bail. He attacked seventy-year-old Alfred Baldock, kicking him in the jaw and robbing him of his £65 pension. Two days later, he set upon a retired Jamaican policeman, Frederick Graver, as Mr Graver was parking his car on the Stonebridge estate in Harlesden, north London. Buchanan asked the older man for cigarettes, and when Mr Graver said he had none, beat him about the head with a three-foot stick he had taken from a skip. Frederick Graver died in hospital three days later.

At the Old Bailey on 18 October 1993, Judge Brian Smedley told Buchanan: 'There is a welter of evidence that you are suffering from paranoid schizophrenia. The doctors are quite satisfied that you remain, and will remain for a substantial period, a grave danger if you are released.' However, he told the court that Ashworth Hospital, in Merseyside, had refused to provide a bed for Buchanan. A doctor there decided Buchanan was not mentally ill under the terms of the Mental Health Act, and if he had been at the time of the attack the illness was 'short lived and drug induced'. Michael Buchanan received four life sentences, for manslaughter, two robberies, and grievous bodily harm, and a further eighteen months for assault.

Released From Prison or Custody

It may be very difficult to predict how mentally ill offenders will behave on release, and it is obvious that their medical notes need to be scrutinised very closely before discharge papers are signed. But of the criminally violent there should be no doubt: custodial sentences should apply until they have achieved a recognised standard of rehabilitation, and the period of their release should be counselled and monitored. These of course are ideals demanding substantial investment. But society deserves better than to have dangerous criminals set loose when they are mindful to kill again, as the following recent cases amply demonstrate.

Malcolm Smith, who had no fewer than 123 convictions including rape, attempted murder and false imprisonment, had served just three months of an eighteen-month sentence before he was released to kill. During custody at Verne Prison, Portland, Dorset, Smith had seen a picture of barmaid Jane Harvell on a cellmate's wall. When he was freed on home leave for four days on 31 May 1992, forty-one-year-old Smith tracked down the girl to the Pelican Wine Bar in Bournemouth where she worked, and arranged to sleep at her flat while she stayed with a friend. When she returned Smith attacked. She was found trussed semi-naked on her bed, choked to death on her own blood with a pillowcase over her head and a cord around her throat. She had a broken nose, three knife wounds to the chest, and had been raped. On 29 July 1993, at Winchester Crown Court, Malcolm Smith was returned to prison for life.

Matloob Hussain had been convicted of murdering his wife, Zaroof Begum, at their flat in Alum Rock, Birmingham, in November 1979. He was released after serving only five years and nine months, but in June 1992 launched a frenzied attack on his sister. Twenty-eight-year-old Ghulam Sugra was beaten to death at her home in Alder Road, Moseley, Birmingham. Hussain was returned to jail by Mr Justice Waterhouse, who described the Home Office's decision to release the murderer as 'remarkable on the face of it', and recommended he should serve at least twenty years.

Nigel Hopton had the distinction of having once been the only man in the British Isles facing execution. He had murdered legal secretary Judith Harris in 1979 at St Helier, Jersey, where the death penalty applied until 1986. His sentence was commuted to life, and he was released in December 1990. But Hopton suffered from psycho-sexual problems which led him on a spree of hunting down women – mostly prostitutes in the Midlands region – for acts of perverted sex. If they refused, he would turn violent. After raping a seventeen-year-old girl in Nottingham and a twenty-six-year-old mother, Hopton was caught and returned to prison for life at Nottingham Crown Court, on 9 September 1993.

Stuart Jobson was out on police bail for alleged violence against his former girlfriend, June Smith. Since the breakdown of their relationship he had remained obsessed and had pestered her until she had had to take out a court injunction against him. Ignoring the conditions of the injunction Jobson followed Mrs Smith to the Texas DIY store in Cheltenham, Gloucestershire, on 4 June 1993. In the car park Jobson leapt from his Ford Capri brandishing a double-barrelled shotgun and, in full view of her daughter and two grandchildren, blasted June Smith at close range. As she slumped to the ground he reloaded and shot her again. Then the gunman turned his weapon on himself, pulled the trigger and fell by the murdered woman's side.

William Woodings had threatened his wife Valerie when she told him she wanted a divorce, and had been told to stay away from her as a condition of bail while awaiting trial at Norwich Crown Court. Instead, on 27 April 1993 he went to the terrace house she rented in Great Yarmouth, and burst through the door brandishing a shotgun. After a five-hour siege, armed police entered the house to find Mrs Woodings shot dead in an upstairs bedroom. Her husband lay sprawled on the landing where he had killed himself.

Adrian Black was also a jilted lover on bail for violence against his sweetheart. In December 1992 he had stormed into Cathy Ainsworth's workplace and dragged her out by the hair, threatening to kill her. Despite strong police objections twenty-two-year-old Black was granted bail. A week later he tricked Cathy into his parents' house in Thatcham, Berkshire, where he blasted her with a shotgun before turning the weapon on himself. Verdicts of unlawful killing and suicide were returned.

Colin Hatch had four convictions for sexual assault on children, culminating in a three-and-a-half year sentence imposed in December 1991 for the false imprisonment, abduction and indecent assault of a fourteen-year-old boy. Senior consultant forensic psychiatrist Anthony Wilkins had pleaded for Broadmoor Hospital to take Hatch, who in his opinion was a homicidal 'menace', but they refused because he was 'not considered to be dangerous enough'. Instead he was ordered to attend a course of psychotherapy sessions at the Portman Clinic – which he failed to do – when he was released on licence in April 1993. He had spent his time in Feltham Young Offenders Institution writing fantasies about abduction, sexual assault and strangulation of the victim. On release Colin Hatch set about putting those fantasies into practice.

On 19 July 1993 seven-year-old Sean Williams rode his mountain bike out of the car park at his parents' public house, The George, in Finchley, north London, looking for a friend. Hatch offered to show him the way, but instead enticed the boy to his apartment on the tenth floor of a block of flats at nearby Norfolk Close. Within fifteen minutes Hatch had assaulted Sean, suffocated him with a plastic bag, put his body in bin-liners, taped them together, and dumped the remains in a lift.

Twenty-one-year-old Colin Hatch was sent down for life at the Old Bailey on 28 January 1994. Judge Nina Lowry told him: 'Life should mean what it says, namely *life imprisonment*. You should never be released back into the community while there remains the slightest danger of you re-offending.'

David Bond was another man to whom that advice should have applied, for he had a history of violent attacks on women and once told police that 'hitting a woman gave him a bigger thrill than having sex'. He committed his first assault when he was fifteen years of age, hitting a girl of his own age around the head with an iron bar in Stretton, Staffs. Three years later, between May and November 1984, he attacked three women in their homes in Burton-upon-Trent. Those attacks earned him five years' youth custody, but he was freed on parole on 12 October 1987. Just three days later he carried out a random attack on Miss Tina Shipston as she walked her dogs beside the river Trent in Nottingham, stabbing her four times and slashing her face. Her left lung was punctured and she was scarred for life, both mentally and physically. Bond, described by a senior detective as a 'walking timebomb', was jailed for eight years at Nottingham Crown Court on 12 May 1988; he had not been charged with attempted murder, but admitted the lesser charge of assault with intent to rob.

At the age of twenty-eight, on 9 February 1993, David Bond was released on parole. He waited until the afternoon of 27 April before carrying out what we can only hope will be his last attack. Deborah Buxton was walking her gundogs by the River Dove near Hatton, in Derbyshire. In a murderous assault almost identical to that on Miss Shipston, Bond struck out at Mrs Buxton with four potentially fatal blows from a brick hammer, and then frenziedly stabbed her from behind with a pair of garden shears, carrying on long after she was dead. That the attack was premeditated was evident, for Bond had ridden his mountain bike around the area for the previous two days looking for a victim, and had stolen the murder weapons from a chapel in anticipation.

David Bond was jailed for life at Nottingham on 20 May 1994, with a recommendation that he should serve a minimum of forty years in prison. After the verdict Deborah Buxton's widower, Ronald, said: 'The awful thing about Debbie's murder is that Bond should not have been out of prison at all. He should never have been given parole with his previous record. It just seems so obvious that he is a danger to women. He proved it time after time. *Yet he was still released to murder Debbie.*'

Guns for Hire

GUNS FOR HIRE

(Guest contributor: John Bevis)

Crime and money have always gone hand-in-glove, and today it is commonplace for guns to be hired to protect 'sensitive' business. The most violent crimes are as often as not related to that most lucrative racket of all – drugs. Over the past twenty-odd years, the drugs trade has spread like a plague across the whole of the British Isles. In Newcastle upon Tyne, described by one resident as 'the roughest place in Britain' where 'if you do anything wrong you have the life expectancy of a hedgehog on the A1', police have been on full alert since six men were shot and two others went missing, believed murdered, in the last two months of 1993. Viv Graham, a seventeen-stone former boxer believed to have run a drugs empire in Newcastle controlling at least 100 bars in the city, was shot dead with a Magnum .357 on New Year's Eve. Manchester's Moss Side, another notorious gangland, saw the murder of twenty-one-year-old Julian Stewart in a drugs-related attack in January 1994. Glasgow has metamorphosed from Mean City to Garden City to City of Culture, but now it is trying to shake off a new identity – City of Violence. The murder rate more than doubled in the first half of 1992 over the previous year, and one single night saw three attempted murders, ten stabbings, and more than a dozen armed assaults. Leeds, Birmingham, Nottingham, Bristol – all have a similar story to tell. Meanwhile in London the tradition of 'keeping it in the family' still holds sway, with the Brindle, Fraser, Arif, Coleman, White and Hiscock clans among the more powerful criminal dynasties controlling the drugs racket. But here they have a new rival – the ruthless Jamaican-based Yardie gangs.

Other international crime syndicates have begun to make their presence known on the streets of London. The Chinese Triads appear to be spreading their wings, while the 'Mafioski' have supplanted the KGB as political terrorists since the break-up of the former Soviet Union. The Mafia itself was said to have been involved in the murder of Domenico Ranno, the Sicilian proprietor of the Donna Ina restaurant in Brixton who was believed to have been selling around a kilo of cocaine a month; Ranno was shot in the head at his home in Helix Road, Brixton, on the morning of 30 November 1993.

Not least, the phenomenon of the 'End Job', once confined to retribution by rival gangsters, is becoming an option for the jealous lover, the 'grass', the businessman who makes one shady deal too many. People who would once have been threatened or 'roughed up', are now more likely to receive a visit from an armed thug on a motorcycle, tempted by the offer of a year's wages for an afternoon's work. It is often suggested that there is in London a 'Murder Incorporated' of full-time professional killers, like the one established by New Yorker Louis 'Lepke' Buchalter in the 1930s. Perhaps the nearest British equivalent was the east London gang run by John Childs and Henry MacKenny in the 1970s, responsible for the disappearance to order of six victims, who were variously shot, stabbed, axed or bludgeoned before being dismembered and burned. But reformed criminal John McVicar remains scornful of stories about teams of highly paid, freelance hitmen roaming London in search of work. If such teams exist, he says, they are at 'the bottom end of the market', and are often convicted. Gangsters in London, he reckons, 'do their own work'. Today's contract killer is more likely to be a heavy criminal involved in drugs, armed robbery or protection, who would be prepared to commit murder if the price were right.

And that right price depends on the job. A clumsy amateur killing might cost £500, but a cool assassination, with all traces covered, would demand a figure closer to £20,000. In 1992 an undercover detective posing as a hitman negotiated a fee as high as £90,000 to kill the unfaithful husband of businesswoman Susan Gill before revealing his true identity. Prices worldwide tend to be lower: in Russia an assassin can be hired for £20, in Colombia for half that amount, while the notorious Mexican Zosimo Montesino, who is alleged to have killed at least 150 people, charged from as little as £3 per job.

The Business of Murder

Terry Maidens was one businessman believed to have been 'taken out' in a contract killing. It was about 7.50 p.m. on Wednesday 26 January 1994, while Maidens was playing with two of his children at their home at Stainforth Close in Whitestone, Nuneaton, Warwickshire, when a biker in leathers and a blue crash helmet knocked at the door. Terry's wife Katherine mistook the visitor for a pizza delivery man – but then she saw the shotgun. The assassin pushed past Mrs Maidens, burst into the sitting room and opened fire, blasting a shot at Terry's head and another into his chest as the dying man fell. The ammunition used was 16-shot Eley Alphamax SP SG, a very heavy duty and lethal cartridge generally used by wildfowlers.

Mr Maidens had been a production manager at Lin Pac Mouldings in Birmingham, where there was reported to have been a clash of personalities between him and an older colleague, Colin Middleton. Exactly what this 'clash' constituted we do not know. What we do know is that Middleton, who had been signed off work at Christmas suffering from stress, held a shotgun licence. And on Friday 28 January his red Suzuki motorcycle was found abandoned on the M9 motorway near Stirling in Scotland. Colin Middleton was arrested in Pitlochry, Tayside, the following day, and on 1 February 1994 was charged with the murder of Terry Maidens.

Another businessman who fell foul of an associate was David Wilson, a Lancashire accountant who had embarked on a deal which he believed would set him up for life. This was fraud on a massive scale, a 213-ton shipload of Mexican-made counterfeit Marlboro cigarettes which were to be sold around the world in a deal worth a comfortable £27 million. But Wilson's partner in crime, a New York-based international fraudster known as Hector Portillo, or 'The Colonel', was double-crossing him. The fake cigarettes did not exist, and it was Portillo's plan to scuttle the empty vessel, or lose it on the African coast, with letters of credit from the duped buyers already paid into his own secret accounts in Zurich. When Wilson got wind of the scheme he faxed Portillo a complaint that he had 'set him up', and threatened that 'one day he would have his day'. That was on 28 February 1992.

By this time a Walter Mitty character, an allegedly debt-ridden alcoholic by the name of Stephen Schepke, was involved. Acting on Portillo's orders Schepke, who liked to describe himself as an international arms dealer, set up a surveillance operation on Wilson's remote home at Withnell, near Chorley in Lancashire. Fancying himself as a double agent Schepke at the same time alerted Lloyd's of London investigators, and the Fraud Squad. When David Wilson revealed he had been interviewed by the Serious Fraud Squad, Portillo arranged to have him 'removed'.

On 5 March 1992 two hired killers burst into Wilson's home. While his wife and two daughters were tied up in the living room, with the TV turned up loud, David Wilson was taken out to the garage where he was shot twice in the head. The two killers were never traced, nor has 'The Colonel' been brought to justice, but the go-between was easy enough to find. At Carlisle Crown Court on 20 October 1993 Stephen Schepke was found guilty of aiding and abetting in the murder, and jailed for life.

A mystery surrounds the disappearance of music business tycoon David Martin, from his £360,000 home at Mosely Hill Farm, Naphill, Buckinghamshire. Martin, an expert in audio systems whose equipment had been used by bands such as Pink Floyd, had sold his company for £1.5 million and set up a helicopter restoration business in partnership with fifty-year-old Colin James. But by September 1992 Mr Martin had ploughed £212,000 into the company for a return of only £20,000, and Mr James was claiming that two helicopters he had bought with his partner's assets had been stolen. On 29 December of that year David Martin went missing. His body has never been found, but in Mr Martin's car workshop detectives discovered bloody footprints which matched a pair of Colin James's exclusive designer trainers. Forensic scientists matched the blood with samples from the missing man's relatives, and said that sprays of blood in the workshop were 'typical of violent injury to someone who is bleeding'. Colin James was charged with the murder, and the case opened at Reading Crown Court on 18 April 1994.

Perhaps the most infamous 'rubbing out' of a businessman was the case of millionaire Donald Urquhart. A former hod-carrier on a building site, fifty-five-year-old Urquhart had made a fortune during the property boom of the 1970s and 1980s and had business connections in tax havens such as Jersey and the Cayman Islands. He was a director of Elstree Golf Club and ran his one-man company, Belgap, from the back of his chauffeur-driven Rover 827 Vanden Plas limousine, which was a 'mini-office' complete with fax and photocopying machines.

Even his golf bag was equipped with a phone. According to his brother Lovat, Mr Urquhart was 'very much a loner' who had recently been 'sensitive', apparently frightened of being attacked in the street.

The bleach-blonde millionaire lived with his Thai girlfriend, Miss Pat Iamspithone, in the penthouse flat of Tenby Mansions, a £4 million apartment block he owned in Nottingham Street, west London. On the evening of Saturday 2 January 1993 the couple had enjoyed a quiet drink at their local, the Queen's Head in Marylebone High Street, and were walking down the street, trying to hail a taxi, when a gunman rode up and opened fire. The killer, wearing a black leather jacket and white crash helmet, pressed the muzzle of his revolver to Mr Urquhart's temple and pulled the trigger twice. As the tycoon slumped to the pavement, the gunman knelt alongside him and fired a third shot at the back of his head. His mission accomplished, the assassin sped away on his motorcycle, a black Yamaha 250cc, registration GRD 505W. Mr Urquhart was taken to University College Hospital where he died in a brain surgery unit after a three-hour operation.

The hunt for the killer was led by Detective Superintendent Bill Scholes, whose team uncovered a tangle of possible leads. It was suggested Mr Urquhart may have made his fortune from money laundering; from illegal gaming-machines; from a drug-smuggling operation based at a retreat he had bought at Holt, on the Norfolk coast, under the assumed name of 'Gerald Gray'; or from dealing in arms. In any event, the killing was a professional job.

On 27 February 1993 a bankrupt builder, who was a self-confessed villain from south London, claimed to have provided the Yamaha motorbike used in the attack. He had been recruited by the gunman, with whom he shared a flat in Croydon. The assassin's surveillance team had followed Urquhart's every move for four months, using cars, a van and the Yamaha, keeping in touch on mobile 'clone phones'. When the murder took place the small-time crook realised he was out of his league, and went to Scotland Yard with his story.

It was not until 9 September 1993 that the police moved in. Seven addresses in London and Rotherham, South Yorkshire, were simultaneously raided at dawn, and four men were arrested. Graeme Nigel West, a builder of Thornton Heath, Surrey, was charged with murder by Marylebone magistrates on 13 September. Geoffrey Heath, of Maltby, South Yorkshire, was charged with conspiracy to murder. Michael Brett, of Purley, Surrey, was accused of plotting the murder, but charges against him were dropped on 17 November 1993. Ten days later Andrew Karn, a salesman from Thornton Heath, south London, was committed to trial at Knightsbridge Crown Court, charged with supplying the killer of Don Urquhart with a gun. At the time of writing, the case has yet to be heard.

Before those arrests had been made, the motorbike hitman had struck again. Forty-two-year-old labourer Tommy Roche was repairing a layby on the Bath Road near Heathrow on Monday 21 June 1993 when the two men roared up on a dark blue 250cc Suzuki motorcycle. The passenger jumped off the pillion, shouted 'Bastard!' at his victim and pumped up to four bullets from a semi-automatic pistol into his chest and stomach. Horrified customers and staff from the McDonald's restaurant opposite the scene watched as the gunman, masked by a full-face crash helmet, walked up to the dying man and finished him off with a shot to the head. A waiter said: 'A manager from this restaurant tried to give him first aid but it was impossible, there was just one big horrible hole in his chest.'

In a stunning revelation, Roche's fiancée Michelle

Davies claimed that the murdered man had once worked as a minder to none other than Donald Urquhart. 'He knew everything about Urquhart but his death was nothing to do with that. Somebody got too greedy. He was involved in a lot of things I can't talk about.' According to underworld sources those ineffable 'things' included a deal in which Roche was said to have accepted a £10,000 deposit on a £1 million cocaine shipment, but failed to deliver the drug. He was also said to have double-crossed a drug gang whom he 'grassed' to the police.

The case aroused renewed concern about the phenomenon of the motorbike assassin. The technique is alleged to have been imported from Colombia, where drug barons first hired motorcycle hitmen in the 1980s. The favoured mounts are fast, lightweight Japanese models, bought cheaply through the second-hand columns and dumped after the job is done. They are the ideal getaway vehicle in traffic-congested cities, and the obligatory full-face helmet provides a natural disguise. It is very difficult to identify the gunman, and few clues are left behind.

The killer of Baron Frederik van Pallandt used a more unusual means of escape – a rubber dinghy. Van Pallandt, remembered as the male half of the singing duo Nina and Frederik was shot dead with his Filipino common-law wife Susannah at their home near the port of Puerto Galera on the island of Mindoro in the Philippines. Police said the assassin, who escaped in Frederik's boat heading for Batangas, was a hired professional. Van Pallandt was believed to have had money difficulties, and it was suggested he had been killed after a business deal went sour.

And it was a business dispute which allegedly led to the murder of thirty-eight-year-old roofing contractor Graeme Woodhatch, who was shot dead at the Royal

Free Hospital in Hampstead, north London, on 24 May 1992. Deith Bridges, a barman, and Paul Tubbs, a roofer, have been accused of hiring Bridges' friend Te Rangimaria Ngarimu at a cost of £7,000 to kill Woodhatch, whom they believed to have swindled them. Ngarimu, wearing a cap, gloves and tracksuit, and carrying a .22 handgun, shot the victim twice in the head and twice in the chest at close range, while he was talking on the public telephone in a hospital ward, where he was recovering from an operation for piles. The killer fled the same day from Gatwick Airport to her native New Zealand, where the money for the execution was waiting for her. But when detectives who interviewed her at her home in Otira, South Island, in August 1993 told her that Bridges and Tubbs had been charged in connection with the killing, Ngarimu was overcome with guilt and returned voluntarily to England where she admitted her part in the crime. The trial of Bridges and Tubbs at the Old Bailey seemed fated when it was first postponed until Ngarimu could be charged, and then later abandoned and the jury discharged on 13 May 1994 after Deith Bridges, who was on bail, was shot in the leg and chest. He had been walking home from the Clay Pigeon pub in Field End Road, Ruislip, west London, when a dark car with two men inside screeched to a halt. One of the men called Bridges' name, then shot him twice with a semi-automatic handgun. Police were treating the incident as attempted murder.

Mistaken Identity?

Professional killers pride themselves on their 'efficiency', but not only are they sufficiently dis-coordinated to kill innocent bystanders, sometimes they target the wrong man. It was hard to draw any other conclusion to the circumstances of the murder of Martin Jacks, a

Cambridge-educated trainee accountant with apparently not an enemy in the world. Mr Jacks was remembered as a charming, self-effacing and popular young man, a Christian and keen sportsman. He had been watching cricket on television on 6 June 1993 when three hooded men kicked his door down, shot him in the thigh with a sawn-off shotgun and left him to bleed to death. They made off in a dark-coloured 'sporty-type' car. Police who were called to the flat in Cortis Road, Putney, south-west London, found Mr Jacks lying in a pool of blood on his sofa. He had been hit in the femoral artery with pellets from a twelve-bore shotgun, and died within minutes.

It was not until one year later, in June 1994, that the public learned the full story – when two men, Arron Bamborough and Roland Thorp, appeared at the Old Bailey charged with Martin Jacks' murder. It had, as suspected, been a case of mistaken identity – in fact the bungling killers had not only got the wrong man in the wrong house but the wrong location as well. It was no surprise to learn that the reason for the murder was related to the drug trade, a point emphasised by Judge Angus Stroyan in sentencing: 'This cruel and merciless murder was a tragic example of death following in the wake of drugs.' Arron Bamborough and Roland Thorp were jailed for life; the third man has not so far been taken into custody. The cruel irony was that Thorp – who was believed to have fired the fatal shot – advanced a defence of mistaken identity.

It was thought at first that the killing of two Department of Transport inspectors at a garage at Bredbury, Stockport, Greater Manchester, was another case of mistaken identity. Alan Singleton and Simon Bruno were investigating stolen MoT certificates, a scam said to be worth £4.5 million a year on the black market – in 1992, no fewer than 120,000 certificates were stolen. The two inspectors went to Chestergate Auto Centre on

22 November 1993, where they were ushered in to an office adjacent to the open-plan inspection bay area. Ten minutes later a man wearing dark clothing and possibly a mask entered the office and opened fire with a twelve-bore double-barrelled shotgun at close range. The emergency services were called at 3.39 p.m., but paramedics arrived to find Mr Bruno and Mr Singleton dead on the floor.

The investigation was led by DS Rod Murray, who thought at first that the inspectors may have been mistaken for the garage's owners, brothers Walter and Thomas Bourke. There had been a long-running vendetta between rival garages in the area, a car-parts shop owned by Walter having been set alight in July 1992, killing a man, and local tyre and exhaust centres fire-bombed in the following year. But on 25 November detectives raided the Bourkes' £250,000 house in Bramhall, Greater Manchester, seizing several guns and a white Ford Sierra Cosworth. Thirty-one-year-old Thomas Bourke was remanded on two charges of murder, while his elder brother Walter was accused of obstructing the course of justice.

Another Death in Drugland

Andrew Birjukove was a bricklayer and self-employed builder from West Wickham in Kent. He also happened to be a small-time crook with convictions for burglary and car offences, who had taken to dealing in drugs. He carried out his business at the Rutland Arms pub in Catford until it was closed down by the brewery, when he moved his pitch to the Two Brewers in nearby Perry Hill. This was a bad move, and Birjukove was warned to take his cocaine elsewhere. It was a warning he ignored at his peril. On the evening of 14 September 1993, a masked gunman dressed in black leapt from a motorcycle and burst into the Two Brewers, where he fired four shots. Birjukove was killed outright while his drinking companion, Mr Bobby 'Red' Campbell, previous landlord of the Rutland Arms, was hit in the back. A third man, Michael Davey, was slightly injured when he gave chase. A customer who knew Andrew Birjukove said that older villains in the area had asked someone from outside the area to deal with him. 'He ignored the warning and came back. It's not so much vigilantes as what you could call pest control. It's to keep the neighbourhood respectable.' On 20 December 1993 police investigators announced they were winding down the hunt for the assassin, having met with a wall of silence.

'The Concrete Overcoat'

Wayne Lomas, a car dealer who had been acquitted of attempted murder in 1985, disappeared from his home in Bristol on 30 August 1988. It was not until five years later, after a number of houses in south Bristol had been raided, that the mystery was solved. Human remains found encased in a one-ton concrete slab under a house in Bristol were identified on 18 October 1993 as those of Mr Lomas, after police and forensic scientists had spent nearly a week digging and chipping away at the concrete using a hammer and chisel. Lomas had been shot, believed murdered in a gangland feud. A forty-eight-year-old man was subsequently arrested in connection with the murder.

An Old Score in Gangland

There has been a change in the way gangland carries out its affairs – a change for the worse. The criminal 'firms' of past decades were interested in status and territory – the Krays in the East End, Billy Hill and 'Spot' Comer in the West End, the Richardsons in south London. Today's successful criminals keep a lower profile and are interested in just one thing – money. According to Detective Chief Superintendent Bill Ilsley, who has led numerous major police inquiries in south London: 'The criminal world has become a lot less stable and it is very worrying. There has definitely been an increase in the number of gangland murders in the last two years. They are basically cold-blooded and it is obvious that a number of them are being done for money.'

James Alfred Moody was an armed robber and gangland heavy, a muscle-bound keep-fit fanatic and member of the infamous torture gang led by Charles Richardson. In December 1980 he achieved notoriety by escaping from Brixton Prison with convicted IRA terrorist Gerard Tuite, an escape which provoked outrage in Parliament and led to the removal of the prison governor. 'Long Jim' Moody evaded capture for thirteen years, and it is suspected that he was involved in contract killings during that time: a former Flying Squad officer said he was 'mad and violent enough'. Certainly there is some evidence that Moody was the man who strode into The Bell public house in East Street, Walworth, south London in August 1991 and shot dead two customers – Stanley Silk, an innocent bystander, and David Brindle. Brindle was none other than the nephew of Francis 'Mad Frankie' Fraser, and it is thought his was a gangland execution in retaliation for the murder of another south London villain, Ahmet 'Abbi' Abdullah of the fearsome Turkish-Cypriot Arif family.

James Moody's past caught up with him on the night of Tuesday 1 June 1993. He was having a drink in the Royal Hotel, Lauriston Road, Hackney, when a man described as about forty years of age and 6ft tall walked in and ordered a drink. He pulled a gun from his pocket and fired four shots into Moody's chest, in front of several other customers, before escaping in a stolen white Ford Fiesta. The car was later found abandoned nearby.

Crimes of Passion

A sensational society murder in Paris resulted in a sixty-five-year-old woman former lawyer being jailed for the contract killing of her daughter's playboy husband. Jacques Perrot, himself a lawyer, married France's best-known woman jockey, Darie Boutboul, in 1982. They were a glamorous couple, but the marriage broke up in 1985 because of Perrot's affairs with other women. He was found shot outside his apartment months after the separation. Police investigators discovered that the mother-in-law, Elisabeth Cons-Boutboul, had defrauded a religious order of more than £1 million, had been expelled from the legal profession, and had lied about the death of her husband. One witness described her as 'the most dangerous woman I've ever met'. She was linked to a blackmailer and gangster, Bruno Dassac, whose body was found in Le Havre harbour in 1989. Whether it was Dassac who had eradicated Perrot we do not know, for Elisabeth Cons-Boutboul swore she would 'rather go to jail than tell the secrets I know'. And on 24 March 1994 to jail she went, for fifteen years.

In a case in America, forty-five-year-old Mary Ellen Samuels has been accused of hiring a hitman to murder her husband Bob, a Hollywood cameraman. Mary and Bob were getting divorced after eight years' marriage, and Mary 'didn't want half the good life – she wanted it all'. After many indiscreet inquiries she hired cocaine dealer James Bernstein, who carried out the murder on 9 December 1988. Samuels celebrated by splashing out on a new Porsche and an apartment in Cancun, Mexico, where her lover photographed her with her naked body covered by $100 bills. But she was not the only greedy one: Bernstein began demanding more money to keep his silence. Mary Samuels hired Paul Gaul and Darryl Edwards to kill Bernstein and dump his body in the woods, but the plot went wrong when they confessed to the police. She stands charged with two counts of murder, soliciting murder, conspiracy and attempted murder.

The Middle East Connection

Adnan Abdul Hameed al-Sane, a millionaire London banker connected to the Kuwaiti royal family, disappeared from his Maida Vale flat on 15 December 1993. Thirty-two hours later his partially burned body was found in a railway arch near Piccadilly station, Manchester. But his head, which had been hacked with a machete and smashed into hundreds of pieces to make it unrecognisable, was not discovered until six weeks later, seventy miles away in a field near the M6 at Cannock, Staffordshire. The head was formally identified after a painstaking reconstruction of its features, made by medical artist Richard Neave of Manchester University, had been recognised by his lawyer.

Friends of the dead man have revealed that he was actively trying to trace three members of his family who were imprisoned in Iraq after the invasion of Kuwait by the forces of Saddam Hussein. Al-Sane had made substantial payments to Middle East middlemen who had promised to find and release the relations, but he was dissatisfied when he received no news of their whereabouts.

A link was made between al-Sane's murder and an incident which occurred in April 1994, when Jordanian investment consultant Ahmed Haj Hassan was shot by two gunmen in the hallway of his London flat in Westbourne Terrace, Paddington. Hassan was a former business partner of al-Sane's, but the relationship had turned sour when al-Sane accused Hassan of illegally transferring more than £500,000 from his bank account. A trial in 1993 was abandoned when the Crown Prosecution

Service offered no evidence, but at the time of his disappearance al-Sane was continuing to press a civil claim against the Jordanian to recover the money.

The Russian Mafia

Ruslan Outsiev was self-styled 'prime minister' of the tiny oil-rich state of Chechenia, a Muslim enclave of the former Soviet Union. In autumn 1992 he came to Britain with his younger brother Nazerbeck to negotiate the printing of currency, stamps and passports for the newly autonomous state. But the Armenian secret service believed Ruslan was intent on selling his country's oil for personal gain, and planning to buy 2,000 Stinger missiles to use against them in the war with Azerbaijan. After he refused to go ahead with the arms deal, the Armenians hired an assassin, allegedly one Ashot Detmendzian, who failed to be granted an exit visa from the USA. Two Armenians living in Britain were recruited in his place. Mkritch Martirossian was an employee of the Armenian KGB, while Gagic Ter-Ogrannsyan ran an export business to the former Soviet Union; he had also been Ruslan Outsiev's translator and guide.

Ruslan and Nazerbeck had been living it up in London, flaunting their wealth on massive restaurant bills, tipping waiters £100 a time, and paying £995,000 cash for a luxuriously furnished flat at exclusive Bickenhall Mansions in Marylebone. Here they enjoyed the services of up to six prostitutes a night; and it was here that the Armenians carried out their assassination.

Removal men calling at the Mansions on Saturday 27 February 1993 were asked to take a refrigerator carton containing 'antiques' to a garage at a house in Pinner View, Harrow. They became suspicious of the 'disgusting smell' emanating from the carton and alerted the police, who broke the box open to find the remains of Ruslan

Outsiev, sealed in polythene and rolled up in carpet, with three bullet wounds in the head. His brother's body was discovered in a locked bedroom at Bickenhall Mansions, killed in the same way; a Beretta pistol with a silencer lay near the body. The two Armenians were arrested when they returned to the Mansions to dispose of Nazerbeck's body, but on 16 June 1993 Mkritch Martirossian was found hanged in his cell at Belmarsh Prison in Woolwich. Gagic Ter-Ogrannsyan stood trial at the Old Bailey, where he received two life sentences on 21 October 1993.

Retribution came soon enough. After Gagic Ter-Ogrannsyan's detention his wife Alison Ponting, a producer with the Russian and Ukrainian service of the BBC's World Service, moved from her home in Chiswick and went to live with her sister, thirty-three-year-old geophysicist Karen Reed, at Willow Way, on the Barnesbury Farm estate at Woking, Surrey. Alison Ponting had received death threats at the time of her husband's trial, and was herself arrested, but not charged, with trying to import a phial of poisonous snake venom from America. There was speculation that the poison was to concoct a suicide pill for husband Gagic, but the alternative theory was that it was a *memento mori* from the Chechenian secret service. After a loaded pistol and map of the area were found in a stolen red Cavalier car, abandoned near the house during a routine police check, a panic button linked to the local police station was fitted at Willow Way. Police officers warned the women not to open the door to strangers.

But Karen Reed did not press the button before she opened the door at 9.00 p.m. on Saturday 30 April 1994. A gunman aged about thirty-five, with short dark hair and wearing spectacles with metal frames, shot Mrs Reed at least four times in the head at close range, killing her instantly. The killing was assumed to be a case of mistaken identity, and Alison Ponting was immediately put under armed police protection.

Yardies

The Yardies are a mafia-style operation originating in the backyards of the ghettos of Kingston, Jamaica. They first surfaced in Britain in the mid-1980s, and are now believed to control nearly all the crack and cocaine dealings in the inner cities of London, Manchester, Birmingham, Bristol and Nottingham. A hard core of probably fewer than 100 members controls numerous acolytes, characterised by extreme violence and almost total lack of loyalty to one another. Their philosophy is 'life is short, but sweet'; their activities tend to promote the first part of that dictum.

Many of the gang members have criminal records in Jamaica, and come to this country on stolen or forged passports. If apprehended at immigration control, they are often granted 'temporary admission' under a change of tactics which followed criticism of the 'racist' policy of keeping suspects in detention centres. They are admitted on condition of keeping in touch with police and staying at a designated address, but 'hundreds' are said to abscond.

A police initiative, Operation Dalehouse, to monitor the activities of the Yardies in south London led to 267 arrests in the eighteen months up to November 1992, when it was disbanded. On 31 July 1993 it was announced that a new taskforce of twelve undercover detectives and immigration officials was to be set up under the leadership of Commander John Grieve.

Yardies go about well-armed and are not reluctant to use their weapons – the most dangerous gang is known as the 'Shower Posse' because they shower their victims with bullets. But the leader of the gang, Christopher Alexander 'Tuffy' Bourne, was destined to die of his own medicine. Bourne, a drug dealer with a criminal record of drug and fraud offences, was shot during a row over control of a crack den in Vassall Road, Brixton, on Sunday 30 May 1993. In all, thirteen shots from at least three weapons sprayed round the flat, and the four bullets which hit Bourne were fired at almost point-blank range. On 25 March 1994, twenty-eight-year-old Raymond 'Emma' Grant was jailed for life with a recommendation that he serve at least twenty years. Three other suspects were cleared of the murder. The trial was described by detectives as a 'breakthrough' because fifty witnesses came forward: in previous Yardie cases possible witnesses had been too frightened to testify.

In August 1993, the badly decomposed body of Glenroy Samuel Wayne Quashie was found at his maisonette in Lee Bank, Birmingham. He had been shot through the head with a single bullet from a Smith & Wesson revolver, within hours of returning from a trip to America. DS Malcolm Ross, leading the investigation, believed the 'mafia-style' execution to be drug-related.

A leading member of a Yardie gang known as the 'Raima Rats Posse' was jailed for life on 16 August 1993 for gunning down two men at a party. An argument had broken out between Leroy 'Scarface' Lesley, an illegal immigrant with a string of convictions, and Andre Blackman at the party in Stoke Newington in November 1992. Lesley had left the bar, been handed a loaded gun by a woman, returned to the bar, pointed the gun at Mr Blackman, pulled the trigger and shot him. Mr Blackman died soon afterwards. His friend Jeff Dixon was also shot, but recovered, while another woman was hit in the thigh when Lesley fired off several shots at random. Leroy Lesley was granted an appeal less than an hour after the sentence had been passed, on the grounds that the case against him did not stand up because his co-defendant, Linneth May Lewis, the woman who had allegedly handed him the gun, had been acquitted.

Not surprisingly the issue of Yardie drug gangs was a

significant subject for discussion at the drugs conference of the Association of Chief Police Officers in June 1994. The conference had the benefit of the knowledge of John Brennan, a former teacher and now a detective sergeant with the South East regional crime squad. Mr Brennan is a specialist in what he prefers to term 'Jamaican crime groups', and wrote his thesis on the subject at Exeter University. He described Yardie activity as 'disorganised organised crime' with no hierarchical structure: 'There are no Mr Bigs, but loads of Mr Bigenoughs.' He concluded: 'One thing is clear: this violent group of international criminals are present and organised in our own back yards.'

Triads

The Chinese Triads are part mafia, part freemasons. They are style-conscious racketeers who make their money through gambling, extortion, prostitution and drugs, but also have secret rituals, codes and initiations that celebrate their somewhat spurious history. This can be traced back 2,000 years, although modern gangs derive from the resistance movement to the Manchu conquerors of the seventeenth century. They supported the republican revolution of 1911 and took control of the thoroughly corrupt Chinese civil service, but were forced underground after the 1949 Communist revolution, retreating to Hong Kong and later to Taiwan.

The fifty or sixty Chinese organised-crime groups boast a worldwide membership of more than 100,000, with Sun Yee On (literally 'New Righteousness and Peace') the largest and most hierarchical. The Triads have for many years operated syndicates in New York, Amsterdam and the UK, but recently they have been spreading their tentacles to green fields like Canada, South Africa, Australia and New Zealand. A dramatic struggle for control of international crime is anticipated in 1997 when China resumes sovereignty over Hong Kong, although the Chinese Minister of Public Security, Tao Siju, has said that he was prepared to work with 'patriotic' Triad gangs in Hong Kong, as long as they were concerned with the territory's prosperity and stability.

Public awareness of the secret societies has been raised in this country by a number of court cases. David Lynch, a twenty-four-year-old passport official, was terrorised into illegally issuing up to 400 passports after three Chinese men held a gun to his head. Brothers Patrick Shu Chai Man and Stephen Kwong On Man, of west London, were alleged to have told Lynch it would be 'worth his while' to issue more passports after he had sold them a first one. He received between £7,000 and £10,000 in cash, was given cars, televisions and videos, and had a flat rented for him. Police caught up with Lynch when two illegal immigrants were found to have full passports authorised by him, and he was jailed for three years.

A murder attempt on a Hong Kong businessman was foiled when the victim fought back despite being shot in the back twice at close range. Ying Kit Lam was believed to be involved in a bid for the leadership of the Sui Fong gang, also known as the Wo On Lok Triads. He was 'horrifically crippled' in the attack which took place 'as an example' in London's Chinatown in September 1991. The gunman, Wai Hen Cheung, was arrested hours later at an address in Manchester, and agreed to give evidence against fellow members of the Triads. Consequently six men appeared at the Old Bailey charged with conspiracy to inflict grievous bodily harm on Mr Lam.

The court was told how Cheung had been initiated as a '49' rank, or soldier, in the Sui Fong in March 1990, after a rival gang member had threatened him. He was ordered to cripple Mr Lam by shooting him twice in the back and 'four or five times in the backside or groin, depending on how he fell'. He was not told to shoot to kill, but if Mr Lam died it would be 'his own fault'. Cheung claimed it took three attempts before he was able to shoot his victim, because he kept losing his nerve. But Jonathan Goldberg QC, representing 'Flying Man' Clifford Wai Ming Tang, described the gunman as 'a sadistic assassin with strong hatreds and uncontrollable violence', who was framing innocent people to protect his bosses and 'jockeying to get the least prison sentence'. Mr Goldberg told the court Cheung was 'obsessed' with firearms; skilled in martial arts and able to kill bare-handed; and guilty of a number of intimidatory attacks, including slashing a man's face with a double-bladed razor to scar him permanently.

After a seven-week trial the jury found five of the accused not guilty, and was discharged after failing to reach a decision on Clifford Tang. Tang and one other defendant, Shui Cheung Wan, were convicted of attempting to pervert the course of justice in trying to stop Cheung from talking to the police, and sentenced to six months' jail. As they had been imprisoned for thirteen months awaiting trial, they were released immediately.

Yakuza

The Japanese equivalent of the Chinese Triads, the Yakuza prides itself on a heroic 'Robin Hood' image, settling disputes more rapidly and discreetly than the normal channels of justice. It claims to have kept hard drugs out of Japan, maintained 'unorganised' crime at minimum levels, and kept inter-gang violence off the streets. Because of this the police have traditionally tolerated its activities. But in 1992 new legislation officially outlawed the Yakuza, by making extortion, money-laundering, gun-running and other mainstays of the society's activities illegal for the first time. This played havoc with the legitimate side of their business which included dealing in property, stockbroking and developing golf courses. In a curious reversal of the normal course of justice, members of the 30,000-strong Yamaguchi-gumi, the largest of the Yakuza, took the National Police Agency to court in March 1993, accusing them of unfair discrimination. The NPA is also considering outlawing two rituals by which Yakuza members distinguish themselves – chopping off the little finger to atone for a blunder, and tattooing the entire body with lurid and intricate dragon and flower designs. The proposed change in law seems likely to prove unenforceable.

Execution USA

THE YEAR ON DEATH ROW

Over the year covered by this edition of *The Murder Yearbook* – 1 June 1993 to 31 May 1994 – there was a slight decrease in the overall use of capital punishment in the United States; a total of twenty-five executions nationwide as compared with twenty-seven in the previous twelve-month period.

However it was, for this writer at least, disappointing to see that yet another state, Idaho, had joined the swelling ranks of the executioners. Individually, Texas was again top of the states' league table with nine lethal injections (the method increasingly favoured across the country). Virginia retained its customary second place, and there are no surprises through the rest of the list; Georgia returned to the fold after a year's 'abstinence'.

Only one execution achieved international media recognition – that of serial killer John Wayne Gacy; some failed to excite even local press coverage and few details are available in these cases.

204*
CHABROL, Andrew J. (20th in Virginia)

A former Naval lieutenant, Andrew J. Chabrol was executed in the electric chair at Greenville Correctional Center at Jarratt, Virginia, on Thursday 17 June. Chabrol pleaded guilty to a charge of abducting, raping and strangling Melissa Harrington, a female recruit, after she had refused his uninvited advances and sexual harassment. Mrs Harrington complained to Chabrol's superior

* Number of the execution, nationally and by state, since restoration of the death penalty in 1976.

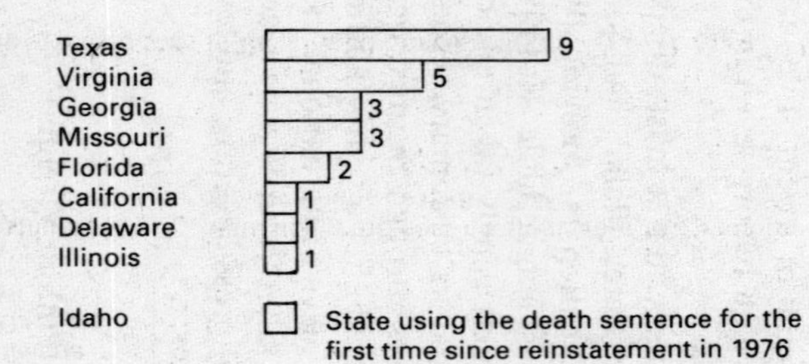

Chart 15 Executions in the United States, 1 June 1993–31 May 1994 (*by State*)

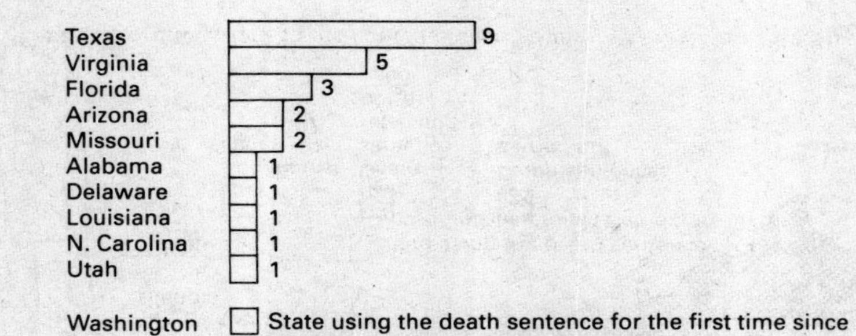

Chart 16 Executions in the United States, 1 June 1992–31 May 1993 *(by State)*

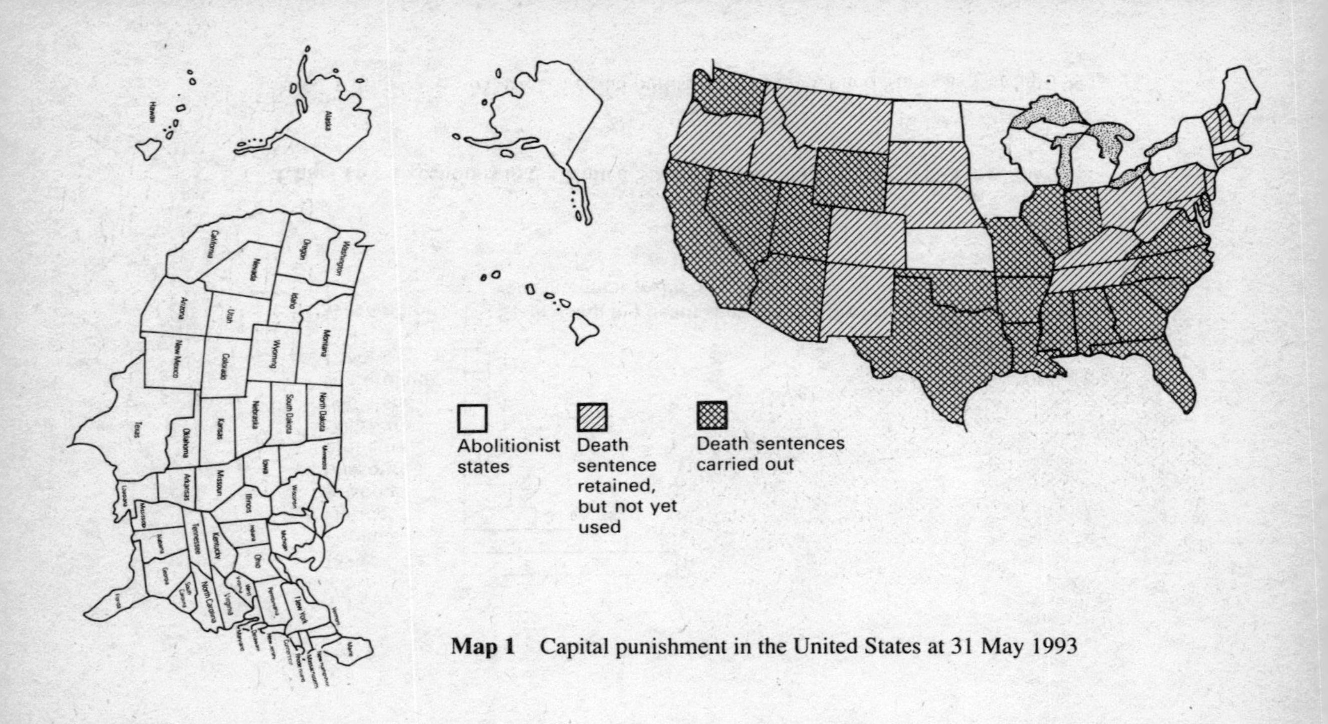

Map 1 Capital punishment in the United States at 31 May 1993

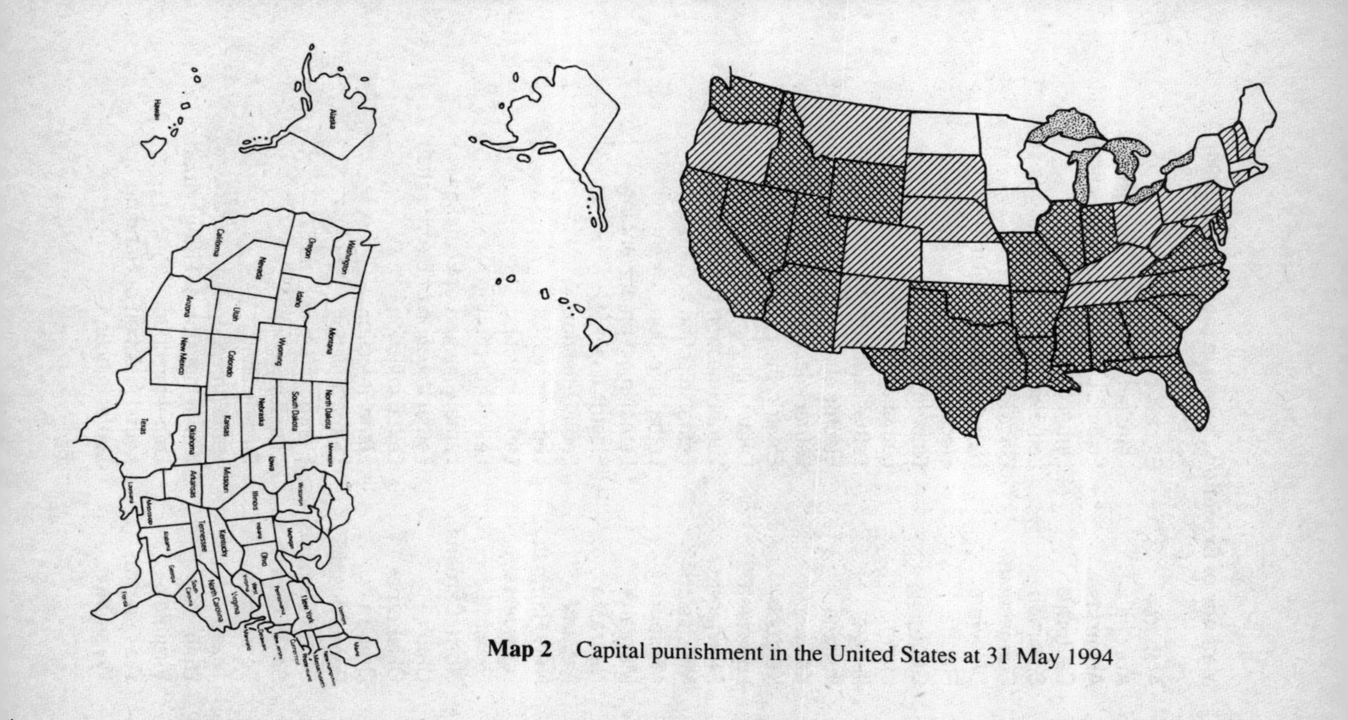

Map 2 Capital punishment in the United States at 31 May 1994

Methods of Execution Current in the US (July 1994)

Alabama	Electric chair
Arizona	Lethal injection or Lethal gas
Arkansas	Electric chair or Lethal injection
California	Lethal gas
Colorado	Lethal injection or Lethal gas
Connecticut	Electric chair
Delaware	Hanging and Lethal injection
Florida	Electric chair
Georgia	Electric chair
Idaho	Lethal injection
Illinois	Lethal injection
Indiana	Electric chair
Kansas	Lethal injection
Kentucky	Electric chair
Louisiana	Lethal injection
Maryland	Lethal injection or Lethal gas
Mississippi	Lethal injection or Lethal gas
Missouri	Lethal injection
Montana	Lethal injection or Hanging
Nebraska	Electric chair
Nevada	Lethal injection
New Hampshire	Lethal injection
New Jersey	Lethal injection
New Mexico	Lethal injection
North Carolina	Lethal injection or Lethal gas
Ohio	Lethal injection or Electric chair
Oklahoma	Lethal injection
Oregon	Lethal injection
Pennsylvania	Lethal injection
South Carolina	Electric chair
South Dakota	Lethal injection
Tennessee	Electric chair
Texas	Lethal injection
Utah	Lethal injection or Firing squad
Virginia	Lethal injection
Washington	Lethal injection or Hanging
Wyoming	Lethal injection

officer, a move which the officer claimed had wrecked both his career and his marriage. Although Andrew Chabrol left the service in 1991, he continued to harbour a desire for revenge and began to keep a computer 'diary' in which he referred to his prospective victim as 'Nemesis'. Shortly afterwards Chabrol and another man took advantage of Mrs Harrington's husband's absence on business to break into their Virginia Beach home. Mrs Harrington was subsequently forcibly removed and taken to Chabrol's house in Chesapeake where she was tied down and raped. When she put up a strong resistance her head was bandaged in parcel tape. After the sexual assault Mrs Harrington was strangled with a length of rope. Claiming that he 'just went berserk', Andrew J. Chabrol refused to appeal against his death sentence, and as a result had a shorter wait between conviction and execution than any of the other nineteen Death Row inmates to be executed since Virginia reinstated the death penalty in 1976. Chabrol's accomplice, Stanley J. Berkeley, was sentenced to three terms of life imprisonment, one each for murder, rape and abduction.

A Navy publication issued at around the time of Andrew Chabrol's execution provides an interesting postscript:

'What is Sexual Harassment?'

Everyone knows that sexual harassment will not be tolerated in the Navy – but what constitutes sexual harassment still seems to be confusing for some sailors and Navy employees.

GREEN – Go

These actions do not constitute sexual harassment. They are typical interactions and common courtesies that happen regularly in an office environment. Some examples:

- Performance counselling

- Touching which could not be perceived in a sexual way, such as placing a hand on a person's elbow
- Counselling in military appearance
- Everyday social interaction, such as saying 'Hello, how are you?' or 'Did you have a good weekend?'
- Expressing concern or encouragement
- A polite compliment or friendly conversation

YELLOW – Slow down to stop

Many of these behaviours fall into the grey areas but others are obvious examples of sexual harassment. Examples:

- Violating personal space
- Whistling
- Questions about personal life
- Lewd or off-colour jokes
- Leering or staring
- Repeated requests for a date after being told no
- Suggestive posters or calendars
- Foul language
- Unwanted letters or poems
- Sexually suggestive touching
- Sitting or gesturing sexually

RED – Stop

These behaviours are always considered to be sexual harassment and, if they continue, punitive action will be taken. Examples:

- Sexual favours in return for employment rewards and threats if sexual favours are not provided
- Sexually explicit pictures, including calendars and posters
- Sexually explicit remarks
- Using office status to request a date
- Obscene letters or comments
- Grabbing, forced kissing, fondling
- Sexual assault and rape

205
STEVENS, Thomas Dean (16th in Georgia)

Thirty-six-year-old Stevens had been sentenced to death in 1977 for the murder of a fellow soldier in Hinesville at Fort Stewart by the rather bizarre means of locking him in the boot of a car and pushing the vehicle into a water-filled pit in Wayne County. The victim, Roger Honeycutt, had been moonlighting as a cab-driver and before he was killed by Stevens and another soldier he had been robbed of $16 and the car radio, and sodomised. Claims by his defence attorney that Stevens was mentally handicapped and had been convicted on perjured evidence were unable to win a last-minute reprieve after several stays of execution. The chairman of the state's Board of Pardons and Paroles concluded his statement: 'Mr Stevens was a willing and active participant who knew the consequences of his actions.' Stevens and his seventeen-year-old accomplice Christopher Burger had decided to rob a cab-driver after drinking all their money away; it was the unfortunate Roger Honeycutt who responded to their call for a car to take them to the airport at Savannah. On the way Mr Honeycutt was forced at knifepoint to stop the car, and undress. According to the prosecutor at Stevens' trial, they then sexually abused him and killed him.

On 28 June Thomas Dean Stevens displayed no emotion when he was strapped into the electric chair at Jackson. He was read a final prayer by the attendant priest, but refused to make any last statement and waived his right to a special meal – instead he ate what everybody else was having, spaghetti with meat sauce, green beans, rolls, peach cobbler and iced tea. Stevens had been scheduled to die at 7.00 p.m., but a delay for a final appeal pushed the time of execution on to 11.15 p.m.

There was the customary visitation from representatives of the campaign against the death penalty who demonstrated outside the Georgia Diagnostic and Classification Center. And there were counter-demonstrations from the pro-capital punishment lobby, one of whom was emphatic that 'this guy deserved to die'. Christopher Burger received a stay of execution from a federal court, and his case remained on appeal until December 1993, when he was judicially executed (see No. 224).

206
DUFF-SMITH, Malcham (60th in Texas)

In a last-minute confession before he was executed, Duff-Smith admitted hiring somebody to kill his mother and three other relatives in order to inherit the family fortune. 'I am,' he said, 'the low sinner of sinners . . . I am responsible for the 1975 and 1979 cases.' Malcham Duff-Smith had been convicted of arranging the death by strangulation in 1975 of his adoptive mother, Gertrude Duff-Smith Zabollo at her home in the exclusive River Oaks district. He had hired Allen Wayne Janecka for $10,000 to do the job and make her death look like suicide. Having squandered the $90,000 inheritance from his mother, Duff-Smith then hired Janecka again in 1979, this time to eliminate his adoptive sister, her husband and their son. The proceeds were expected to be in the region of $500,000. In 1979 Malcham Duff-Smith was indicted but never tried on the three later charges, and had throughout vociferously protested his innocence. It was only when he was actually lying strapped to the gurney awaiting lethal injection at Huntsville on 29 June that he finally spilled the beans. As for Janecka, he was convicted of the murder of Duff-Smith's nephew but the finding was overturned on appeal; he awaits retrial for the murder of Mrs Zabollo.

207
HARRIS, Curtis Paul (61st in Texas)

On 1 July, thirty-one-year-old Curtis Harris died by lethal injection at Huntsville. Harris had been convicted with his brother Danny (see No. 210) of bludgeoning to death twenty-seven-year-old Timothy Merka in what became known as the 'Good Samaritan Killing'. The Harris brothers flagged down their victim on the night of 11 December 1978 when their stolen car broke down on a country road. Danny held on to Mr Merka while Curtis beat him to death with a tyre lever before robbing him and driving off in his truck. Curtis Harris's attorney had appealed unsuccessfully on the grounds that the jury had not been selected properly, and had not been given the opportunity to consider evidence that as a result of childhood beatings Harris had become brain damaged.

208
BLAIR, Walter Junior (9th in Missouri)

On 21 July 1993 Missouri's longest-serving Death Row prisoner was executed by lethal injection at Potosi. Thirty-two-year-old Blair was sentenced to death for a contract killing committed in 1979. He had been accused of accepting $6,000 to kill twenty-one-year-old Katherine Jo Allen, a Kansas City art dealer, to prevent her testifying at the rape trial of a man named Larry Jackson. In his defence Blair had alleged that another man, Ernest Jones, was the real killer; perhaps it was no coincidence that Jones was the chief prosecution witness against Blair. During his twelve and a half years on Death Row, Junior Blair had frequently said that he would rather die than continue to live in prison, and a mural painted by him at the end of one of Death Row's four wings incorporates the words: 'Death is certain – Life is not.'

209
LASHLEY, Frederick (10th in Missouri)

When he was convicted of the murder of his foster mother in 1981, Lashley was just seventeen years old. Mrs Janie Tracy was not only his foster mother, but also a cousin, and had raised Fred from the age of two. Fifty-five-year-old Mrs Tracy had been recovering from a brain operation when Lashley, after taking out the light bulb to plunge the room into darkness, waited for her to come in, smashed her skull and stabbed her to death; the proceeds of this endeavour were less than $15. At Lashley's trial his attorney tried to make a defence of the fact that he was under the influence of PCP ('angel dust') at the time. When, after twelve years on Death Row, the appeal system ran out, opponents of the death penalty claimed that it would be unjust to execute a person who was only seventeen when they committed their crime.

Frederick Lashley was executed by lethal injection at Potosi Correctional Center on 28 July; before he died he said he bore no grudge against any of the people involved in the execution, and realised that they only had a job to do.

210
HARRIS, Danny (62nd in Texas)

Harris who, in 1978, in company with his brother Curtis, killed a 'good Samaritan' driver who pulled over to help them, was executed by lethal injection at Huntsville on 30 July. Making a last-minute plea, Harris's lawyer, John Hotigner, said that his client was not the same person after fifteen years in jail: 'The seeds of goodness have grown in him.' On his own behalf, Danny Harris claimed: 'I have peace, I have strength. I have courage, the comfort of Christ, the grace of God.' In response Bill Turner, District Attorney of Brazos County, commented:

'If facing the death penalty caused him to reckon with his maker, so be it. I applaud him for that. But that doesn't make me think he's any less dangerous.' Curtis Harris was executed on 1 July (see No. 207).

211
JERNIGAN, Joseph Paul (63rd in Texas)

In July 1981 seventy-five-year-old Edward Hale arrived at his home in Dawson, about sixty miles from Dallas, to find he had an uninvited and unwelcome visitor – Joe Jernigan, who was in the middle of burgling him. At his subsequent trial, Jernigan confessed to stabbing and shooting Mr Hale and was sentenced to death. An accomplice, Roy Lamb, was paroled from a thirty-year sentence two years ago. Thirty-nine-year-old Joseph Paul Jernigan was taken into the death cell at Huntsville just after midnight on 5 August. Asked by the warden if he had any final words to say, Jernigan remained silent but nodded to his brother Bobby who was there as a witness. It is recorded that Joe Jernigan coughed six times and his head and shoulders jerked as the lethal cocktail of drugs was pumped into his left hand; he was pronounced dead at 12.31 a.m.

212
HOLLAND, David Lee (64th in Texas)

In July 1985 David Holland robbed the savings and loan office managed by twenty-nine-year-old Helen Barnard. During the course of the raid Mrs Barnard and one of her tellers, Diana Jackson, were forced into the bank's vault and shot dead with a .45-calibre handgun. Holland escaped with around $8,000. Holland, a bank security officer, was identified on a videotape recording of the robbery and sentenced to death for the Barnard murder; he was also charged with killing Mrs Jackson but never tried. Fifty-five-year-old David Holland was executed by lethal injection at Huntsville, and was pronounced dead at 12.16 a.m. on 12 August. He declined his right to make a last statement.

213
KELLY, Carl (65th in Texas)

'I am an African warrior, born to breathe and born to die.' So ran the final statement of thirty-four-year-old Carl Kelly. As the lethal chemicals were injected into his arm, Kelly's last words were: 'I feel the poison flowing.' Carl Kelly, along with his accomplice Thomas Graves seized eighteen-year-old Steven Pryor from behind the counter at the Waco branch of 7-Eleven and forced him at gunpoint to his car parked out back. There they found David Riley, a vagrant, asleep in Pryor's car. Kelly and Graves robbed their captives of $30, drove them to a remote area, shot them and threw the bodies over a 60ft cliff. Kelly was picked up by police while he was, rather unwisely, driving Steven Pryor's car; in the boot was Carl Kelly's wallet. As if this were not incriminating enough, Pryor was a diabetic with a rare blood group – identical to that found on Kelly's shoes.

After fourteen years on Death Row he was dispatched at Huntsville on 20 August. Thomas Graves, who pleaded guilty to the killings as well as another shooting the previous week, was sentenced to life imprisonment, the result of a plea bargain.

214
CANTU, Robert (66th in Texas)

Twenty-six-year-old Cantu was executed by lethal injection at Huntsville on 24 August. He had been sentenced to death for a robbery which resulted in murder in 1984, when Cantu had been just eighteen years old. In his defence he claimed he had been nowhere near San Antonio at the time of the incident; however, one of the surviving victims identified him.

215
MASON, David Edwin (2nd in California)

On the same day Robert Cantu died at Huntsville, David Mason was led into the gas chamber at San Quentin. Mason was sentenced to die for the murders of four elderly women in 1980, and the strangling of a fellow prisoner in 1982. Mason also confessed to a sixth killing but was never put on trial.

Despite the fact that David Mason is only the second prisoner to be executed in California since restoration, the state has the highest Death Row population in the country.

216
DUROCHER, Michael Alan (32nd in Florida)

Whether or not Durocher deserved to be executed is part of the eternal debate; but certainly *he* thought he did. Indeed, he insisted on it, writing to the state governor begging him to sign the death warrant: 'I am a believer in capital punishment and I respectfully request that justice be done.' When Governor Lawton Chiles obliged, Durocher sent him a letter of gratitude. Mr Chiles' enthusiasm may have had something to do with Michael Durocher's criminal record which, if not unsurpassed, was certainly formidable. In 1983 he murdered his partner Grace Reed, her five-year-old daughter Candice, and their six-month-old son Joshua; their bodies were not discovered until 1990. He was also under sentence of death for shooting a man dead in an armed robbery in 1986, and was serving life for bludgeoning a room-mate to death two years later.

Despite the fact that Durocher himself had consistently refused to lend his voice to an appeal, representations were made on his behalf by groups opposing the death penalty. So irritated was he by this interference that Michael Durocher sought and was given a Florida Supreme Court ruling that he could waive all appeals, and that a state agency which represents Death Row inmates had no right to represent him. On 25 August Michael Alan Durocher was granted his wish: at daybreak he was executed in the electric chair at Starke.

217
WILKERSON, Richard James (67th in Texas)

Just before he was given the lethal injection at Huntsville on 31 August, twenty-nine-year-old Richard Wilkerson said in his final statement: 'I'd just like to say I don't hate nobody. What I did was wrong. I just hope everybody is satisfied with what's about to happen.' What Wilkerson did that was wrong was go out with two friends and kill eighteen-year-old Anil Varughese, the manager of an amusement centre who had sacked Wilkerson from his job two weeks previously. One of the other killers is presently on Death Row awaiting execution and the third, who was only sixteen years old, was sentenced to life imprisonment. All three were suspects in other deaths that resulted from the subsequent robbery but were never put on trial.

218
DESHIELDS, Kenneth (3rd in Delaware)

Sentenced to death for the murder of his employer Elizabeth Reed of the Sussex County Landfill Company, in 1984, Deshields was executed by lethal injection at Smyrna on 31 August. Although his family maintain that Kenneth Deshields was only sentenced to death because he was black and his victim was white, Deshields' last words were: 'It ain't worth it; it ain't worth taking a life.'

219
JAMES, Johnny (68th in Texas)

James, thirty-nine at the time of his execution, was sentenced to death for kidnapping forty-seven-year-old Barbara Mayfield from BJ's Lounge near High Island, about fifty miles south of Houston, in October 1985 and killing her. Mrs Mayfield owned the bar and had at one time employed James. James shot his victim in the foot to immobilise her and stuffed her into the boot of his car, driving fifteen miles to the town of Winnie. Here he held up a convenience store, stole $300 and dragged the shop assistant into the car at gunpoint. In a secluded spot James forced the two women to engage in sexual acts with each other, and raped and sodomised the shop-girl. He then shot both his captives twice in the head with a .38-calibre pistol before dumping them at the side of the road. Unfortunately for him one of his victims survived and identified Johnny James as their attacker. James was executed by lethal injection at Huntsville on 3 September and was pronounced dead at 12.17 a.m.

220
WISE, Joe Louis Sr (21st in Virginia)

Wise was sentenced to death for bludgeoning, shooting and drowning forty-three-year-old William H. Ricketson during the course of a robbery in 1983. Mr Ricketson was a maintenance worker at the Mecklenburg Correctional Center, and his body was found hidden beneath soil and bricks in a pit in Mecklenburg County. Wise was arrested the following day when he was driving his victim's car. Thirty-one-year-old Joe Wise Senior went to Virginia's electric chair at the Greensville Correctional Center at Jarratt on 14 September.

221
BONHAM, Antonio (69th in Texas)

In 1981 Bonham beat sixty-two-year-old college teacher Marie McGowan to death with a brick, raped her and then ran over her with her own car. Arrested a week later after police found his fingerprints on the victim's car, Bonham claimed he merely abducted Mrs McGowan in order to steal the vehicle. The jury clearly thought otherwise and took just thirty minutes to decide on the death penalty. In a not entirely new line of defence Antonio Bonham's lawyer at appeal maintained that he was given the death sentence because he was a young black who could not afford a lawyer at his trial. Mr Michael Chatton also had some harsh words to say about his theory that blacks were being kept off juries. He concluded: 'Mr Bonham's appeal for clemency raises again the issue of racial discrimination in the application of the death penalty.' None of which made a scrap of difference, and Antonio Bonham received a lethal injection at Huntsville on 28 September.

222
GUINAN, Frank J. (11th in Missouri)

Forty-seven-year-old Frank Guinan was put to death by lethal injection at Potosi Correctional Center on 6 October. He had been sentenced to death for two murders committed while behind bars.

Guinan was originally serving a forty-year sentence for robbery and assault with intent to kill; in 1981 while he was doing time he and a cellmate, Richard Zeitvogel, stabbed John McBroom with knives made from a pair of scissors – the two men claimed that McBroom was an informer. Sentenced to death for this crime, Guinan got into a fight with a fellow Death Row resident in 1985; Robert Baker was stabbed more than fifty times by Guinan and died of his wounds. In interviews before his execution Frank Guinan maintained that it had been Zeitvogel alone who had killed McBroom; he claimed that he had walked into the cell and seen Zeitvogel stabbing him: 'I told Rich to stop, but it was too late.'

Richard Zeitvogel is currently on Death Row.

223
COOK, Anthony (70th in Texas)

'I just want to tell my family that I love them, and I thank the Lord and Saviour Jesus Christ for giving me another chance and for saving me.' These were the last words of thirty-two-year-old former electrician Anthony Cook before he died by lethal injection at Huntsville on 10 November. Cook had been on parole less than a fortnight after serving a fraction of his eight-year sentence for theft when he and Robert Moore, another parolee, abducted thirty-five-year-old law-school graduate David Dirck Van Tassel Jr in 1988. The kidnappers drove Mr Van Tassel to a park fifty miles away where Cook shot him four times in the head, robbed him and stole his car.

At the subsequent trial Robert Moore testified against his accomplice and received a fifty-year prison sentence. Cook was sentenced to death. While he was waiting on Death Row, Anthony Cook underwent a religious conversion, the result of which was that he wanted to block appeals being made on his behalf and to have his sentence of death carried out. According to District Attorney Hollis Lewis: 'He [Cook] sent me a letter basically saying he could not persist in the appeal where they were alleging that a co-defendant [Moore] actually pulled the trigger. He said: "I am the one who did it. I can no longer lie about it." ' Before the killing Anthony Cook had been in and out of prison most of his life, receiving sentences for crimes as varied as theft and burglary and aggravated assault.

224
BURGER, Christopher (17th in Georgia)

In 1977 Burger and his accomplice Thomas Stevens (see No. 205) were responsible for the brutal murder and sexual assault on cab-driver and fellow soldier Roger Honeycutt. At the time Christopher Burger was just seventeen years old; at the age of thirty-three, when the death penalty was carried out on 7 December 1993, Burger became the first person in thirty-six years to be executed in Georgia for a crime committed as a minor. The attorney who fought for a commutation of Burger's sentence to life without parole told of a brutal childhood which taught Burger violence as a natural part of life. In a last desperate appeal to the state's Board of Pardons and Paroles, she described his early life. His mother constantly cursed him, Ms Andrea Young said, and his father beat him regularly and viciously. When he was seven years old, Chris Burger's parents divorced and he spent the next ten years of misery being knocked back and forth between them like a football. At the suggestion of his mother's new partner, the boy took to using drugs and landed in a juvenile detention centre. When he was released at the age of seventeen he joined the US Army and was posted to Fort Stewart where he encountered Thomas Stevens, then twenty years old.

Despite these appeals for mercy Christopher Burger's execution went ahead. After the Supreme Court had delayed proceedings for almost three hours in order to review the case to see if there were 'extenuating circumstances that might warrant further action', the justices rejected the request for a stay at 8.53 p.m. Meanwhile, the condemned man had spent much of the day receiving visits from about thirty people – friends, members of his family, including his mother, and members of the clergy. It was reported that he ate little of his specially requested meal of unleavened bread and water.

The main local paper, the *Atlanta Constitution*, described the execution: 'Burger was ashen-faced and nervous as six prison guards led him from his holding cell into the death chamber shortly after 9.30 p.m. and strapped his arms and legs into the chair at the Georgia Diagnostic and Classification Center. In his last statement – before the leather mask was placed over his face – he asked for forgiveness and requested one final prayer: "I'd like to say I'm sorry . . . I'd like to say I'm sorry to anybody and everybody I've ever hurt," he said, his cheeks twitching. "Please forgive me." Warden Walter Zant pronounced Burger dead at 9.51 p.m. – nine minutes after 2,000 volts of electricity shook his body and caused his fists to clench and turn purple.'

225
PHILLIPS, Clifford X. (71st in Texas)

On 15 January 1982, Mrs Iris Siff, managing director of the Alley Theater in Houston, Texas, was working late filling out a government grant application form, when she was strangled. Her assassin was Clifford X. Phillips, a former security guard at the theatre who had been dismissed a few weeks earlier for falling asleep on the job.

It was not the first time Phillips had come to the notice of the police or the courts. He had already served a seven-year stretch in New York State for killing his three-year-old son in 1970 by forcing water down his throat. The child's body was found stuffed in a suitcase.

He had also been accused of beating his daughter so savagely and persistently that she had lapsed into a vegetative state. Predictably, in the case of Mrs Siff's murder, Phillips' defence attorney dragged out the old chestnut of racism – claiming that because the victim was white and the jury was all white, and Mr Phillips was black, he could not have a fair trial. Just hours after the Supreme Court refused to block the execution, Clifford Phillips, fifty-nine years old, was executed at Huntsville by lethal injection on 15 December. He made a barely coherent last speech, offering love to his wife, thanks to Allah, and remorse to his victim and her family.

226
PRUETT, David Mark (22nd in Virginia)

Pruett, who confessed to the rape and murder of his best friend's wife, was executed in the electric chair at Greensville Correctional Center, Jarratt, on 17 December. It was in 1986 that David Pruett was convicted of the sexual assault and stabbing of thirty-five-year-old Wilma Harvey at her Virginia Beach home the previous year. Mrs Harvey's husband had given Pruett a job as a chef at the restaurant he managed. At the same time as confessing to killing Mrs Harvey, Pruett also told detectives that he had been responsible for the murder of Deborah McInnis in 1975; Miss McInnis had been a fellow-worker at the Kentucky Fried Chicken restaurant at Virginia Beach. Pruett was convicted of first-degree murder and robbery in this case just four months after receiving the death penalty in the Harvey case.

227
WELLS, Keith Eugene (1st in Idaho)

According to Wells' own statement in an interview with the *Idaho Statesman*, he walked into a bar at Boise in

1990 and had been drinking for a couple of hours when 'I knew someone had to die.' Using a baseball bat he had brought with him, Wells first clubbed to death bar patron John Justad as he walked out of the toilet, and when barmaid Brandi Rains came to see what was going on, he beat her to death as well. Wells admitted: 'I was a predator on the prowl for prey.'

Convicted and sentenced to death, Keith Eugene Wells strenuously opposed any appeals on his behalf, apparently believing that he was possessed by demons and could only rid himself of the curse by dying. He got his wish on 6 January, when he had the doubtful double honour of being the nation's first victim of judicial execution in 1994, and Idaho's first since the death penalty was reinstated in 1976. Wells died by lethal injection at the Idaho Maximum Security Institution. It was reported in the *New York Times* that: 'As the execution . . . went ahead inmates pounded on the walls and stomped on the floors.'

The last execution in Idaho had taken place on 18 October 1957, when thirty-five-year-old Raymond Allen Snowden, an itinerant labourer, was hanged for the murder and mutilation of a woman he met in a bar.

Twenty-one people currently reside on Idaho's Death Row.

228
BARNARD, Harold (72nd in Texas)

Fifty-one-year-old Harold Barnard was convicted of killing sixteen-year-old student Tuan Nguyen at the 7-Eleven convenience store owned by his father in Galveston, Texas. Despite the fact that the boy and his father had filled a bag with money for the robbers, when Barnard shot Tuan Nguyen in the heart with a sawn-off shotgun, he and his three accomplices fled empty-handed. They were arrested half an hour later driving a stolen car. At the trial Mr Jack Brock, the state prosecutor, told the jury: 'There was absolutely no provocation, and the robbery had apparently been completed and Barnard had the money in his hand. This is a case that is appropriate for the death penalty.' The jury had no trouble agreeing with him. In his defence it was argued that Harold Barnard was suffering from paranoid delusions, and whether or not this is the case, fellow-prisoners will attest to his volatile state of mind, often heaving heavy objects around and going into screaming sessions that can last days. Or rather *could* last days; Barnard was executed by lethal injection at Huntsville on 2 February.

229
WATKINS, Johnny Jr (23rd in Virginia)

Whether he appreciated it or not, and he probably did not, Johnny Watkins Jr added a footnote to the legal history books. After eighty-six years of executions in Virginia's electric chair, Watkins' on 3 March was the last; as from 1 July, condemned inmates will be put to death by lethal injection.

The state's solid oak electric chair was installed at the Virginia State Penitentiary at Richmond in 1908. When that prison closed in 1991, the chair was removed to the newly built Greensville Correctional Center, fifty-five miles south at Jarratt. In total, 258 men and women have been executed in Virginia's chair, and there have been some ugly incidents when executions have gone wrong. For example in the case of Wilbert Lee Evans [see *Murder Update* by Brian Lane, Robinson Publishing, 1991, London] in 1990, and Derick Lynn Petersen in 1991 [see *Murder Yearbook* by Brian Lane, Headline, 1993 Edition, London]. The procedure should be simple – as simple anyway as such a cumbersome process can be: the condemned killer is strapped into the chair and his face covered with a leather mask. Once the button is pushed, the chair delivers a 1,825-volt shock for thirty seconds, followed by a 240-volt surge for sixty seconds. It then resets itself over a span of three to five seconds and repeats the cycle.

In the case of Johnny Watkins Jr things went smoothly, and the thirty-two-year-old double murderer did not struggle, complain or make a final speech. Watkins had been convicted of fatally shooting Betty Jean Barker during a robbery on a convenience store on 14 November 1983, and Carl Douglas Buchanan in a similar raid on 22 November of the same year.

230
WEBB, Freddie Lee (73rd in Texas)

Webb was executed by lethal injection at Huntsville early on the morning of 31 March. He had been convicted of killing a man and abducting his wife during a robbery at a restaurant in Corpus Christi.

231
HANCE, William Henry (17th in Georgia)

On Thursday 31 March, after once again angrily protesting his innocence, William Hance was executed in Georgia's electric chair. It was following the murderous activities of the so-called 'Stocking Strangler' Carlton Gary, that a scribbled note was received by a Georgia newspaper in March 1978. The message was that a black woman would be killed every thirty days unless the 'Strangler's' toll on elderly women stopped and the crimes were solved; the man signing himself 'chairman' of the 'Forces of Evil' also demanded a ransom of ten thousand dollars. Within days the decomposed body of prostitute Brenda Gail Faison was found in a shallow grave outside Fort Benning army base. Two other women, also black, were known to be missing, so it was a wise precaution to assume that the 'Forces of Evil' had already begun to kill.

Painstaking inquiries by the military CID came up with the information that one of the camp's soldiers had been seen drinking with Gail Faison shortly before her disappearance. His name was William Henry Hance. Following a telephone tip-off, army police also found the bodies of the two other missing women – Mrs Irene Thirkeld and Private Karen Hickman. During intensive interrogation, Hance confessed to all three killings. He was first indicted by the civilian authorities for the murder of Gail Faison and with extortion arising out of the ransom demand. At his trial he was convicted and sentenced to death. Hance was later tried for the remaining two murders before a court martial, and was convicted and sentenced to two terms of life imprisonment. However, these sentences were not ratified by a military review board and Hance's convictions were overturned. In view of his already existing death sentence, the army decided not to retry him.

William Hance's journey to the electric chair enjoyed several moments of controversy, not least when a woman juror at his 1984 sentencing trial claimed that she was coerced into voting for the capital penalty. The final appeal on his behalf contended that Hance was mentally retarded and was thus protected by a 1988 state law that bans execution of the retarded. However, there was insufficient medical evidence to support his claim and, albeit after some delay, William Hance went defiantly to his death. In his final statement he claimed: 'Right at this very moment I can prove my innocence. I was trying to find a judge and attorneys to prove my innocence. There was no motive. There were no witnesses. There were no clues.'

232
BEAVERS, Richard (74th in Texas)

Beavers was convicted and sentenced to death for killing a man and then shooting his victim's wife in the head. The thirty-two-year-old inmate died by lethal injection at Huntsville on 4 April.

233
STEWART, Roy Allen (33rd in Florida)

Executed 22 April.

234
ANDERSON, Larry (75th in Texas)

Executed 26 April.

235
SPENCER, Timothy Wilson (24th in Virginia)

Executed 27 April.

236
ROUGEAU, Paul (76th in Texas)

Executed 3 May.

237
GACY, John Wayne (2nd in Illinois)

Everybody knew it was going to be the Big One; after all they had waited fourteen years for 10 May 1994, the day when John Wayne Gacy was going to fry (actually he wasn't, he was going to be injected with a lethal cocktail of drugs – but that didn't stop the revellers carrying placards reading 'Say goodbye, the time has come for you to fry').

John Wayne Gacy was arguably America's most notorious serial killer and certainly one of the most prolific multicides. Between 1972 and 1978 the man the press later came to know as the 'Clown Killer' sexually abused, tortured and then strangled thirty-three young men and boys and hid their bodies around his home and garden near O'Hare International Airport outside Chicago. When it was announced that, the appeal process finally exhausted, Gacy was to be executed, the whole atmosphere around the Stateville Correctional Center at Joliet, Illinois, suddenly took on more the atmosphere of a carnival than a solemn occasion on which one of the country's most appalling monsters was to suffer the ultimate sanction of the law. Urged on by media hungry for increases in circulation and viewership – Walter Jacobson, anchor-man with WFLD-TV, who had won the coveted TV witness ticket to see the execution, was reported as saying: 'This is just the kind of break we needed for our ratings' – a veritable fever of eager anticipation gripped Chicago. As many as a thousand people occupied a floodlit field close to the prison, many wearing clown costumes in parody of Gacy's *alter ego* as Pogo the lovable clown, throwing confetti and streamers, others wore black 'grim reaper' hoods and danced about yelling and singing slogans and rhymes. Among the most popular of these were: 'Turn that frown upside down – they have just fried the clown' and 'Goodbye Gacy' to the tune of *Hello Dolly*. The only comparatively serious gesture was made by one group who lined up thirty-three body bags in the street in Chicago, one for each of Gacy's victims; however, even these had acquired their own little knots of partygoer placards bearing the familiar words 'Goodbye, the time has come for you to fry'. T-shirts were available from street vendors: 'No Tears For The Clown'.

But if the denizens of Chicago's retentionist campaign were having fun, John Wayne Gacy seemed hardly a scrap less jolly – being described by his attorney Greg Adamski as 'chatty and talking up a storm'. The execution was set for 11.00 p.m. (5.00 a.m. London time) though eleventh-hour bids for a reprieve caused a minor delay in the procedure. Nevertheless Gacy remained calm, protesting his innocence to the last and claiming in a television interview that: 'I am the thirty-fourth victim. I believe that after I'm executed the state will find out that they have killed an innocent man.' And he was clearly revelling in the one thing that had become almost as much a drug for him as it had been for a nation that had turned him into, if not exactly a national hero, then at least a character or major celebrity. It is said that Gacy received more fan mail than any other prisoner on Death Row – an incredible 27,000 letters to each of which he obligingly replied. Television interviewers and presenters were queuing up for the privilege of an on-air chat. In a final chilling paragraph to an interview with Gacy conducted by Alec Wilkinson for *New Yorker* magazine, the newsman seemed to put his finger on how Gacy had remained aloof through all his long years in captivity: 'He seemed unaware that he was in prison because he was a criminal. He seemed to think that I had come to see him because he was famous.' This necessary fantasising had also been observed by Gacy's lawyer when he said of Gacy's calm: 'I think he denies the reality.' Attorney David Keefe continued: 'There probably isn't even a real Gacy. When you cut away the artifice, there probably isn't even a person there at all.'

So if he no longer exists, who exactly *was* the monster America loved to hate, and how did he become Death Row's most notorious inhabitant? It *ended* like this:

At nine o'clock on the evening of 11 December 1978, fifteen-year-old Robert Piest went to a chemist's in his home town of Des Plaines, Illinois, to talk to a building contractor working on the shop about a holiday job. He was supposed to go straight back because it was his mother's birthday and the family were giving a party. But by 11.30 Robert had not arrived and Elizabeth Piest and her husband contacted the police.

The name of the building contractor was John Wayne Gacy – a name already known to the police since, earlier in the year, twenty-seven-year-old Jeffrey Rignall had reported being approached by a plump man with a flashy car and invited to join him in the vehicle to smoke some marijuana. The fat man had rendered Rignall unconscious by pushing a chloroform-soaked handkerchief into his face, and had then driven him to a house where he was beaten with whips and raped. Rignall regained consciousness in Lincoln Park where he had been dumped, but he could tell the police little about his attacker and they were not much help. Eventually it was Rignall himself who went on a trawl of the city and found the Oldsmobile, but even then the authorities were slow to call on the owner, John Wayne Gacy, though he was a familiar name to them with a record of arrests for various sex and violence offences against young boys.

When officers paid a visit to 8213 West Summerdale Avenue, Des Plaines, the unpleasant smell led them to discover seven bodies in various stages of decomposition under Gacy's house, along with parts of several others; eight more corpses were dug out from the garden and the garage. In all, remains of twenty-eight bodies were found around the house and five Gacy had thrown in the Des Plaines river – including that of Robert Piest.

Gacy had been born in Chicago on 17 March 1942. As a child he was hit on the head by a swing and thereafter suffered from fainting fits. He graduated from business school and became a star shoe salesman. Despite two failed marriages and a violent temper, he was a man who made a great effort to be liked, and was a popular children's entertainer known as 'Pogo the Clown'. Then Gacy set up a business as a renovation contractor and he used this to attract young men eager for work – many were subjected to rape and thirty-three lost their lives.

Despite the several confessions that he made while in custody, admitting to killing thirty-two teenaged boys before, during or after sex (he had lost count, there were thirty-three), John Wayne Gacy did not give evidence at his trial. On 12 March 1980 the jury rejected his defence plea of insanity and convicted him of murder with a recommendation for the death penalty. And now he was going very reluctantly to pay the price that the law had determined was appropriate to his crimes. Not that John Wayne Gacy appeared to notice. He ate a hearty last supper of fried chicken and fries, followed by strawberries, washed down with Coke – an ironical choice for a man who had once owned the franchises on three Kentucky Fried Chicken outlets in Iowa.

As the time approached for him to die, Gacy, now a rather tubby fifty-two-year-old, was puffing away at a cigar and joshing with prison staff and the Roman Catholic chaplain – for all the world like a man getting ready for a party. As the star of the show was being brought into the 10ft x 8ft execution cell, the audience of forty-two people representing journalists, police and legal officers and prosecution attorneys filed into the observation room where they would watch the procedure through a plate-glass wall. Obliging to the last, John Wayne Gacy climbed smiling on to the special padded stretcher and offered himself for pinioning at the ankles, wrists, chest and hips – and was linked through an intravenous needle with the execution machine. He was even observed to wink at one of the guards and remark, with a smile on his face: 'You can kiss my ass.' Those were his last words before the three drugs – sodium thiopentone, an anaesthetic, pancuronium bromide to stop the breathing, and potassium chloride to stop the heart were pumped into the vein at minute intervals. At least, that was the theory. In reality it became one of a growing list of bungled executions being reported from Death Row. In this case, the anaesthetic tube functioned and Gacy was mercifully rendered unconscious. According to one witness, 'he gave a huge sigh, then he swallowed and went quiet. Then his eyelids closed.' However, according to prison warden Howard Peters, 'there was a clogging in the [second] line' and the poison was blocked. As guards pulled a blue curtain across to prevent the observers witnessing the scene, the tubing of the apparatus was 'rerun'. Then the curtain opened again and the execution continued. It took eighteen minutes to kill John Wayne Gacy – twice as long as it should have done. Life was pronounced extinct as 12.58 a.m. (6.58 London time).

In a basement room at the prison twenty-three relatives of Gacy's victims huddled around a television set waiting for the news. There was no hysteria as there was outside the prison, just a few tears. Karl Cahoon, whose brother died at Gacy's hands, summed up the feeling when he said: 'Everybody has lost today. We lost our relatives. His family lost their father. He lost his life. There's a lot of losing going around.' Meanwhile, the revellers were still in festive mood, enjoying themselves blowing out the candles of the handful of people demonstrating against the death penalty and finishing off with a few rounds of 'Turn that frown upside down, they have just fried the clown.'

Appendices

Appendix 1
Serial Murder Update

Introduction

TO CENSOR OR NOT TO CENSOR

A debate that has smouldered for many years now – whether true crime is suitable subject matter for 'entertainment' (that is to say movie and television treatments and reconstructions) – has erupted more than once over the past year and the general received wisdom, albeit from those with loudest voices, seems to be that it is not suitable.

But whatever the cinematic virtues and vices, it seems that the subject of serial murder still has a long life ahead of it. Indeed, no less venerable a film institution than the London Film Festival found space in its 1993 version to incorporate a special 'mini-festival' of movies about serial killers and their black deeds. There were six films in all (imaginatively chosen because the list could have been far longer with old chestnuts such as *Silence of . . .*, *Henry . . .*, and *Dirty Weekend*; they could also presumably have included a few 'blasts from the past' – how about *Arsenic and Old Lace*?). The films were *Painted Heart*, *Kalifornia*, *White Angel* and *One Night Stand*; and two deserve special mention for interest quotient – *The Hawk*, which reverses Helen Mirren's adopted role as killer-catcher in the 'Prime Suspect' series to one of a wife whose husband may or may not be the serial killer. *Genghis Cohn*, in many respects unique among the selection, centres on a Jewish comedian who comes back to avenge himself on his Nazi executioner; the film tends to compare the modern concept of serial murder with historical issues such as Nazism. The fact is that, as in every sphere of human endeavour, there will be the responsible and the irresponsible, there will be the good, the bad and the ugly.

Whatever I feel on the matter, of one thing I am certain – that, regardless of its effect on the *individual*, the escalating tendency to elevate murderers (and particularly serial killers) to cult status can only serve to undermine the morality of the *society* that tolerates it. It is impossible (and undesirable) to control the thoughts and feelings of the individual in respect of his or her likes and dislikes, but it would seem irresponsible to allow them access to material marketed *solely* to feed a prurient lust for the horrific.

Take Charles Manson – once described as the most dangerous man in America – who with his 'family' literally butchered at least seven and almost certainly many more innocent victims during the 1960s. From the time mad Charlie and his equally crazy followers were put away he had a following; he still has a following, most particularly among youths who were not even born at the time of the Tate/LaBianca slaughter. There are Charlie Manson appreciation societies – *fan clubs* – and to service them there are Manson T-shirts, Manson posters, Manson bubble-gum cards (a whole series), a disc by the appropriately named Birdmen of Alcatraz of a homage to Manson, *Song for Convict Charlie*, and it is rumoured that Axl Rose, leader of the band Guns'n'Roses, is planning to record one of Manson's inept songs. And I am indebted to Robert Leedham of the *Guardian*'s 'Guide' for his perceptive view of the merchandising of mass murder, and for reminding me that one Trent Reznor (of a band with the unlikely name of Nine Inch Nails) recorded his last offering in the house in Cielo Drive where Mad Manson hacked to death Sharon Tate and her friends.

The unlovely Reznor told Robert Leedham: 'I can understand in some ways the empowerment it must give someone to kill someone . . .'

Much the same is true of most of the more notorious serial killers whose exploits are finding their way into comic books and on to posters; and it is possible to purchase a variety of sets of portraits of these multicides in the form of 'trading' or bubble-gum cards. The cards originate in the United States, but are available in Britain. One particular set of these 'trade cards' – those published by Eclipse Enterprises Inc. – enjoyed a very controversial introduction to the world of true crime. According to the editors of the series they were not only foully misrepresented in the media ('deluged with dozens of reporters every day for six months')* but 'received more than 10,000 pieces of hate mail . . . mostly from Christian groups'. Going, as things seem to, from bad to worse True Crime Trading Cards encountered the biggest blow of all – to their purse. A number of the States of the Union proposed to ban the cards – Arkansas, Florida, Michigan and New York. Even Canada joined in, halting shipments of the cards at customs under an 'obscenity' clause of the Tariff Act. Inevitably the hysteria died down, leaving only Nassau County, New York, with a new law forbidding the sale of trading cards 'depicting a criminal' to a person under seventeen years of age (punishable by one year's imprisonment).

But the story did not end there. Even the subjects of the cards themselves were laying into Eclipse Enterprises. Ken Bianchi (who with his cousin Angelo Buono became the 'Hillside Stranglers') demanded almost $7 million for having 'his likeness appropriated

* Quotations have been taken from the Introduction to *True Crime: Serial Killers and Mass Murderers, Vol. 2.*

for commercial purposes'. Apparently Kenneth has tried this one before, with several publishers, and failed in his lawsuits.

Because of what they describe as 'a promise we made to card collectors that the original cards would not be reprinted', Eclipse have reprinted the cards in booklet form . . . to be banned? In the words of the editor, 'We'll see.'

Some of these madmen do not even have to wait for immortality. During the siege of 'Fort Apocalypse' at Waco the battle had hardly got under way before the souvenir stalls had set up to service the thousands of sightseers who flocked to the tiny Texas town: posters, car stickers of the 'I have been to Waco' variety, and any number of T-shirt designs based on the theme.

Weird
Asshole
Come
Out

was one of the less patronising slogans. Had he known – and perhaps he did – David Koresh would certainly have approved of the publicity (though not of being deprived of a cut of the profits); after all was the 'Lamb of God' not himself just before Armageddon in the process of negotiating a fat fee for book and movie rights to the siege?

Talking of profits from notoriety, it was reported by the *Daily Mirror*'s New York correspondent Alan Hall that Jeffrey Dahmer, the 'Milwaukee Cannibal', 'is now trying to auction off his grisly assortment of personal possessions, including the fridge where police discovered human hamburgers made from his victims'. And he should have little difficulty raising a good price if reports coming in at the beginning of March 1994 are anything to go by.

The report originated from the Columbia Correctional

Institution in Portage, Wisconsin, where Dahmer is serving his 957–999-year sentence, and was relayed via the *Milwaukee Journal*. According to that newspaper the Institution is being inundated with love letters, fan mail and sizeable sums of money – including one gift of £3,900 from a woman in London. Another female correspondent apparently wants to teach Jeffrey about Jesus, and enclosed £240 along with a wad of religious texts, and a nun with whom he corresponds on the subject of art was quoted as saying: 'He did awful things but way deep down he isn't a mean kid.'

There is neither any law to stop people sending prisoners money nor to prevent the inmates receiving it. What has pinpointed this case is that, although the courts awarded Dahmer's victims more than $30 million in compensation they have so far not received a cent. Meanwhile the 'Milwaukee Cannibal' has amassed an estimated $9,000 in gifts, which he spends, according to prison governor Jeffrey Endicott, on comics, records and items from mail order catalogues.

Axl Rose seems to have left Dahmer alone – for the moment anyway – and it was left to rapper Eazy-E to record for posterity his adulation of Jeffrey 'The Cannibal' Dahmer.

Another favourite monster hero was still cashing in on his horrific record of multicide just weeks from his execution. John Wayne Gacy, convicted of the sadistic sex murders of thirty-three boys and young men, went electronic. In collaboration with a telephone message company, Gacy recorded his final declaration of innocence and for less than a couple of dollars anybody in America could phone 1-900-622-4229* to hear Pogo the 'Evil Clown' claim, among other things: 'The state wants

* For the benefit of the curious it should be said that this number is no longer valid.

you to believe this fantasy. It does not hold water. It raises doubts who John Wayne Gacy is . . . he is the thirty-fourth victim.'

But John Wayne Gacy was not just relying on the few bucks he drew in from the jammed phone lines; Pogo was also an amateur artist – not in the conventional sense of course. Jolly John's subject matter included himself, Mad Charlie Manson, Adolf Hitler, witches, demons, skulls, his own house where the murders were committed (ones which show the cavity under the floor where he stored his victims are a favourite), and pretty much anything ghoulish.

Needless to say the daubs sold – and sold well. Ed Vulliamy, writing from Nebraska for the London *Observer* in late April 1994 described Gacy's ascent from serial killer to art celebrity. It would seem that, like the telephone message, the marketing of the paintings began in a cheapskate sort of way – in fact they were offered in the ads section of *Psycho Killer* (whatever that may be!) for around $75. That is until an entrepreneur named Arthur Deco (Art Deco – geddit?) moved in, befriended Gacy and took over the business side of things. Labelling the psycho's paintings 'art brute', Deco made hundreds of thousands of dollars selling John Wayne Gacy's pictures to the rich and famous around Beverly Hills. Then Jimmy Tuoronto muscled in on the scene, ousted Deco and took over the business. At the last estimate the paintings, described by one art gallery as 'so expensive because they're unique', were fetching up to $20,000. One collector, quoted by Vulliamy said: 'I have always been fascinated by the dark side . . . I'm interested in the idea of sex crime and murder, but my fantasies are more tame.' They would be, he is a librarian.

In the wake (no joke) of Gacy's execution (see p. 249) a businessman named Joe Roth spent $7,300 on twenty-five of the killer's paintings and a bonfire party at which they were ritually incinerated. The event, at Naperville, Illinois, was attended by around 300 people, reportedly including a number of relatives of Gacy's victims. 'I think being here today and being able to toss that stuff on the fire finally gave them some satisfaction,' Mr Roth explained.

INSIDE THE MIND OF THE SERIAL KILLER

Running parallel to the customary hysteria of the tabloids, however, there have recently been a number of serious attempts to analyse and come closer to an understanding of the mind of the serial killer.

The phenomenon of serial murder, while not by any means a modern development in homicide, has at last begun to attract serious study.* It was in the United States in the 1970s that this new and increasingly prevalent *type* of murderer was identified – one who kills *apparently* randomly and without *obvious* motive. An awareness of the need to make some positive effort to analyse and combat this baffling phenomenon coincided with the establishment of the FBI's National Academy at Quantico, Virginia, where senior instructors founded what was called the Behavioral Science Unit. In response to the virtual impossibility of applying the time-honoured techniques of homicide investigation, FBI agents began work on a system of 'psychological profiling' which would use the disciplines of the behavioural scientist, the psychologist and the psychiatrist to help analyse evidence, both tangible and intuitive, collected by officers at the scene of the crime. The profile is crafted by the careful assessment of elements such as victim trait, witness

* For one detailed study see *The Encyclopedia of Serial Killers*, Brian Lane and Wilfred Gregg, Headline, London, 1992.

reports and the method and location of the killings. The profile attempts to indicate physical and psychological characteristics resulting in a 'portrait' of the suspect and his behaviour patterns. For obvious reasons a considerable element of instinctive guessing is involved, and no law enforcement officer would dismiss a suspect from his investigation simply because he did not fit the profile. However, profiling has proved increasingly accurate in narrowing the field of inquiry.

The man who established the Behavioral Science Unit at Quantico was Robert K. Ressler, a former military man and at the time a special agent working out of the FBI's Chicago office. In 1974 Ressler joined the academic staff at the FBI National Academy teaching such subjects as abnormal psychology and, later, hostage negotiation techniques. It was while Bob Ressler was in England at an international seminar at the Bramshill police academy that he coined the term 'serial killer'. In his excellent autobiographical study of his work at Quantico,* Ressler describes the occasion: 'At the time, killings such as those of "Son of Sam" killer David Berkowitz in New York, were invariably labelled "stranger killings". This term didn't seem appropriate to me, however, for sometimes killers do know their victims. Various other terms had been used, but none hit the nail on the head. I took the opportunity [at Bramshill] to attend the other seminars and lectures. In one of them, a man was discussing what the Brits called crimes in series – a series of rapes, burglaries, arsons, murders. That seemed a highly appropriate way of characterising the killings of those who do

* *Whoever Fights Monsters*, Robert K. Ressler and Tom Shactman, Simon & Schuster, New York, 1992. The title is taken from a phrase in Nietzsche's *Thus Spake Zarathustra*: 'Whoever fights monsters should see to it that in the process he does not become a monster. And when you look into an abyss, the abyss also looks into you.' Words which Ressler finds particularly appropriate to the dangers of his own and his colleagues' researches.

one murder, then another and another in a fairly repetitive way, and so in my classes at Quantico and elsewhere I began referring to "serial killers". The nomenclature didn't seem to be a big deal at the time; it was part of our overall effort in trying to get a handle on these monstrous crimes, of seeking ways of comprehending them so we could move more quickly toward apprehending the next serial killer.'

In early 1978 Ressler and John Conway initiated a series of interviews with seven of America's most notorious murderers – Sirhan Sirhan (who assassinated Senator Robert Kennedy), Charles Manson, Tex Watson (one of Manson's 'family'), Juan Corona (multiple killer), John Frazier (multiple killer), Herbert Mullin (multiple killer) and Edmund Emil Kemper (multiple killer). It was the first time ever such extensive interviews had been undertaken, and was the foundation of what Ressler called the Criminal Personality Research Project. The Project added a huge store of useful knowledge on the background and motivations of serial killers over years of offender interviews. In 1981 the CPRP and other facilities established by the Behavioral Science Unit were put under a combined project name, the National Center for Violent Crime Analysis. This in turn absorbed the work done by another pioneer of scientific crime analysis, Pierre Brooks, under the name Violent Criminal Apprehension Program, the name now given to the combined project – and so VICAP was born.

VICAP's main aim was to make available, via computer records, information on the *modus operandi* of unsolved violent crimes nationwide, which could be tapped into and compared by the VICAP personnel with the hope of identifying a serial killer operating across state borders. The problem is that such a scheme relies upon the committed cooperation of all states in reporting their unsolved crimes; it has not, Ressler confesses, been a 100 per cent success. However, he presents powerful arguments that the scheme could reduce the 25 per cent of homicides which are unsolved to between 5 and 10 per cent: 'Here's my reasoning. VICAP doesn't all have to do with serial murderers, who might be traced because, for example, we are able to match the pattern of knife wounds on victim A in Massachusetts to those on victim B in New Hampshire, giving the police more of a lead on the killer. A lot of other crimes would feed into it. For instance, say that you had a single homicide-by-gun in New Jersey. The bullet was found but not the killer; the information was entered into the VICAP computer though. Say that two years later, in a bar in Texas, a man was arrested for an attempted rape and a gun was seized from him. Running that gun's ballistic particulars through the VICAP computer might turn up a match, and the man arrested in Texas could be tied to the unresolved single homicide in New Jersey.' It is a convincing argument, and whether or not all the states of America can be persuaded to collaborate, strong interest in the system has been shown by countries as far apart geographically and culturally as Britain and Korea.

Robert Ressler retired from the FBI in 1991; but he has by no means retired from law-enforcement activities. He has a busy schedule of lectures on criminology and hostage negotiation, but is also in great demand as a consultant in the preparation of psychological profiles, and most recently he was an expert consultant in the trial of Jeffrey Dahmer, the 'Milwaukee Cannibal'.

Against all common expectation the picture of the multicide that emerges is not one of a bulging-eyed psychopath with slavering lips and more tics than an alley cat. Indeed, few convicted serial killers have been found insane – even the most ugly crimes, such as those of Jeffrey Dahmer, were the result not of madness but of sociopathy, a total dehumanisation of the victims to little more than objects.

In his own thoughtful, academic study of POP (Psychological Offender Profiling)* David Canter, an expert in behavioural science and professor of applied psychology at Surrey University, gives this chilling warning: 'Even the most depraved serial murderer is not an alien being driven by processes totally beyond normal experience. If he were it is highly probable that the police and others would have become aware of him long before the crimes became a series.' It is Professor Canter's level-headed dismissal of the media mythology surrounding offender profiling, where the police 'expert' confidently predicts the colour of the multicide's socks, that is the value of his book, because psychological profiling is of immense value in cases of serial rapes and murders. As he says: 'Criminals write their own stories, psychology may help us to read them.'

An excellent example of this approach, and one of David Canter's first and most successful investigations in collaboration with Scotland Yard, was the case of the man who had become known as the 'Railway Rapist'. After a series of violent rapes committed close to railway lines in north London and the Home Counties between 1982 and 1985, the crimes of the 'Railway Rapist' changed rapidly to those of the 'Railway Killer'. In December 1985 nineteen-year-old secretary Alison Day was dragged off an East London train and taken to a block of garages in Hackney where she was garrotted. Seventeen days later Miss Day's body was found floating in the river Lea. Three months later Maartje Tamboezer was murdered on her way to the shops in West Horsley, Surrey. Although he had tried to burn clues off the body,

* *Criminal Shadows: Inside the Mind of the Serial Killer*, David Canter, HarperCollins, London, 1994.

the killer-rapist had left semen stains and a set of footprints at the scene of Miss Tamboezer's murder. The link was finally made with the activities of the 'Railway Rapist' and information was immediately entered on to the computer-based files of the so-called 'Operation Hart' set up by teams of officers from Scotland Yard, Surrey, Hertfordshire and the Transport Police.

It was not in time to save the life of Mrs Ann Lock, who disappeared on her way home from the television studios where she worked in May 1986; her body was not found until July. Meanwhile, forensic experts had been busy eliminating suspects from the 'Operation Hart' file by matching body fluid samples lifted from Maartje Tamboezer's body; thus the register was reduced from upwards of 5,000 to 1,999. A man named John Duffy was number 1,505, and although he was interviewed by detectives he refused to provide a blood sample. What was more, he bribed a friend to 'mug' him and then sought safety in a psychiatric hospital to recover from the 'trauma'.

At this time POP was a relatively unknown technique – in Britain at least – in the arsenal of weapons being made available by the rapidly emerging science of forensic psychiatry, but increasingly frustrated by their own lack of progress, the police next enlisted the professional help of David Canter. Professor Canter painstakingly constructed a projectural profile of the 'Railway Killer' based on analysis of police witness statements and details of scene-of-crime evidence – in other words, how, when and where the killer struck. From this information Canter was able to provide a profile consisting of seventeen main points. The analysis was to prove positive on thirteen of those observations. For example, it was David Canter's belief that, with the increasing confidence that evading capture had given him, the killer was venturing further from his home ground – spreading his wings as it were. If this were true, then the 'Railway Killer', or 'Railway

Rapist' as he was then, committed his first three crimes close to home – around the Kilburn/Cricklewood area of north-west London. Professor Canter was also able to predict correctly that the killer was married, childless (a source of great anguish as it turned out) and surrounded by domestic disharmony (not surprising for a man who tied his wife up before sex and frequently bragged that 'rape is a natural thing for a man to do').

While the police were waiting for David Canter's report, the 'Railway Killer' struck again. This time the victim was a fourteen-year-old girl who was blindfolded before her ordeal. During the inevitable struggle the mask slipped and she must have got a good look at her attacker. Why the rapist did not kill this girl is inexplicable, given his former *modus operandi*. Once the psychological profile had been run alongside the computer file of 'Operation Hart' it came up with the name that officers had been waiting a year for: John Francis Duffy. After a short period of surveillance Duffy was arrested at his mother's home where scene-of-crime officers found enough forensic evidence to build a watertight case. Duffy was eventually sentenced to seven life sentences with a recommendation that he serve at least thirty years.

For Professor Canter it was the first of many successes, and in the wake of the trial he was recorded as observing: 'A criminal leaves evidence of his personality through his actions in relation to a crime. Any person's behaviour exhibits characteristics unique to that person, as well as patterns and consistencies which are typical of the sub-group to which he or she belongs.'

Another academic survey of great interest was provided in August 1993 by Alan Leonard, senior psychologist at Wormwood Scrubs Prison and printed in the journal of the British Psychological Society. The study had been carried out by a team of psychologists into the backgrounds of a group of forty-four serial rapists (average 3.5 offences) selected from ten prisons around Britain and twenty recidivist robbers (average 3.8 offences). The main thrust of the study was to assess the viability of psychological profiling in the apprehension and treatment of offenders. The broad results were that serial rapists (who, like John Duffy, frequently turn to murder) are more likely than any other offender to have been physically abused as children (54 per cent of rapists and 19 per cent of robbers). Indeed family life in all the cases studied had been disrupted, often resulting in the separation of parents. Forty-three per cent of serial rapists did not have natural parents at the time of their first offence, and more than one in three had spent time in local authority care. True to the common profile of the serial rapist (and the serial murderer for that matter) most of the individuals in the rape category had strangers as their victim trait. One final statistic is that 39 per cent of rapists come from an ethnic minority group, compared with 20 per cent in the robbery category. The link between childhood trauma and serial aggression is consistent with the experience of the FBI statistics, putting the percentage as high as 70 per cent.

Meanwhile, Dr David Lykken of the University of Minnesota has just completed a thirty-year study programme seeking to support his theory that a high proportion of the most dangerous serial offenders (killers, rapists and those convicted of frequent violent assault) were born with a low genetic capacity for fearfulness and have failed to develop a healthy sense of guilt and empathy with their fellow beings.

At Washington's Georgetown University, Dr Jonathan Pincus added a further dimension when he reported that as many as 90 per cent of all the violent criminals sent to him for observation suffered some sort of neurological abnormality – notably of the brain's frontal lobe, which keeps in control the limbic system which governs aggression and sexual urges.

Another key factor linking the psychology of serial killers is what is referred to as disassociation – an emotional withdrawal from the rest of humankind. In this the serial multicide has an aspect also common to mass, or spree, killers – they have often been described as 'loners', and not infrequently this desire to cut off is also related to childhood trauma. It is this feature too that fuels the desperate need of most multicides to dominate, to acquire the power over life and death. The early years of a potential multicide's activity will often emphasise this, with acts of gratuitous cruelty to animals and smaller children, and an inclination toward arson. It is subsequent to this that the serial killer develops his individual fantasies – frequently of a sexual nature – and begins to act them out, starting perhaps with pornographic literature and videos, graduating to sexual molestation and, at an unpredictable point when the desire for greater stimulus, greater power, becomes overwhelming, committing the ultimate gesture of domination – murder. That this thrill loses its potency is testified by the fact that the frequency with which the multicide needs to 'top up' frequently escalates. It has rightly been compared (by expert on serial killing Brian Masters) with the prognosis of a drug addict.

One thing is certain, although serial murder has bedevilled humankind for as long as we can trace, it is escalating, and whatever interpretation we attach to the fact, unless society and its law enforcement officers find a way of identifying the potential multicide before he can become a national menace, the victim counts will continue to grow.

Much the same conclusions were reached in a lengthy study of 200 cases of serial murder undertaken by Dr Eric

Hickey of the California State University. The end product was an absorbing film titled *To Kill and Kill Again* which, while concentrating on an overview of the mind of the murderer – again we encounter concepts such as disassociation and warning signs such as fire-raising and cruelty to animals – pivoted on the case history of a single, typical serial killer. Yes, it was Jeffrey Dahmer again. Although the film was responsible and rational, scientific rather than sensational, it did have one desperately worrying moment. Producer Patrick Fleming had, not unreasonably, sought an interview with Jeffrey's father, Dr Lionel Dahmer. Through his agent, Dr Dahmer declined to appear in the film – not as one might have thought because he wanted to forget, but because 'it would interfere with his own Hollywood plans'. And so we come full circle!

Case Studies

THE BACKPACK MURDERS
The Case of Ivan Milat

Murder is no longer a rarity, if indeed it ever was, but to link seemingly unconnected missing person reports and corpses found in 'suspicious circumstances' to a series or 'serial pattern' requires all the skills of an experienced police force. That those travelling abroad (from wherever to wherever) are especially vulnerable is well known, and when two British women, Caroline Clarke from Northumberland and Joanne Walters from mid-Glamorgan, disappeared while hitch-hiking in Australia in April 1992, it was a tragic repeat of a familiar story. Caroline and Joanne had met in Australia and they teamed up to hitch-hike around the south of the country. They paid a visit to Tasmania and subsidised themselves by working as fruit pickers before returning to Sydney. In April they had left a backpackers' hostel heading for the south-east of New South Wales. It was not until September that their remains were found by a jogger, buried in the appropriately named Executioner's Drop.

In October of the following year two more corpses were unearthed in the same stretch of remote Belanglo Forest, sixty-odd miles south-west of Sydney. The two nineteen-year-olds, James Gibson and Deborah Everist from Melbourne, had not been seen since 1989. As one newspaper reported: 'It has triggered fears that a serial killer may be at large.'

Then on the first day of November a fifth body, identified by forensic dentistry as that of twenty-year-old German national Simone Schmidl, was discovered in the same location; she had vanished in January 1991. The following day the body count rose to seven when an intensive search revealed a male and a female skeleton, later identified as twenty-one-year-old Gabor Neugebauer and his twenty-year-old girlfriend Anja Habschied, German visitors who had disappeared two years previously. Anja had been decapitated. At the same time Sydney police announced that an earlier victim, Fraulein Schmidl, had died from multiple stab wounds – as, according to forensic tests, had the other victims.

Simultaneously another announcement offered a reward of £250,000; it was made by New South Wales Premier John Fahey for information leading to the capture of the man described as 'Australia's most wanted criminal'. Meanwhile, Duncan Chappell, director of the Australian Institute of Criminology, expressed concern that the so-called 'Backpack Killer' did not fit the normal psychological profile of a serial murderer, in that he killed across genders and killed more than one victim at a time. Despite the difficulty of searching such a vast and remote area of woodland and scrub more than 300 police officers were drafted in to comb the entire area inch by inch for clues and other possible burial sites, and files on missing persons across Australia were reopened.

True to their word the police launched the biggest murder hunt in the country's history, and by the second week in November 1993 already had a list of suspects. On the 15th of the month the *Sydney Morning Herald* announced that they had passed on to detectives the name of an escaped schizophrenic who as early as January had telephoned the news desk claiming that he and two accomplices had murdered the British backpackers Caroline Clarke and Joanne Walters. According to the newspaper the man said: 'I was best friends with the guy who did it. We took the girls; I had a knife and my friend had a rifle [Caroline Clarke had been shot ten times in the head].' The informant apparently boasted of the wonderful sensation of stabbing another human being in the head. Although the man was considered dangerous when he fled from a psychiatric hospital, the police did not regard him as a serious suspect and he was released after being questioned.

However, progress was being made on the forensic evidence gathered from the area around the killer's personal graveyard. Cartridges fired from a .22 Ruger had been found near the body of twenty-two-year-old Caroline Clarke, and these were being tested against some spent cartridges taken from an isolated farmhouse outside Sydney.

By the end of November a possible eighth victim was provisionally added to the list. The investigation team sifting painstakingly through missing persons and unsolved murder records had turned up the name of Diane Pennacchio, a twenty-nine-year-old Australian mother who had disappeared after leaving a bar near Canberra, having told friends that she planned to hitch-hike home to Queanbeyan. Her body had been found in a wood in 1991; she had been stabbed to death. Although the burial site was more than 100 miles from the location of the backpackers' cemetery, police revealed (for the first time) that all the victims had been interred in a very distinctive way. All eight corpses had been placed face downwards alongside a fallen tree trunk with their hands placed behind their back. Then a triangular canopy of sticks had been built over the body and covered with ferns.

Even so, despite the unabated intensity of the investigation and the huge expenditure of manpower and resources, the backpacker taskforce continued to be frustrated in their search for a suspect. When the break came, at the end of February 1994, it was as unexpected as it was lucky. Two British hitch-hikers, responding to accounts of the investigation reported in the press, had some valuable experiences to relate. A twenty-four-year-old woman, who was not named, told police she had been backpacking in the New South Wales outback in January 1990 when she accepted a lift in a truck. Before they had travelled far, the man began to act strangely, and with remarkable presence of mind the hitch-hiker leapt out of the vehicle in the Belanglo State Forest. As she ran into the woods, the driver of the truck fired a gun at her, but missed. Another British backpacker, a twenty-five-year-old former sailor, later identified as Paul Onion, told officers that in 1990 he had been travelling in the same area when he had been offered a ride by a man who pulled a gun out of the glove compartment. As Paul fled the man shot, missed, and then sped off with the tourist's passport, camera and private papers. Mr Onion, blessed with a good memory, was able to identify not only his assailant from New South Wales police mugshots, but also his car.

A low-key police surveillance was carried out over the next few months, and at the end of May 1994 officers pounced. Following a series of seven dawn raids carried out on 22 May by armed officers from the New South Wales Protection Group three men were taken into custody – one, a forty-nine-year-old truck driver later named as Ivan Milat, was charged with armed robbery and discharging a firearm, and the others, one of them Milat's brother Walter, were charged with drug and firearms offences. Also seized during the raids was a staggering arsenal of weapons – sixty assorted guns, 7,000 rounds of ammunition, swords, machetes, and a crossbow and arrows – and a couple of old backpacks. Most significant was the recovery of a rare type of .22-calibre Ruger of the type used in the backpack murders.

While detectives from the Homicide Squad questioned Milat, other officers were digging over the land around his house at Eagle Vale. So confident were police that they had at last got their man that they rang the parents of Caroline Clarke and Joanne Walters. At police headquarters, gun-fanatic Ivan Milat had been charged with the offences relating to the attacks on the two Britons who escaped with their lives. He appeared before a court on 23 May, did not plead and was understandably refused bail. As he was driven off in the police van, Milat shouted: 'I didn't kill no one, mate, I didn't kill no one.' The two other men picked up at the same time were bailed. Meanwhile, members of the so-called Task Force Air, set up to investigate the backpack murders, were combing every inch of a remote farm near the Wombeyan Caves to the north of the Belanglo Forest, collecting dozens of spent cartridge cases.

On 30 May 1994 Ivan Robert Marko Milat, described as a 'road mender' and former trucker, was charged with the deaths of seven backpackers. As he stood in Campbelltown Local Court, Sydney, to hear the charges read out to him, Milat showed no sign of emotion. His solicitor said afterwards: 'Mr Milat has instructed me that he is not guilty of the charges of murder that have been pressed against him today.' Mr Marsden continued: 'The media and publicity hype over the past two weeks is prejudicing my client's right to a fair trial.'

Meanwhile, the rest of the family were standing solidly behind him. Brother Wally, in an exclusive interview for *Today* newspaper, claimed: 'I am convinced Ivan is innocent and is no monster.' While his mother told reporters: 'He would never give rides to strangers and backpackers . . . he believes they will dirty his car.'

However, prosecutor Mr Ian Lloyd QC told the court that parts of a Ruger rifle wrapped in a plastic bag had been found hidden in the lounge of Milat's bungalow, and ballistics tests had linked it with cartridge cases found at the scenes of two of the killings.

Ivan Milat is scheduled to appear in court again on 28 June, too late to be reported to this volume. It will be the culmination of Australia's most sensational instance of serial murder and its most extensive murder investigation.

THE MONSTER OF FLORENCE
The Case of Pietro Pacciani

It was not until the latter days of November 1993 that Pietro Pacciani, a sixty-eight-year-old farmer who worked a smallholding at Viccio di Mugello in the hills above Florence, was finally taken into custody and charged with the crimes attributed to the phantom 'Mostro di Firenze'. Although he had been the subject of part of the investigation into the activities of the Monster, Pacciani was at first thought to be too physically weak at five feet four inches to have carried out the killings, and too simple to be responsible for the taunting letters that the killer sent to the police.

However, in 1989, acting on an anonymous tip-off, the

Florentine police rekeyed Pacciani into their computer, and again it pushed his name to the top of a list of 100,000 potential suspects. Significantly, the Monster of Florence was active in the years between Pacciani's prison sentences – first for the murder of his girlfriend's lover in 1951, when he found them together and stabbed him to death in a fit of jealousy; and then his imprisonment in the mid-eighties for regularly raping his two daughters.

The first of the Monster's 'couples' series took place in the year of Pacciani's release, 1968. It was a hot August night when a man and his mistress were shot dead with a .22-calibre automatic pistol while engaging in sex in their car parked close to a disused cemetery fifteen miles from the centre of Florence. Ironically, the woman's husband, Stefano Mele, confessed, was tried, and wrongly convicted of the murders and, in March 1970, sentenced to thirteen years' imprisonment. On 14 September 1974 another couple were killed in their parked car, with a gun proved by forensics to be that used in the 1968 killings. Both these latest victims were found naked, and their bodies bore unusually shaped bruises which pathologists later suggested were caused by the handle of a scalpel; the woman had, in addition, been sexually violated with a vine stalk.

It was not until 6 June 1981 that a third couple were shot, and the woman's sex organs mutilated. True to the pattern of many serial killers, the frequency of the murders would escalate – further killings took place on 22 October 1981, and on 19 June the following year there were two double murders on the same day. Two homosexuals were shot dead while sleeping in their van on 9 September 1983, and it is with the benefit of hindsight that this would most logically be explained by the fact that one of the German men had long 'hippie-length' hair which may have made him look superficially like a woman. Two more couples were killed on 29 July 1984 and 8 September 1985. In both the latter incidents, the mutilation of the women's bodies included removal of the left breast.

Despite intensive police investigations no suspects immediately emerged, and more curiously still in this type of crime, there were no more killings consistent with the Monster's pattern.

Then, in November 1993, the newspapers were spreading jubilation – the Monster had been caged at last. At the end of April the following year Pietro Pacciani stood before a judge and ten-strong jury in the Florentine high court charged with sixteen murders – all of which he strenuously denied.

According to the prosecutor, Pacciani's madness dated back to that time in 1951 when he caught his girlfriend with her lover. He stabbed the young man more than fifty times and then forced the girl to make love with him beside the corpse. Pacciani says that he has never lost the memory, never lost the picture in his head: 'I saw Miranda's left breast uncovered, and that sparked my jealousy.'

Frequently in tears as he was mobbed by the news photographers and television cameramen, Pacciani shouted at them: 'I am innocent. I am a lamb who is treated as a scapegoat.' But at least the trial gave an eager Italian public the opportunity to watch their own favourite monster on television, because the legal process was relayed around the nation. And who knows, their home-grown serial killer could even make it to the big screen – notable among the celebrities packed into the small court was Thomas Harris, whose *Silence of the Lambs* has become a multi-million-dollar industry. Harris, a frequent visitor to Florence by all accounts, is reported as saying that he finds the Monster case fascinating but the trial boring.

Adding to the general atmosphere of shocked excitement as the trial opened were rumours that anonymous letters had been sent to the court and to the defendant's attorneys containing what at first glance looked like strips of skin. Forensic tests are being undertaken to determine whether they came from the same body as the similar relic sent to a lawyer following the last murder/mutilation. As Pacciani had been in jail for a year awaiting trial the implication is obvious.

As the trial progressed, the prosecutor delivered some strong forensic ballistic evidence in that a bullet found on Pacciani's land matches all the sixty-seven removed from the victims' bodies and vehicles. This 'needle-in-a-haystack' find was the result of a determined twelve-day search of their suspect's home and garden by local police in April 1992. They also found a notebook, made in Germany, which almost certainly belonged to one of the German tourists who were killed.

The trial is expected to drag through summer, nobody seeming to want to let go of what the press have (inaccurately) claimed to be the first trial of a serial killer Italy has known (what about the 'Devil of Turin' in 1987, and the 'Ludwig Murders' in the 70s and 80s?). As for the Monster of Florence, we must wait and see.

THE HOUSE ON CROMWELL STREET
The Case of Frederick and Rosemary West

(Guest contributor: John Bevis)

Cromwell Street, Gloucester, was for many years a safe, tranquil residential family backwater, a desirable place to live. But the past few decades have seen it subjected to the 'inner-city syndrome' of decline as prosperity has moved out, and its once-proud villas have become shabby and uncherished, places where 'drifters, dropouts and teenagers who had been kicked out of home could look for bedsits'. Standing out like a rotten tooth is No. 25, a bleak three-storey semi-detached town house, with ugly cracked concrete-rendered walls and sickly lime-green window frames. The forbidding façade is relieved only by an incongruously jaunty wrought-iron house number plaque, and a rusty horseshoe nailed over the front door. God bless this house.

During the 1970s the upper floors of the property were divided up into half a dozen of the cheapest bedsits in town, remembered by a former boyfriend of one of the many young girls who lodged there as 'pretty basic, with kids coming and going all the time. You'd never question it if someone moved on.' Presiding over those comings and goings was landlord Frederick West, a builder by trade, who had carried out extensive home improvements in the twenty-two years of his occupancy. He had added a single-storey extension to the rear of the property, without getting planning permission, had converted the cellar into two bedrooms; and laid a patio terrace over the forty-by-fifteen-foot rear garden, enclosed on one side by a tall screen of cypress trees, and on the other by the walls of the adjacent Seventh Day Adventist Church.

Mr West was paid a visit by Gloucester CID on Thursday 24 February 1994. A woman detective had pressed for a search warrant after suspicions were aroused by a telephone call imparting 'certain information'. That information, believed to have come from a member of the West family, related to the disappearance of Frederick and Rosemary West's sixteen-year-old daughter Heather, last seen at Gloucester DHSS office on 29 May 1987. Her uncle, Graham Letts, remembered Heather as 'every mother's dream child, pretty, polite, well behaved and helpful. She was lovely, a butterfly.' But she had become 'withdrawn and quiet' in the months before she vanished. Her parents had not even reported her as missing, as they insisted she had left home 'with a lesbian in a blue Mini' of her own accord: 'she had always been a loner'. But now detectives had been told something which made them believe that if she had left home, she had not gone very far.

The first place to look was the garden. The red and grey stone-composition flags of Fred West's cherished patio were lifted, a mechanical digger was brought in, and the excavations began. An 'archaeological-type dig' was masterminded by Professor Bernard Knight, the distinguished Home Office pathologist from Cardiff University, who laid out a grid over the whole of the site to ensure that every inch was investigated. Under the supervision of Detective Superintendent John Bennett a team of thirty officers worked in relays, digging the rain-sodden soil and sifting each shovel-load through a sieve to search for clues. The workforce dug down through the dark brown topsoil to the heavy blue clay beneath, labouring overnight in pouring rain under the glare of arc lights. On the second day a trowel struck a hard object near the extension; loose soil was scraped away, and a human skull was revealed. The mystery surrounding Heather West's whereabouts had been solved.

The dead girl's parents were immediately arrested. 'I didn't kill her,' shouted Fred as the couple were driven away in an unmarked police car, at 11.20 a.m. on Friday 25 February. After questioning Rosemary West was released on bail without charge; but by the following Monday, when her husband appeared before Gloucester magistrates to be formally charged with murder, two more bodies had been found in the garden. They were both adults, both were wrapped in pink blankets, but identification was to prove difficult due to the decayed condition of the remains. Police believed they may have lain in Fred West's back yard for as many as sixteen years.

On 2 March a police spokesman announced that one of the bodies had been positively identified as Shirley Ann

Robinson, a one-time lodger at Cromwell Street who was last seen in 1977. She had been something of a drifter, allegedly living a life of petty crime and moving between her home town of Melton Mowbray, Leicestershire, to Wolverhampton and Bristol, which goes some way to explaining why she had not been missed. At the time of her death she was eighteen years old, and heavily pregnant. Her baby had died three weeks before Shirley was due to give birth, and its pathetic remains were found buried near the mother's body. According to Liz Brewer, a contemporary Cromwell Street lodger, Ms Robinson was bisexual, and the father of her child was none other than her landlord – Frederick West. If that was not enough, at the very same time Rosemary West had also been pregnant – pregnant with another man's child. Ms Brewer elaborated: 'The Wests had told Shirley they had an open marriage. Neither minded the other having lovers, and they all seemed to be getting on with it and both women were waiting for their births, with Shirley's due first. Fred didn't seem to mind his wife expecting by another man.' But then one morning 'someone told me Shirley had gone to visit relatives in Germany because she couldn't cope with the tense situation. I was told she probably wasn't coming back.'

This, of course, was manna to the tabloids. 'Pregnant Lesbian is Horror Garden Victim', barked the *Sun*. There was endless speculation as to how many bodies might eventually be unearthed in the 'Garden of Evil' or within the adjacent 'House of Horror'. Locals cashed in on the camera crews who flocked from as far as Japan and the United States, charging hefty facility fees for filming from windows overlooking the site, and offering cups of tea and rolls at the sort of prices you might pay at the Ritz. One local lad was even promising souvenir T-shirts with the slogan 'Freddy's Back: Nightmare on Cromwell Street'.

The next five days lived up to the most macabre

conjecture. The bodies of two more females were uncovered in the cellar of the house between 3 p.m. and 3.30 p.m. on Saturday 5 March, and detectives hinted they were now searching for nine more bodies. They thought there were five buried in the house, and two in a field near West's former home at Much Marcle. 'We believe at least some of the victims had been sexually molested and died after being strangled', one newspaper reported a (strictly unofficial) police source as saying. 'A number of the victims may have been dismembered in the bath before being cemented into the building. We understand some were lodgers who had lived in the house over the past twenty years. Others could be local young women who have gone missing over two decades.'

By this time floorboards and fittings had been ripped out, the bath and sink removed from the downstairs bathroom, and no less than 200 tons of soil excavated from the garden, which was beginning to resemble the Somme battlefield. The police operation had been stepped up, with thirty detectives and forty uniformed members of the force assigned to the case; besides the army of officers involved in sifting through the fabric of 25 Cromwell Street, there was another team cross-checking the missing-persons files to bring to light unsolved cases of young women in the area. At the top of the list were Mary Bastholm, a fifteen-year-old waitress last seen as long ago as 1968, waiting for a bus, and Lucy Partington, a student at Exeter University, who had disappeared in December 1973. A massive police operation at the time had failed to trace her.

Sunday 6 March. Victim number six, a young woman, is found under the cellar. 'How Many More?', the *News of the World* wants to know. Police harness a revolutionary new tool to assist them, at a cost of £2,000 a day. Ground Penetrating Radar, developed by ERA Technology in Leatherhead, Surrey, was being used for the first time in a murder investigation, and was to prove of invaluable assistance. This high-tech device was developed during the Falklands conflict to locate landmines, and uses radar signals to scan underground cavities and disturbed layers of earth to a depth of two to three metres. The contours are plotted on a video monitor, which displays subterranean air pockets as conspicuous red zones. A more than passing resemblance has earned the machine its nickname 'The Lawnmower', and it has come to symbolise the perspicacity of the Gloucester investigations.

Meanwhile, investigators had broken into a chimney breast and the bathroom floor, using pneumatic drills. And the basement had been dug in places to a depth of five feet, undermining the very foundations of the house. A hasty call to Readymix cement company brought fourteen tons of concrete to the house, where it was pumped into the cellar to underpin the structure.

Monday 7 March. Victim number seven is found under concrete in the cellar. 'They've Lost Count of the Bodies', gasps the hysterical *Sun*. The Ground Penetrating Radar has located four of the bodies, and indicates further areas of disturbance which will have to be excavated. Officers are to be offered stress-counselling, for as a police source put it: 'It is a gruesome task working in the heat of powerful lights with exposed remains all around. The cellar is now a crypt full of excavated bodies.' In fact 'bodies' was something of a misnomer; due to their decomposed condition police were classifying the finds as 'sets of remains'.

Tuesday 8 March. Victim number eight is discovered buried four feet beneath the bath on the ground floor. West's brother-in-law, Graham Letts, reveals that he had helped lay the foot-thick concrete floor one day in the summer of 1987. 'Now I know what was underneath I feel sick. I'll be haunted to my dying day by the thought of what I did.' Sergeant Jim McCarthy, in overalls and rubber boots, is filmed bringing a box of human remains draped in black cotton out of the house to a waiting police van. In the space of five minutes the pitiful scenario is repeated another four times.

Wednesday 9 March: Contractors start to fill in the garden, their search complete. Indoors, victim number nine is found buried six feet under the floor behind a false wall in the downstairs bathroom. She is informally identified the following day as fifteen-year-old Carol Ann Cooper, who was last seen on 10 November 1973. Carol, 'a lovely, intelligent girl', had been in care at The Pines children's home in Bilton Road, Worcester, since her mother died when she was nine. She was on a weekend visit to her grandmother, Alice Tonks, at the time of her disappearance, and spent her final evening at the cinema with her boyfriend. Carol was last seen getting off a bus less than half a mile from her grandmother's house in Warndon.

Detectives had by then also sealed off West's former home at No. 25 Midland Road, just 300 yards from Cromwell Street. And at the same time a plain wooden stake was planted in a cornfield known as Fingerpost, on the road between Much Marcle and Dymock, where further remains were believed to have been buried. A permanent guard was mounted on the spot. Speculation was running riot as to the number of possible other sites, it now being suggested that as many as thirty properties where West had lived or worked might have to be searched. Accountants were ringing alarm bells that the massive operation might exceed the Gloucester constabulary's budget, and indeed its first seventy-two days were to cost an estimated £600,000. Gloucestershire is one of the country's smaller forces with just 1,150 officers, and its £50 million annual budget is already stretched by the cost of security for three royal residences in the county.

By 11 March Frederick West had been charged with eight murders. Throughout the investigation he had been questioned by relays of detectives, who found him to be co-operative 'some of the time'. They were thus able to piece together the bare bones of the story of his life.

Frederick Walter Stephen West had been born in 1942 at Much Marcle, near Hereford, the son of a wagoner. As a young man he lived with his parents and two brothers at No. 1 Moor Court Cottages, a tied cottage in the village, and developed a powerful physique working with his father Walter as a farm labourer. Fred took a job as a lorry driver and met his first wife, blonde eighteen-year-old Catherine 'Rena' Costello who hailed from Coatbridge, Lanarkshire, when she was working as a waitress at the New Inn at Ledbury. They were married at Ledbury Registry Office on 17 November 1962 and had two daughters, Charmaine, born on 22 March 1963, and Anna-Marie, born on 6 July the following year. After an interlude in Lanarkshire where Fred found work as an ice-cream salesman, and a brief residency at 25 Savoy Street, Glasgow, where Rena is alleged to have worked as a prostitute, the Wests moved back down south, living at plot 25 at a caravan park at Bishop's Cleeve, Cheltenham. But the marriage had 'effectively terminated' after the birth of the girls, and in 1970 West told friends Rena had taken up with an engineer and returned to Lanarkshire. She was never seen again.

By the time of his wife's disappearance, West was having an affair with a girl twelve years his junior, fifteen-year-old Rosemary Pauline Letts. Her disapproving parents put the girl into care in an attempt to stifle the relationship, but when Rosemary attained the age of responsibility on her sixteenth birthday she moved in, responsibly or not, with Fred at the local caravan site. On 17 October 1970 the couple were blessed with a daughter,

Heather. They later set up home at a two-storey pebble-dash house in Midland Road, Gloucester – coincidentally another No. 25 – together with Fred's daughter Anna-Marie, who went on to live with Fred and Rosie until about 1980, was married in 1986 and still resides in Gloucestershire. The other daughter from West's first marriage, Charmaine, had been voluntarily placed in council care in 1969, but was now returned to her father. She appears to have gone missing shortly after; West reportedly told Anna-Marie that Charmaine had gone to join her mother in Scotland.

Fred made an honest woman of Rosie on 29 January 1972 at Gloucester Registry Office, where he gave his marital status as 'bachelor', and three days later the Wests moved into yet another No. 25, Cromwell Street, which they bought from property developer Roger Zygmunt. The fecund couple went on to bring up a family of ten children. There was the irresistibly named Mae West, born in 1973; Stephen, in 1974; and Barry, in 1981. At least two of Rosie's other children – Tara and Louise – came from a relationship with another man and were of mixed ethnic origin. Finally there were two younger daughters, named Rosemary and Leanne. Unfounded reports have suggested that Fred West may have fathered as many as twenty-four children by different women; to date there seems to be little evidence to back this up. The Wests supplemented their income by taking in lodgers for many years, but this enterprise seems to have ceased towards the end of the 1980s.

Friends and neighbours remember Fred West as polite and friendly, 'a really nice, quiet bloke' if somewhat 'regimental', a devoted father who loved to take his children to the seaside at Weymouth. He had a mop of black curly hair and sideburns, and was forever dressed for work in his blue overalls. West was a hard worker who gave loyal service to his employers: Gloucester Wagon

Works, Dowmac, and finally Carsons Contractors. And he zealously applied his do-it-yourself skills at home, creating a temple of Melamine and Formica. The front room downstairs he turned into a bedroom, which was frequently used by Rosemary. Under the carpet of this room was a trap-door leading down to the cellar, converted by West in 1987 into two partitioned rooms where four of the children slept. The first floor, which was out of bounds to the children, featured another bedroom, with lace-canopied bed, and a sitting room with an L-shaped bar fully stocked with spirits and optics, a television and video. On the top floor a bedroom, kept under lock and key, was fitted out with a four-poster bed with the unusual accessories of spotlights and a concealed microphone.

Rosie West's brother Graham Letts was a frequent visitor to the house, and he remembers how 'There was something eerie about the atmosphere there. The children were always immaculately turned out, their manners were impeccable. But they were so subdued it was unnatural. Even with nine or ten children around you'd hear a pin drop. My wife Barbara and I thought it was because Rosie was so strict with them. The message was clear – if you don't do as I say you'll regret it.'

According to Graham Letts, his sister 'seemed to be using the same tactics' to discipline her children which their own mum and dad had employed. The seven Letts children had been kept on a tight rein and were 'not encouraged to have many friends'. Rosemary's elopement with Fred, whom her parents had 'disliked from the outset', was no doubt in part an act of rebellion. The marriage endured through thick and thin, but apparently went through a difficult time in the early 1990s. Sister-in-law Barbara Letts claims that in 1992 Rosemary took a cocktail of tablets and drink in a suicide bid, and was only saved at the last minute because she managed to stagger downstairs. Her son Stephen raised the alarm and she was taken to hospital where her stomach was pumped.

Mr Letts was shocked to discover that his sister was leading a double life as a prostitute who worked under the name 'Mandy Mouse' and boasted of running a 'slick operation' from 25 Cromwell Street. There was a telephone in every room, even in the bathroom, and a special doorbell for the constant stream of £40-a-time clients to the house. And according to Rob Williams, who dated daughter Mae West and lived at Cromwell Street in the early 1990s, Rosemary West was a 'nymphomaniac', an exhibitionist who would sometimes parade in front of lodgers in the nude. She and Fred allegedly lived for sex, and had a collection of hard-core porn videos, including films of themselves having sex with each other and with other people. Mr Williams said he was shocked to come home one day to find Fred and Rosie's other children, aged between eleven and fifteen, watching blue movies.

The press and media were probing into every aspect of the Wests' private life, and not surprisingly Rosemary West felt obliged by 'horrendous and extensive speculation' to make a statement through her lawyer Leo Goatley that she wanted to 'disappear and start a new life'. Mr Goatley said: 'She has been subjected to mental trauma and shock,' and added that he had written a complaint about reporting of the case to the Attorney General. On 26 March Mr Goatley announced that his client, who had been relocated by police to a 'safe house', was considering suing the police for compensation for damage to her home. And Fred West, too, felt he was being persecuted. When detectives took him in disguise to his former home he complained bitterly that they were 'ruining his twenty-two years of DIY'.

All of the remains so far unearthed from the West household had been taken to Home Office pathologist Bernard Knight's laboratory at the Wales Institute for

Forensic Medicine in Cardiff. Professor Knight is one of the most respected experts in his field. He has conducted painstaking forensic work on some notorious murder cases, including the death of Vatican banker Roberto Calvi, whose body was found hanging below Blackfriars Bridge; nurse Helen Smith, who died in controversial circumstances in Saudi Arabia; and he helped identify fifteen-year-old Karen Price, whose skeleton was found in a Cardiff garden eight years after she was killed. In his spare moments the professor has used his expert knowledge to write ten thrillers, including *The Thread of Evidence* and *The Lately Deceased*, under the pseudonym Bernard Picton.

We do not know in what condition the remains arrived at the pathologist's laboratory, but since some had been buried for more than twenty years they would obviously have been very decomposed. How would Professor Knight set about identifying the victims and their cause of death? He could match DNA profiles with those of living relatives; facial reconstruction is possible, either by physically building up a face on a plaster cast of the skull, or by doing much the same thing using computer graphics; further identification may come from ear-rings, buttons, buckles, shoes and scraps of clothing found with the corpse. The cause of death may be determined by examining the bones in the upper neck, for hanging; the hyoid bone at the base of the tongue, for strangling; the integrity of the skeleton, for butchery; and chemical analysis of soil surrounding the remains, for cases of poisoning.

One member of Bernard Knight's team was Dr David Whittaker, reader in oral biology at the University of Wales college of medicine, and consultant forensic adviser to the Home Office. It is interesting to realise how much data his examination alone might glean. The doctor's first job would be to determine the duration of interment by Fourier Transform Infrared Spectroscopy. This provides invaluable ageing data from the analysis of absorption patterns of infra-red light on the skull. The gender would then be determined, by examining the verticality of the forehead and bone ridges above the eyes – both more pronounced in males – the shape of the lower jaw, and the size of the area where the major neck muscle is attached. As a further check, sex chromosomes may be extracted and analysed from tooth pulp. Age at death can be gleaned from tooth development, in cases of those under twenty years old; after that age tooth growth ceases, and individuals would be aged by assessing how much of the tooth's membraneous structure had become saturated with tooth mineral. Dental records would then be prepared from the remains, and compared with the records of missing persons. Finally, a technique of superimposing still and video pictures on the skull and jaw features of the remains would check for a good fit.

By 8 April detectives were able to announce that all of the nine bodies found at Cromwell Street had been identified. All were young women aged between fifteen and twenty-one, and no fewer than four had last been seen waiting for buses. These included one, Carol Ann Cooper, who had already been named; another was Lucy Katherine Partington, the Exeter University student who had headed the police file of suspected victims. Lucy had been visiting her mother at Gretton, near Winchcombe, Gloucestershire, and was standing at a bus stop when she was last seen on 27 December 1973. Shirley Hubbard was the next bus-stop snatch victim; she was a fifteen-year-old schoolgirl who vanished on 14 November 1974 after leaving her work experience job at Debenhams, in Worcester, to catch a bus to her foster parents' home at Droitwich. And eighteen-year-old Juanita Mott went missing on 11 April 1975 after failing to catch the bus home to

Newent, twelve miles from the county town. She had not been reported missing.

Other victims included Lynda Carol Gough, a seamstress working at Gloucester Co-op, last seen just two weeks before her twentieth birthday in April 1973, after leaving her parents' home to move into a flat in Gloucester. The disappearance had been reported to police and her distraught parents had made concerted efforts to trace her. Swiss-born Therese Siegenthaler, a sociology student at Woolwich College who lived in Caterham Road, Lewisham, south London, was twenty-one years old when she went missing. She was last seen on 15 April 1974, leaving home to hitch-hike to Ireland via the Holyhead ferry. When her friend Edith Simmons told her to be careful, she had said: 'I can take care of myself; I am a judo expert.' Finally, the third body in the garden was identified. This was seventeen-year-old Alison Chambers, a Youth Training Scheme placement at a firm of solicitors in Gloucester. She had run away from her home in south Wales, and her disappearance in September 1979 had been reported to the Missing Persons Bureau, but not to the police. In her last letter to her mother she revealed that she had been staying with 'a big family'.

The focus of activity moved to Letterbox Field on Stonehouse Farm at Kempley, near the Hereford and Worcester border, on 28 March. The press circus was charged £50 a day to park in an adjacent field, and to cater for their 'earthly' needs farmer's wife Juliet Watkins set up a caravan cafe christened The Dig Inn. One can only hope its bacon sandwiches were more tasteful than its name. The site was scanned by the Ground Penetrating Radar 'lawnmower' and a part of the field enclosed under a blue and white inflatable tent. On 10 April, after 160 tons of soil had been removed from a trench 135 feet long, human remains were discovered in a makeshift grave three feet below the surface. This was the last resting place of Catherine 'Rena' Costello, Frederick West's long-lost first wife. She had gone missing at the age of twenty-four; her remains were unofficially identified on 14 April 1994, which would have been her fiftieth birthday.

The remorseless murder probe was extended to the eighteen-acre Fingerpost Field at Stonehouse Coppice, just a quarter of a mile from Letterbox Field, when on 13 April DS John Bennett announced: 'We are going to search an area 25ft by 25ft, and we have reason to search there.' It was surmised that somebody with detailed information about the burials had overcome an initial reticence, which had necessitated the 'overkill' operation in the back garden of Cromwell Street, and was by now co-operating very closely with detectives. Certainly Fred West was questioned for no fewer than seventy-eight days, before being moved from police custody to prison on 17 May 1994. But information relating to Stonehouse Coppice was a little out of date: Fingerpost Field had been used as a dumping ground for top soil over the years, and tons of earth had to be removed before the original ground level was reached. And then on 18 April an underground spring flooded the nine-foot hole.

Excavations continue at the time of writing, and Anna McFall, who vanished in the early 1970s at the age of twenty-two, has been named as a person the police would like to trace.

Fred West's former home at 25 Midland Road had been under police quard since the first body was found, and was by now overdue for a search. Police were particularly anxious to find out what had happened to West's daughter by his first marriage, Charmaine, who had disappeared in 1971, aged eight. A survey of the property was commenced on 20 April, and the garden was searched but nothing was found. The inquiry moved indoors on 4 May, when the kitchen floor was excavated. And there, the following day, under a thick layer of concrete, in a heavy mass of rubble, the police found what they were looking for. Charmaine West's remains were gently lifted from their resting place by PC George Sharpe, who carried them in a box draped in black cloth to a waiting van.

Since the initial shock of the early discoveries, the newspapers had become rather blasé about the case, and it seemed the police operation would steamroller on, turning up another body every now and then, the only thing unknown being the final tally. But then on 21 April 1994 there was a bolt from the blue. Rosemary West was charged, jointly with sixty-seven-year-old William Smith, of raping an eleven-year-old girl and assaulting a seven-year-old boy, causing actual bodily harm. The offences were said to have been committed between January 1972 and 6 July 1976. Mr Smith was released on bail, but Rosemary West was remanded. It is rare for a woman to be charged with rape, but if the woman actively assists or encourages another person to commit rape, and that person is found guilty, she can also be convicted. It was beginning to look as if Mrs West's 'slick operation' would demand very close scrutiny.

The charges against Rosemary West multiplied like cancer cells. On 23 April she was charged with having sexual intercourse with the same girl without consent along with another man, sixty-four-year-old Whitley George Purcell, between 6 July 1976 and 6 July 1980. Three days later she was charged with murder, the murder of Lynda Gough; on 28 April, the murders of Carol Ann Cooper and Lucy Partington; on 3 May, Therese Siegenthaler; on 5 May, Shirley Hubbard; on 16 May, Juanita Mott; on 19 May, Shirley Robinson; on 24 May, Alison Chambers; and finally, on 26 May, the most awful charge of all, the murder of her own daughter Heather. Fred West stands accused on all nine of those charges, as well as the murders of two persons not yet officially identified whose remains were found at Midland Road and Letterbox Field – a total of eleven murders.

On 26 May Fred West's younger brother, John Charles Edward West, was accused of raping two young girls between 1 January 1975 and 1 January 1980. One of the girls was aged seven or eight, and the other between eleven and sixteen. And Rosemary West appeared charged with one of the same offences.

One of the extraordinary things about this case is that so many of the murder victims could have disappeared without trace for so many years. But at any one time in Britain, there are no fewer than 250,000 people listed as missing. A third of that number are children under eighteen. The only organisation set up to combat the problem nationally is the Missing Persons Bureau in Richmond, Surrey, funded by donations and staffed by volunteers, and lacking even the resources for a computer database. Each year the Bureau deals with about 30,000 calls, and finds in the region of 750 missing people. They are of all ages and classes, although middle-aged men and girls in their mid-teens are slightly more likely than other groups to vanish – usually due to stress, illness, drug problems, pregnancy, professional or emotional pressures. Janet Newman of the Bureau said: 'People from the same families used to live virtually on top of each other in the same streets, villages and towns. But that has changed. People get busy and move two or three times. That means relations miss out on a large slice of their lives before gradually losing all contact.' It is those people, with a transient lifestyle who have drifted away from their families, who are the most vulnerable – as the 'killing for company' case of serial killer Dennis Nilsen illustrated only too graphically.

The Missing Persons Bureau was inundated with calls during the Cromwell Street investigation, and one of the happiest aspects of the case was that five missing women were reunited with their families. In March 1994 it was announced that the Home Office was to allocate £90,000 a year to a new, and long overdue, national missing persons' bureau with a full-time staff of three to be based at Scotland Yard. This would be an interim step to a fully integrated national police database on missing persons, part of the national police computer network to be launched within two years.

Frederick and Rosemary West are likely to have to remain in custody for at least a year before their trial is heard. Until that time the questions of how, and why, so many young women died in Gloucester, and whether either or both of the Wests were implicated in those deaths, will have to remain unanswered. What we know for certain is that a great deal of harrowing information relating to the manner of death will be revealed at the time of the trial, and since so many of the victims were abducted young women it is likely that a sexual motive will be suggested. And there seems no doubt that the scale of the murders committed over such a very long time, the apparently casual manner in which they were dispatched, above all, the contrast of the ordinary family home with the horrors which lay within its very foundations, will earn the House of Horror a place in criminal history alongside the crimes of John Reginald Christie and Dennis Nilsen.

Those two cases, in which murder victims were kept within the home, may shed some light on the problem of what to do with the Wests' house. The closest parallel is perhaps 10 Rillington Place in west London, the infamous charnel house where the bodies of six strangled women were found in 1953. The road was renamed Ruston Close soon after their murderer, John

Christie, had been hanged at Pentonville, and the terrace of Edwardian houses was later demolished to make way for a housing estate. On the other hand 23 Cranley Gardens, the three-storey 'semi' in Muswell Hill where Dennis Nilsen dismembered many of his victims, was sold soon after his conviction and divided into flats, all of which, included Nilsen's, are still happily occupied. And 25 Argyle Street, Oxford, where university student Rachel McLean was found strangled under the floorboards in 1991, continues to be rented as student accommodation.

But even if, as seems prudent, Cromwell Street is renamed, No. 25 was pretty well torn apart during the investigation. After the excavations inside the property and garden were complete, a mechanical digger ploughed up the front patio on 5 April 1994. A police spokesman stated: 'We have always said we will carry out a 100 per cent search of the house and this is what we are doing.' They returned to the back of the house on 15 April and ripped apart Fred West's DIY project, the building extension. A blocked-up well containing a ten-foot depth of water was discovered beneath the extension, and police sent a diver down, head first, with an underwater camera, but he found nothing. On 25 April Rosemary West, against her husband's wishes, put the 'dead res' up for sale, boarded up, bricked up, structurally precarious, and full of evil memories. The sale would have to be 'strictly sight unseen', as Leo Goatley, Mrs West's solicitor, put it: 'You would need a sledgehammer to get in.' Offers were invited in the region of £50,000, and no less a man than Michael Winner gave the dump his blessing with the words: 'Any young bargain hunter should snap it up.' But most of us would consider the house and garden of No. 25 Cromwell Street, Gloucester, to be one do-it-yourself project too far.

Postscript

Having been separated since Frederick was taken into custody followed by Rosemary, the Wests met in the magistrates' court at Gloucester for the first time on 30 June 1994. It was hardly a touching reunion – for Rosie at least. As he entered the dock, West reached out his hand and brushed his wife's neck, bending to speak a few words to her; she appeared to ignore him, and only once during the relatively brief formality did she even glance at him. Fred West seemed, on the other hand, to be looking around with great interest – proving that even magistrates' courts are more entertaining than prison cells. It was West's eighth appearance in court and his wife's sixth, but their first together. The court was reminded by counsel that Mr and Mrs West stood jointly charged with the murder of nine young women. Separately, Frederick West is further charged with the murder of his first wife and their daughter, and Rosemary West with two counts alleging unlawful sex with an underaged girl, and assault. As the couple rose to leave the court, West again tried to touch his wife and she again ignored him.

STICKS AND STONES
The Case of Joel Rifkin, the 'Chainsaw Ripper'

It was just another motoring accident for the Long Island highway patrol. It was a nuisance, but routine; sure the truck that had wrapped itself round a telegraph pole had some weird stickers on it – the one on the bumper read: 'Sticks and stones may break my bones but whips and chains excite me' – but there were a lot of crazies in New York. Besides, this guy *looked* OK. Funny smell coming from the pick-up though. Lifting the edge of the tarpaulin bundle in the back the officer soon realised why. Before anybody could do anything but gasp in horror, the driver held out his hands to be cuffed and said: 'I killed her, I killed her – she was a prostitute.'

That was on 28 June 1993. According to his own story, two days before, the scruffy, overweight man with thin hair and a droopy moustache had been cruising the red-light district of Manhattan in his mother's Toyota. When he turned on to Allen Street, just beyond the Williamsburg Bridge, he kerb-crawled until he saw what he wanted; her name was Tiffany Bresciani, twenty-two years old, lately from Metairi, Louisiana, via Hollywood. It would be her last night walking Allen Street. Not that Tiffany had the least suspicion, not until she had exchanged her body for her client's money and felt his hands closing around her throat. Another thing Tiffany Bresciani would never know is that she would be the victim that cut short the career of the Ripper, a serial killer who had claimed the lives of several prostitutes in New York. Tiffany's body was driven five kilometres (about three miles) back to the more salubrious district of East Meadow, where it was offloaded into a wheelbarrow in the garage of a house in Garden Street. There she would remain until the early hours of Monday 28 June when the assassin carried Tiffany's already decomposing body into the back of his road-weary Mazda pick-up and headed south to find a suitable burial ground. The truck had travelled some few miles along the Southern State Parkway when a highway patrol car noticed that it had no registration plates. Not exactly a hanging offence, but officers Sean Ruane and Deborah Spaargaren had a job to do, and when the Mazda ignored their loudhailer order to pull over, they gave chase. It was a chase that ended in Mineola with the pick-up in collision with a telegraph pole; ironically it was just in front of the Nassau County Courthouse. The rest we know.

What the police didn't know when they got him back to headquarters at Republic airport was the extent of their prisoner's catalogue of carnage; that would emerge over the following six hours.

The man's name was Joel Rifkin, a thirty-four-year-old unemployed gardener – or 'landscaper' as he described himself – and the story that he told defied belief. In all there had been seventeen killings in three years, or at least that is all Rifkin could recall; all of them hookers, picked up around Allen Street. Surprisingly, this was something of a bombshell for the detectives interviewing Rifkin. They never even knew they had a serial killer *to* look for. In the twilight world of prostitution – one of the riskiest trades around – girls came and went, many of them rootless drifters with no known family to report a disappearance. But now the search teams had something to go on – Joel's memory.

The first killing was in 1989, and the next not until the following year; according to Rifkin he chopped their corpses into pieces for easy disposal. On the location of these victims Joel couldn't be more helpful than to say that he thought one was dumped in a canal around New York and the other in New Jersey. In the summer of 1991 the slaughter began in earnest. There was Barbara Jacobs, who was parcelled up in a carton and tossed into the Hudson river. Then twenty-two-year-old Mary DeLuca, a drug addict whose family had reported her missing from home; on 1 October her decomposed body was found by a scavenger on a waste tip near West Point. Meanwhile, on 23 September a black cabin trunk was found floating gently downstream where the Harlem river passes Randall's Island; inside was the body of Tun Lee, a thirty-one-year-old prostitute and drug addict. It was December before Joel Rifkin felt the urge to kill again, and threw her body, encased in a steel oildrum in the Harlem. In January Joel bought another oildrum to dispose of yet another victim, this time in Newtown Creek; it was found bobbing up and down in the scum and debris three months later.

By that time Joel Rifkin had also killed Maryann Holloman, a thirty-nine-year-old crack addict, and tipped her body off the Verrazano–Narrows bridge out on Coney Island. It was not until July that the dismembered parts were washed ashore. Lorraine Orvieto was twenty-eight years old, well brought up, expensively educated, and a manic depressive who had taken to cocaine and then to prostitution to finance her habit. In December, Joel Rifkin put her corpse into a metal drum and dumped it in the same spot as Maryann Holloman.

During the course of 1992, Rifkin eclipsed the lives of a further six victims. Among them were twenty-five-year-old Iris Sanchez, whom he strangled, then driving her body to Kennedy airport. Just off the Rockaway Boulevard, he hid it under a discarded mattress – where it remained until Rifkin was arrested and directed the police to his victims' last resting places. Anna Lopez was thirty-three, a high-school dropout and long-time substance abuser who had gone on the game to support her coke addiction and her three illegitimate children. After strangling her, Rifkin left her body in some woodland on the Interstate 84 where it cuts through Putnam County. It was found there a few days later.

During the early summer Joel Rifkin strangled and dismembered a so-far unidentified woman and threw her head, arms and legs into the Hudson; at the end of July the headless torso was found wrapped in a plastic bin bag at FDR Drive and 123rd Street. With a final burst of energy Rifkin fitted in a further three butcheries by the end of the year – one, according to his confession, was dumped in West Nyack, though the body has not yet been found. She was followed by thirty-one-year-old Mary Catherine Williams, like the other victims a crack addict and prostitute, who went missing from the East Village and was found in December on scrubland in Torktown. Around early November Joel Rifkin picked up Jenny Soto on her beat working Allen Street; her body washed up on the rocky shore of the Harlem by Lincoln Avenue and 132nd.

The new year saw a fresh crop of killings. In February 1993 judge's daughter Leah Evans disappeared. Although Leah was something of a latter-day hippy with a fondness for booze, she was, according to the police, not on drugs and not known as a prostitute. Like many serial killers, Joel was beginning to lose sight of his victim trait. In many ways the parallels with England's Peter Sutcliffe were inescapable – Sutcliffe too progressed from killing prostitutes ('Just cleaning up t' streets') to killing women who *might* have been prostitutes – in other words any female who happened to be on foot on the street after dark. Unsurprisingly Rifkin quickly earned the press soubriquet 'Joel the Ripper'. Joel was clearly feeling productive because Leah Evans was only the first victim of the month. We do not know who the second was – just a collection of body parts scattered around the Hampton Hills Golf Club at the eastern point of Long Island.

There were seventeen in all, though detectives feel there may be more. Joel just can't remember. All he knows is that he started picking up whores just after getting his driving licence; of one thing he is emphatic – he always paid before he had sex and he *always* left the money with the corpses.

It was perhaps understandable that it was a shock to the police to find that a serial killer had been operating without their even suspecting. After all, Rifkin had been dispatching what many would class as New York's dross – hookers and junkies. Who cared? He had also been careful to dispose of his victims over a wide geographical area, so that the already overstretched police resources around the precincts never got to link the murders together.

The effect on Joel's adoptive mother, Jeanne Rifkin, and on their neighbours in the genteel suburb of East Meadow (aptly described by one journalist as 'a place of deeply competitive shrubbery') was devastating. Local police recalled a close-knit, almost secretive family, keeping themselves very much to themselves. Joel was remembered by neighbours as a quiet child who had been born in 1959 and was shortly thereafter adopted by Bernard and Jeanne Rifkin. When Joel was three years old the family (including by now an adopted daughter, Jan) moved to East Meadow where Bernard Rifkin became a pillar of the local community until his untimely death from cancer in 1987. Taking the service at Bernard's funeral, Joel was moved to say: 'Though my father did not give me life, he gave me love.' And this is typical of the face Joel Rifkin showed to the world. However, already by adolescence the young Joel was having difficulty relating to his peers, he became withdrawn and reclusive, making himself a perfect target for the Woodland Junior High bullies, who nicknamed him 'Turtle' and 'Lard-Ass.' In fact, truth to tell, Joel had an utterly miserable time of it at school. In her perceptive article on the Rifkin case in *New York* (9 August 1993), Jeanie Russell Kasindorf quotes one of Joel's contemporaries as saying: 'I feel bad that we picked on him. Now, in a way, I'm saying to myself – although I'm not blaming myself – maybe all the abuse he took in high school led to it . . .'

From high school, Rifkin drifted in and out of various local colleges and courses, still withdrawn, still painfully shy in the company of any girls except the prostitutes on whose services he was increasingly relying. Joel moved out of East Meadow just after his father's death and into a flat on West 49th in Manhattan. This independence lasted only a couple of months before Joel was back at home with his sister and mother and still desperately trying to improve himself at college, this time in the field of ornamental horticulture – gardening. It didn't last, and according to his own confession, he compensated for failure at Farmingdale by embarking on multiple murder. The rest we know.

When detectives searched Joel's room at the Rifkin home they found all the corroborating evidence they needed – like many serial killers, Joel could not resist taking a souvenir from his victims, and the room was littered with ladies' underwear and jewellery, make-up and personal documents; more horrible were the blood-stained saws, machete and chainsaw with which Joel Rifkin had dismembered his victims before disposing of their bodies across Connecticut, New York and New Jersey. One police spokesman is reported as saying: 'A lot of serial killers are timid. They take trophies to show they're in control.'

Meanwhile, police search teams with bloodhounds were acting on Rifkin's directions and attempting to retrieve as many of the victims as possible. By 1 July nine bodies had been found, though it is still doubtful whether we will ever know the true extent of the killings. Joel himself was engaged on the series of preliminary appearances at the Mineola Court, Long Island, which would ultimately lead to his indictment at the High Court.

Joel Rifkin awaits his trial in Nassau County Correctional Institute on Long Island, where he has, according to recent reports (mid-April 1994) entered into a feud with mass killer Colin Ferguson (see page 346) after a brawl over Rifkin's loud use of the public telephone. In subsequent altercations, Ferguson, a militant black, was heard to yell at Rifkin: 'I wiped out six devils [white people], and you only killed women'; to which Joel repeatedly responded: 'Yeah, but I had more victims.'

Updates in Brief

Austria, Czechoslovakia and United States
Jack Unterweger

It was the trial everybody had been waiting for. In fact the authorities had been waiting two years to get Jack Unterweger into the dock; he had made fools of them more than once, but this time they had got him. It wasn't only the law that was waiting, though; Jack was something of an international celebrity – a charismatic serial killer whose motivations were fuelled by violence and whose reign of terror spanned three countries and two continents; a fugitive on the run from law enforcement officers who, when he was eventually caged, became the darling of the Viennese literati for his prison cell poetry and his autobiography.

Surprisingly, Unterweger was a native of Austria, for that country has spawned few serial killers (though the trial in Vienna in 1991 of four nursing assistants and their conviction for the serial murders of at least forty-two of their elderly patients shocked Austria and served to show that few places are safe from the multicide). What comes as no surprise is Unterweger's background – a history of family neglect and abuse shared with the majority of serial killers.

Jack was born the illegitimate son of an Austrian mother and a soldier with the visiting American forces. In infancy the child was abandoned by his parents and spent his formative years being shuffled around various relatives who, when they got fed up with him, had him committed to one institution or another. By the time he entered his teenage years, Unterweger was already into prostitution and petty crime; in fact he was to claim much later that his early introduction to pimping and subsequent motivation for murdering prostitutes was because his mother was a prostitute. Despite being a bad mother she was nothing of the kind.

The first of Jack Unterweger's known murders took place in 1976. The victim was eighteen-year-old Margaret Schaefer, who Unterweger claimed was a prostitute but almost certainly was not; she was beaten and strangled with her own bra. Twenty-four-year-old Jack landed a life sentence. And in many respects that's what it was – certainly his own life was about to change dramatically. In the same way that some offenders find religion in prison, Jack Unterweger found literature. Over the following years he wrote reams of poetry, a novel and an autobiography, and edited the prison magazine. In short, Jack was a reformed character – he was even allowed out to attend literary parties with an increasing circle of influential Viennese intellectuals. In 1990 Jack Unterweger was considered to be so reintegrated into the society he had wronged that he was let out on parole.

And so it might have remained, with Jack going onward and ever upward towards literary stardom and the cult of media personality. There was just one impediment, he still liked killing people – or so the prosecutors at his trial claimed. In October of the year of his release the first of the prostitutes Jack Unterweger is said to have killed was discovered dead; in the first few months of the following year, 1991, a further six Austrian women were found murdered. In the summer of the same year Jack made a cultural visit to the United States – which coincided with the murder of three prostitutes in Los Angeles. It looked as though the literary celebrity still had his night job. On his way back to Austria Unterweger stopped off in Prague, where Blanka Bockova, another prostitute, met an untimely death. Because of his previous conviction for murder, the Austrian police already had Jack Unterweger high on their list of suspects for the local murders, and when he arrived back from his literary travels detectives were waiting to speak to him. Jack was delighted to help, desperate to help, unfortunately he could give them no information – he was an author not a policeman. Unterweger was questioned, released, and questioned again with almost comic regularity – not that it worried Jack, he was in the limelight.

Then the investigating team took a chance; they applied for a warrant to take him into custody. In February 1992 a team of officers roared up outside Unterweger's Viennese apartment closely followed by the television crew they had invited along for publicity. And it was publicity they got, though not the kind they anticipated – Jack had done a runner!

Despite half the police forces in Europe taking part in the hunt, the fugitive remained at large through Switzerland, over the border into France and up to Paris for a few days, whence with calm confidence Jack headed for Florida. There he was arrested by the Miami police and locked up while he fought extradition – and nearly won. Finally, though, Jack Unterweger, unbowed, was packed off back to Austria where his trial opened in the southern city of Graz at the end of May 1994. He faced eleven indictments for murder, representing the tally from Austria, the United States and Czechoslovakia.

The legal process lasted thirty-two days during which experts sought to prop up the uncomfortable fact that the prosecution's case was based almost entirely on circumstantial evidence. For example, the *modus operandi* was always the same: victims were picked up in local red-light districts, driven to remote spots where they were strangled with their own underwear before being hidden in woodland. It is an indicator that nobody with a passing knowledge of criminal psychology could ignore; it was spelled out by an FBI expert in offender profiling – all the deaths resulted from the same hand. And was it merely coincidence that in each case Jack Unterweger could be placed in the area? Perhaps it was, because Jack had been protesting his innocence for a couple of years – was still protesting his innocence. There were just two, albeit rather shaky, pieces of forensic evidence. The clothing of one of the victims was found to have picked up red fibres from a scarf owned by Unterweger, and a hair discovered in his car was 'almost certainly' from the woman murdered in Czechoslovakia. Hardly what anybody could call a watertight case. As for Jack, his last words before the jury retired to consider their verdict were: 'I was a greedy, ravenous individual, hungry for life, determined to rise from the bottom . . . it wasn't me!'

The jury, however, thought otherwise – or at least some of them did. Of the panel of eight, two found him innocent. He was found not guilty on two of the eleven counts because the bodies of the victims were so badly decomposed that no convincing evidence could be offered to the court.

And that appeared to be that. The authorities had put Jack Unterweger where they felt he belonged, and his fan club could hardly wait for his next literary venture from behind bars. Jack himself, still loudly proclaiming his innocence, was bundled off to serve his life sentence.

That life sentence did not last very long. Just hours after being locked up, Jack Unterweger was found hanging in his cell at the end of an *ad hoc* rope cobbled together from his shoe-laces and a track-suit cord.

England
Beverley Allitt

Nurse Beverley Allitt, a severe sufferer from the rare psychological illness Munchausen Syndrome by Proxy was convicted at Nottingham Crown Court in 1993 of the thirteen charges against her. It was always difficult to tell during that lengthy legal process who cut the more sympathetic and tragic figures, Allitt herself, clearly emotionally and physically unable to cope with anything at all or the bewildered and grief-stricken relatives of her victims. Just one thing was absolutely certain – that a National Health Service savagely and cynically deprived of human and financial resources by a government hell-bent on decimating even the most basic medical care can be held directly responsible for the series of blunders, oversights, wrong diagnoses and mislaid and misinterpreted information. On Ward Four, the children's ward where Bev Allitt worked, the budget had first been cut and then frozen. By 1991 there were only two trained nurses on the dayshift and one on nights.

It was during fifty-eight days in the spring of that year that a series of mysterious deaths, illnesses and injuries struck Ward Four like a plague. The first incident, on 21 February, resulted in the death of eight-week-old Liam Taylor; the last was on 22 April when staff lost their battle to save the life of fifteen-month-old Claire Peck. Between these dates there were no fewer than twenty-six inexplicable failures of medical treatment, four children died, nine were injured; of those who survived some will never fully recover. Although there were clearly worries expressed by staff and supervisors, there were neither time nor facilities enough to carry out the day-to-day hospital work, let alone launch full-scale investigations. By the second week in April the pattern was becoming so plain that it was shouting – but still nobody dared admit the obvious, that there was a murderer loose on the children's ward. How long the supervisors would have remained blinkered is a matter for debate; but it was a potentially lucky day for a lot of sick infants when Dr Nelson Porter, a hospital consultant, heard a lecture at a conference on the subject of Munchausen Syndrome by Proxy, a personality disorder which manifests itself in the uncontrollable urge to draw attention to the sufferer, often by causing injury either to themselves or to those in their care. It is most often noted in the cases of mothers with small babies and children; and in hospitals. Now it all made sense and Dr Porter, to his credit, demanded instant action, including calling in the police. The hospital authorities were not so enthusiastic – after all it was Friday evening, best wait till Monday. Which is the day Claire Peck lost her life. For Dr Porter it was the final straw. He had spent the weekend tirelessly investigating the catalogue of suspicious cardiac arrests in children and now sent anything – blood, samples from the drip, samples of anything that had been in contact with Claire Peck – for immediate analysis. The result came through that evening, a very unusual result, a result so unusual that Alan Wills in the pathology lab had run the tests four times. Each time it was the same: the reading on the scale for potassium had gone off the top of the scale. Claire had died with more than 10 millimols of potassium per litre in her blood. Now the police were called in.

It was Detective Superintendent Stuart Clifton whose unenviable task it was to sift through the confusing medical evidence detailing overdoses of insulin, reports, staff rotas. Staff rotas. There was a key there to the mystery that was unavoidable – one name turned up every time there had been an incident; the name was Beverley Allitt. Allitt was taken into custody on 21 May 1991. While she was being questioned another police team was searching her room, where they found the ward's allocation book in her wardrobe. In the end Bev was released, though as a precaution she was sent on leave. By 26 July 1991 the police case was felt to be sufficiently strong to charge Beverley Allitt with murder. This was blocked by the Director of Public Prosecutions taking immediate charge of the case – at the insistence, it is rumoured, of a government who feared that the final blame might be laid at the door of the Department of Health. But by this time Bev's closest friend (in fact her *only* friend) Tracy Jobson, a fellow nurse, had begun to get frightened. The games had become too dangerous. So Tracy paid a visit to the police and talked to them about the time they worked on a geriatric ward together and had started bumping off the elderly patients. In November 1991 Beverley Allitt was formally charged with four counts of murder, eight of attempted murder and eight of causing grievous bodily harm.

It is difficult to know what anybody hoped to get out of the trial. It opened at Nottingham Crown Court on 15 February 1993. When she appeared, Bev Allitt had lost five stones in weight as the result of a form of anorexia. She had been held in Rampton Psychiatric Hospital and had returned to a childhood habit of hurting herself – scalding herself with water, eating broken glass, and other attention-seeking stunts.

After a trial lasting almost two months, during much of which time Bev Allitt had been too ill to attend court, the jury returned on 11 May 1993. Following sixteen hours' deliberation, they began to present their verdicts piecemeal; four days later the process was complete, and on 25 May Mr Justice Latham sentenced Allitt to thirteen life sentences, four on charges of murder and nine for grievous bodily harm. Beverley Allitt was returned to Rampton and an intravenous drip.

The question throughout was whether the government, and Health Secretary Virginia Bottomley in particular, had the courage to launch a public inquiry into what went wrong in the Grantham and Kesteven and what could be done to prevent a similar disaster. To considerable anger and frustration – particularly on the part of relatives of the victims – the government possessed no such courage, and promised instead 'an official inquiry to be held in private'.

Suicide

It was quite clear that the case of serial killer Beverley Allitt would not be out of the news for very long. And so it proved. Over the months following the trial Bev Allitt's physical condition improved, though clearly her mental health remained fragile. At the end of August 1993, there were reports that Allitt had been rushed from Rampton to nearby Bassetlaw Hospital in Worksop. Officials from Rampton kept a constant vigil as staff at the hospital treated self-inflicted wounds caused by Allitt opening out steel paper-clips and forcing them into her body. She was returned after treatment, and though it is no secret that Bev Allitt has threatened suicide before no more information became available on this incident.

Confession

October brought another development when Beverley Allitt confessed to Lincolnshire detectives that she had committed three of the murders with which she had been charged and six other attacks. It proved to be a half-measure, because although Allitt had previously denied all the charges neither the police nor her solicitor were willing to divulge the names of the victims. All the official police statement would confirm was that: 'An application was made to interview Beverley Allitt at Rampton Hospital with a view to providing more information for the inquiry . . . As a result she has now admitted to committing nine of the attacks she was charged with.' Although understandably disappointed that families were not given names, the mother of one of the victims was reported as saying: 'I am quite relieved she has at long last confessed. It will put a few people's minds at rest now that the right person was convicted.' The police team under Detective Superintendent Clifton plan to interview Allitt again.

The inquiry

With the results of Sir Cecil Clothier's private inquiry imminent, two of the doctors expected to feature boldly in the criticisms decided to try to draw the flak before it came. Dr Nelson Porter and Dr Charithnanda Nanayakkara, senior paediatricians at Grantham and Kesteven General, were expected, probably quite unjustly, to be made scapegoats for the failings of the system. Significantly, both men were made 'redundant' shortly after the case, when the hospital had a 'shake-up of paediatric services'. On 27 January Dr Nanayakkara told a specially convened news conference: 'We experienced an extraordinary set of circumstances which no other paediatric unit in the country had ever experienced or could reasonably be expected to experience. Any comments or judgements on our actions must be set in this context and not with hindsight.' As well as once more adding his voice to the uproar demanding a *public* inquiry with the opportunity of cross-examination, Dr Porter criticised the Clothier inquiry for its secrecy and for the fact that no paediatrician sat on the board. It was no surprise that Sir Cecil was soon in print admonishing the two doctors for speaking so frankly (and publicly), claiming that their words were 'a most injudicious and regrettable attempt to influence the outcome of an inquiry conducted in the public interest'.

The findings of the Clothier inquiry were made known to that interested public on 11 February 1994. And it was as most people who had taken an interest in the wider issues of the Allitt case had suspected – an unashamed whitewash of discredited and terminally faulty government health policy. One typical headline (from the London *Evening Standard*) read: 'The Great Baby Killer Whitewash; fury over nurse Allitt report'. The *Guardian* offered the opinion that the report 'blames everyone except the real culprit, the system'. Of course, Drs

Nanayakkara and Porter were, as they had anticipated, the scapegoats – the former 'played down the possibility that someone was harming children'; the latter 'took feeble and indecisive steps'. There were other criticisms of the hard-pressed staff of course, in fact of almost everybody – except Mrs Bottomley and the Department of Health. There were, for example, **sloppy appointment procedures**, a way of saying that Beverley Allitt should never have been employed in the first place; **inadequate staffing** without actually addressing the responsibility for that inadequacy; **overworked doctors** (in the case of senior paediatricians such as Dr Porter and Dr Nanayakkara a norm of around 104 hours a week, but during holiday and emergency periods up to 168). In one of the most fatuous statements ever to be made in a government-sponsored inquiry Sir Cecil Clothier QC stated in his introduction to the report that 'the dreadful lesson we have learned is that no matter how numerous and skilful the staff of a hospital may be a malevolent, cunning and deranged person can nevertheless contrive to commit his or her crimes'. It was another red herring, but the demonisation of Beverley Allitt and the dismissal of understaffed hospitals must have warmed Mrs Bottomley's heart.

By 14th February the public had been able to add their views, via the correspondence columns of the press. One of those who wrote a long and detailed letter to the *Guardian* was a D.M. Onions SRN. Where had we heard that name before? It was in Clothier's list of criticisms of Grantham and Kesteven General: 'Mrs Moira Onions, clinical services manager: did not properly check that Allitt was fit to be employed.' Mrs Onions responded passionately in defence both of her staff and of her own position in relation to the reports criticism of her engagement of nurses.

The general finding of the report, then, was that

individuals should be blamed for the killings in Ward Four – certainly not the health authority, and heaven forbid, the Ministry of Health.

By way of something more positive, the Clothier report put forward twelve child safety recommendations – most of which, such as the sufggestion that post-mortems should be carried out by a specialist paediatric pathologist wherever death is unexpected or clinically unaccountable, would seem to be the minimal expectation of any adequately funded and co-ordinated national health service.

But if Mrs Virginia Bottomley had been given her scapegoats, the parents of Beverley Allitt's victims did not even get a copy of the report. It was just one final scandal in a seemingly endless series of mishandlings. Parents had been assured that advance copies of the Clothier report would be dispatched by courier on 11 February. As the hours passed, one mother telephoned the Grantham and Kesteven General to inquire: 'I was told rather impatiently that our copies of the report had been lost.'

Robert Mawdsley

Beneath the loud headline 'Britain's Own Hannibal', the *Star* newspaper (29 July 1993), in an exclusive story not picked up by even the other tabloids, related the case of forty-year-old Robert Mawdsley, apparently kept in secure isolation in a steel-lined cell resembling that occupied by the fictional cannibal Dr Hannibal Lecter in Thomas Harris' *Silence of the Lambs*. Mawdsley was convicted of murder in London in 1974 and confined in Broadmoor's secure hospital in Berkshire. Three years later he and another inmate took a fellow prisoner hostage and strangled him. Mawdsley then sawed the man's head open and threatened to eat his brains.

Transferred to Wakefield Prison, he then executed fellow inmates William Roberts and Stanley Darwood and was put in solitary confinement, telling prison officers: 'I adore the sight of blood.'

Too tough even for the notorious Wakefield jail, Robert Mawdsley was transferred to a specially designed 'suite' of cells at Parkhurst on the Isle of Wight. Three of the old cells have been knocked together providing a lavatory and shower room, a living room with cardboard furniture and a concrete bed-base, and a television room where Mawdsley watches the set from behind a panel of armour-plated glass. He is considered so dangerous to staff that meals are passed through a gap between the tungsten steel bars and the doors. Ironically, Mawdsley is a former member of Mensa and has an IQ rating approaching genius; he is also said to be a talented and obsessive artist, having decorated the walls of his cell with drawn circles – all exactly the same size.

Netherlands
Arie and Dinie Van Baak

In the middle of January 1994 a Dutch couple were put on trial in the central town of Zutphen charged with the murder of five babies carried by their daughters, twenty-five-year-old Evelien and twenty-six-year-old Jolanda. The infants were the products of an incestuous relationship lasting fourteen years. Arie and Dinie Van Baak, who had already been imprisoned for incest in 1991, also faced indictments on subjecting the girls to at least nine abortions.

Russia
The 'Russian Rippers'

Since the Soviet Union opened itself up to closer scrutiny by the outside world – and indeed by its own people – we have learned a great deal about the extent of crime in Russia and its former republics. What has been most revealing to criminologists is that the pattern of serial murder recorded in the West, and particularly in America, has its parallel in Russia.

The first notable example was the case of Nikolai Dzhumagaliev, the killer cannibal known as 'Metal Fang' on account of his white-metal false teeth, who created a reign of terror in the republic of Kazakhstan during 1980. Although he had already served a jail sentence for manslaughter, Dzhumagaliev appeared to be the perfect gentleman, presentable, clean-shaven and neatly dressed. He enjoyed escorting attractive women on strolls by the river in Alma-Ata where he worked on a building site. But, having lured his prey to a lonely spot on the river bank, Metal Fang raped and hacked the woman to death with axe and knife and then lit a fire and cooked the victim. It was always on the evening following one of these sorties that Dzhumagaliev's friends would be invited to a supper of roast meat.

Metal Fang was eventually discovered when two drunks he had invited home for a snack found a woman's head and intestines in the kitchen. Dzhumagaliev was charged with seven murders, but the court found him not responsible for his actions and committed him to a mental institution.

Nikolai Dzhumagaliev escaped from custody while being transferred to another institution in 1989; no public announcement was ever made of Metal Fang's escape lest it cause panic. He was recaptured at Fergana, Uzbekistan, in August 1991, after earlier being reported for trying to proposition women in Moscow.

Perhaps the best known Russian serial killer was another cannibal – Andrei Chikatilo, the 'Rostov Ripper' – who was active between 1978 and 1990.

In 1978 the first known victim, a teenaged girl, was

found dead in a wood outside Rostov, a busy port at the south-eastern corner of what was once the USSR. Over the succeeding years the list of those who disappeared grew longer, and the discovery of mutilated remains punctuated the normally quiet life around Rostov with increasing regularity; in one year alone there were eight deaths in a single month. The killer's approach was always the same. With the uncanny sixth sense of the natural predator, he could pick out the weak and vulnerable on the edges of society's groups, trawling the streets and railway stations for the homeless drifters who were unlikely to be missed, singling out the solitary child on his way to school.

Despite a manhunt that extended from Rostov to Siberia led by experienced detectives seconded from Moscow, the police still seemed helpless in the face of a catalogue of carnage which had by now spread to the neighbouring republics of Ukraine and Uzbekistan. Then, in 1979, a man was picked up in an isolated wooded area, but persuaded the police that he was simply an innocent hiker; after taking his name and particulars they allowed him to go on his way. The same man was taken into custody five years later, having been picked up close to the scene of one of the murders carrying a length of rope and a knife in his briefcase. A blood test proved in the laboratory that the man's blood group differed from that of the semen samples recovered from the bodies of some of the victims, and the suspect was released. What the Russian police, with their basic grasp of forensic procedures, did not know is that in extremely rare cases secretions from different parts of the body can have different serological groupings. Andrei Romanovich Chikatilo was one of those rare cases.

It was not until November 1990 that a police officer stopped Chikatilo in the street after spotting bloodstains on his face. When another body was found and the officer reported the incident of the bloodstains Chikatilo was put under heavy surveillance. On 20 November the police saw him approach a young boy at a railway station and arrested him. Under questioning Andrei Chikatilo readily confessed to an unbelievable fifty-five brutal murders, though as he was the first to admit, 'there may be more'.

The trial of the fifty-four-year-old former teacher and one-time Head of Supplies of the Rostov locomotive repair shop opened in Rostov's own very unceremonial court on 14 April 1992. In the centre of the threadbare room a huge iron-barred cage had been built around the dock. Inside sat Andrei Chikatilo, chained like a wild beast, the baying crowds of his victims' families surrounding the cage, screaming for his blood. The two-volume indictment listed thirty-five child victims – eleven of them boys – and eighteen young women.

There was never any likelihood of Andrei Chikatilo being found not guilty of the crimes with which he was charged – after all, he not only confessed in detail, but he led police searchers to forest locations where many of his victims still lay buried. What was in dispute was his sanity, and therefore his culpability. If, as the prosecutor claimed, Chikatilo was sane at the time of his killings then he faced death in front of a firing squad. On behalf of his client Mr Murat Khabibulin agreed that Chikatilo *could* tell right from wrong; however, knowing right from wrong is a different matter from being able to *control* his actions. In the end it was decided by the Moscow-based Serbsky Institute (Russia's leading institute of psychiatry) that Andrei Chikatilo was responsible for his actions.

It was not until 15 October 1992 that Judge Leonid Akubzhanov announced his sentence, accompanied by further wailing, flailing and gnashing of teeth from the by now well-rehearsed onlookers. Fifty-two of the fifty-three murders had been successfully proved and it took the judge an hour and a half to read the verdict, making constant references to the brutality of Chikatilo's murders: 'He ruthlessly and cold-bloodedly dismembered his victims, pulling them apart while they were still alive.' Finally Judge Akubzhanov intoned the sentence: 'This court cannot do other than sentence you to what you deserve for these terrible crimes – Andrei Romanovich Chikatilo, you are sentenced to death.' Chikatilo was so angered by what he obviously considered a gross miscarriage of justice that his rantings and ravings now mingled with the general pandemonium of the court: 'I fought in Afghanistan,' he reminded the jeering crowd, 'I was a partisan who defended the barricades; I fought for a free Russia.' Then he was taken from the iron cage for the last time and returned to prison.

Andrei Chikatilo's lawyers had already started the appeal process; if it failed, it would then require the intercession of President Yeltsin himself to save the Ripper from execution. It was not until 15 February 1994 that the 'Rostov Ripper' faced the implementation of his death sentence. President Yeltsin had rejected a plea for clemency, and Andrei Chikatilo stood before his executioner in a prison at Novocherkassk, near Rostov-on-Don in southern Russia. The customary method for carrying out the death penalty is with a single bullet in the back of the head.

In the wake of the Chikatilo trial, two useful books were published on the case – Peter Conrad's *The Red Ripper* (Virgin True Crime, London, 1992) and *Hunting the Devil* by Richard Lourie (Grafton, London, 1993). As well as being an exhaustive study of the 'Rostov Ripper' case, Lourie's book gives an account of Vladimir Storozhenko, another Russian serial killer rarely heard of in the West. Storozhenko was, like Chikatilo, finally run to ground by Inspector Issa Kostoev of the Russian Attorney General's Office.

For two years between 1979 and 1981 the city of

Smolensk had been terrorised by a series of twenty rapes and brutal assaults on women which had left a dozen dead. The problem was that having got Storozhenko into custody, Inspector Kostoev knew that he had no chance of bringing charges of murder against him without a confession, and the likelihood of that was slim indeed. 'Storozhenko was a tough guy who had already done time, and who wore the tattoo of a snow leopard on his shoulder, insignia of the Russian outlaw. The tattoo on his chest, a pale-green angel with its wings extended in flight, looked like a needle-and-thread job done in prison. Kostoev could read the signs, he knew about the snow leopard, he knew about men like Storozhenko with their muscular necks and reckless bravado . . .' (*Hunting the Devil*).

In the end by appealing to his prisoner's macho arrogance, the policeman secured his confession; he suggested to Storozhenko that a man such as he might be more use to the secret service alive than dead: 'Sometimes they sentence a man to death and then use a false execution certificate. He gets a new name, sometimes even a new face through plastic surgery, and then he's sent abroad.' It worked like a charm, as Kostoev instinctively knew it would.

At around the same time Andrei Chikatilo was awaiting his trial, another so-called 'Russian Ripper' was standing in a metal cage in a Moscow courtroom facing charges of murder. Alexander Timofeyev, or 'Jack Potroshitel' (Jack the Ripper), had been on a maiming and killing spree in the northern sector of the Russian capital for three months before police arrested him. The association with London's notorious Jack the Ripper was an appropriate one. Timofeyev approached women on quiet streets and, after engaging them in some small talk, pulled out a knife and began slashing and stabbing at their bodies; frequently this savage attack was preceded or followed by rape. It seems that the act of slashing was the important element for Timofeyev, the drawing of blood, because he left his victims where they fell and ran off without checking whether or not they were dead. Many did survive, and in March 1992 they at least had the satisfaction of giving evidence in court against their attacker.

Another case of serial murder in Russia also coincided with the Chikatilo trial. In October 1992 the newspaper *Isvestia* reported that a serial sex-killer with the enigmatic soubriquet 'The Boa' had been taken into custody. The first murders took place in 1986 at Odintsovo, a town about twenty-five miles south-west of Moscow. The victims were teenagers who had been mutilated and sexually assaulted. Although there are currently ten named victims in the police investigation the prosecutor's office admits that the number may grow. The only information revealed about 'The Boa's real identity is that he is a thirty-three-year-old single man.

More recently, in February 1993, a serial killer is reported to have killed ten women in Moscow and Ukraine. The detective heading the investigation on the killer called 'M' said the man was in his early twenties and believed himself to be a 'hyper-sexual'. Inspector Mikhail Slinko added: 'He thought women would faint with desire for him; sadly they seldom did.' Instead 'M' decided to transfix his victims in a more reliable way – he skewered them to wooden poles.

South Africa
The 'Station Strangler'

Although like most nations South Africa has not been free from the curse of serial murder, it has not suffered an epidemic such as that which bedevils the United States. Daisy de Melker was hanged in Pretoria in 1932 for poisoning her son and probably, though it was never proved, a couple of husbands; Salie Linevelt sexually assaulted, robbed and bludgeoned to death four women in 1940 and was hanged; and during 1953–5 Elifasi Msomi, a native of Richmond, Natal, butchered fifteen men, women and children, later claiming that it was not he but the 'tokoloshe' – the bogey-man of tribal folklore – that had been responsible. More recently, from 1986 to 1989 Louis van Schoor, a white former policeman turned security guard, shot dead thirty-nine blacks and wounded about sixty more, all of whom he claimed were 'resisting arrest'.*

However, not even this had prepared blacks in the townships for the reign of terror of the man who came to be known and feared as the 'Station Strangler' because his earlier victims in the late 1980s were found by the railway track. Although it is now thought that the killer claimed the first of his upwards of twenty-two victims in 1986, police were sure the murders had stopped in 1992. However, it was not until January 1994 that the full extent of the crimes was realised. Around the middle of the month two corpses, that of twelve-year-old Jeremy Smith and the other an unidentified eleven-year-old boy, were uncovered from shallow graves in the Cape Town township of Mitchell's Plain. The fact that Jeremy Smith had suffered the loss of an ear seemed to indicate that he had been tortured, and his torn fingertips were testimony to the courageous struggle the child had put up. The following week three more bodies of boys around twelve years of age were discovered, and only days later, no fewer than six further disinterments from the scrub-covered area around Mitchell's Plain each yielded the body of another sub-teenage boy – all were of mixed race,

* For greater detail on all these cases see *The Encyclopedia of Serial Killers* by Brian Lane and Wilfred Gregg, Headline, London, 1992.

and all had been sodomised, bound and strangled. The only clues found by the police were a set of false teeth and a mocking note, clearly from the killer, reading: 'One more; many more in store.'

In no time hysteria had gripped the native community, and while mothers kept their children away from school, the menfolk patrolled the streets armed with whatever rudimentary weapons they could lay their hands on. When pupils at one nearby primary school complained that a suspicious-looking man had been loitering around the playground, a group of adults chased him into the bush. They lost their quarry, but found two more decomposing bodies of young boys, fully clothed but with their trousers pulled down. Law and order minister Hernus Kriel offering a substantial reward for information said: 'The reign of terror must be ended. This killer must be brought to justice.'

As tension rose in the township police made strenuous efforts to curb the spread of armed vigilante groups, though the radical Pan-Africanist Congress party urged local people to join in a mass hunt for the elusive strangler. The PAC also accused the police of not taking the murders seriously because the victims were not white. Unfortunately this inflammatory election rhetoric simply exacerbated the anger of the crowds and one unfortunate man was chased through the streets by a mob and trapped in a sewer pipe from where he was rescued by police officers only to be then beaten to death. The feelings of local mothers were summed up by one township woman reported as saying: 'They must hand him over to the women so that they can deal with him, or give him to the gangs so that they can torture him. They mustn't just kill him.'

Also accusing the police of dragging their heels was Ibrahim Clayton, head of the Islamic school, who argued that it was their colour that was against the victims:

'When four white girls went missing the police acted quicker. They put their pictures on milk cartons. One of the grievances is that since the first killing in 1986 the police were slow to act. The response is great now, but how many are dead? Twenty? It's too late.'

But at least nobody could accuse the police of not acting now. Police Colonel Leonard Knipe, leading the investigation, claimed: 'South Africa has never seen a sexual deviant killer on this scale. In all my career I have never come across anything so horrific.' It was a measure of the determination of Colonel Knipe's team that within a week of this statement a man had been held on suspicion, and so incensed were the crowd of 500 township dwellers that the police were obliged to use tear gas and shotgun fire to disperse the mob. Which was a good thing for the suspect – he was found not to be connected with the crimes of the 'Station Strangler'.

However, in the middle of April it was announced that another man had been taken into custody and detained by the police after a week's observation. Police would say only that he was in his late twenties and a former psychiatric patient. Four days later, when he appeared in court, it was learned that the scar-faced teacher who was an enthusiastic body builder, was named Norman Simons and that he was twenty-seven years old. As Simons was led from the heavily guarded court at Kuilsrivier to undergo psychiatric examination, forensic scientists were analysing evidence to be presented at a future trial.

Spain
Antonio Angles

Typical of the sociopath whose crimes escalate in severity, Antonio Angles Martin, called latterly the 'Beast of Valencia', was on police records simply as a convicted drug dealer and known psychopath who had escaped from prison after being allowed out to attend the Valencia fiesta. Then on 13 November 1992 three young girls, Miriam Garcia and Desiree Hernandez, both fourteen years old, and Antonia Toni Gomez, fifteen, left their homes in the village of Alcacer on the east coast of Spain to hitch-hike together to their local school dance. There was nothing unusual in this in a country known for its affection for children, and especially in small villages adolescents are accustomed to walking at night – these trips even have a name, *paseos*. The girls were last sighted at 8.30 at Picassent, near Valencia, getting into a large white car. Inside the vehicle was a man, later identified as twenty-six-year-old Antonio Angles, and at least one other male.

Over the following eleven weeks an intensive search for the girls and any information on their whereabouts or fate proved fruitless. A nationwide poster campaign with pictures and descriptions of the girls with the caption 'Help Us To Find Them' in several languages resulted in hundreds of calls, none of which advanced the investigation. Detectives spread their net worldwide with officers even travelling to North Africa with the thought that the girls might have been abducted for the white slave trade. Miriam Garcia's father took the unusual step of visiting London to seek the help of Scotland Yard.

And the mystery might well have remained on the books of the international police for many more weeks, months even, had not torrential rain at the end of January 1993 removed a layer of topsoil. Which is how a local beekeeper saw Antonia Gomez's watch lying in the mud. As he reached down to pick it up, he pulled the hand it was on with it. The subsequent exhumation showed that each of the girls had been bound with their hands behind their backs and they had been buried one on top of the other. Pathologists later established that all three victims had been murdered on the night they disappeared. It is known that the girls were sexually abused and tortured before being shot in the back of the head, but no further details have been released. But if the killers had been brutal, they had also been very stupid, as scene-of-crime officers were quick to realise the significance of a medical prescription in the name of Angles carelessly dropped in the *ad hoc* grave. It had not belonged to Antonio himself but to a brother who was not slow to lay the blame for the killings squarely on the shoulders of his sibling and another man. The hunt was on for Antonio Angles.

By this time, however, the squalid Antonio had heard on the radio that the bodies had been found, and after plundering his mother's life savings he fled. What happened next, what Angles' itinerary was, is still a mystery – the only person able to tell us for sure is still at large. However, it is believed that Angles hijacked a car to take him to Madrid and over the border into Portugal. From Lisbon he may have hidden among the containers on the merchant vessel *City of Plymouth* bound for Dublin in the Irish Republic. Certainly a stowaway was found aboard the ship and locked in a cabin until it docked on 24 March. When representatives of the Garda arrived to arrest him Antonio Angles had disappeared – apparently via a porthole, for a knotted rope was reportedly discovered dangling from the side of the ship and one of the life-jackets was found discarded in Dublin harbour. What is more likely is that the wily Angles simply waited for his opportunity in hiding and walked off the ship when it berthed, then picking up another vessel bound for Britain.

That was the available information in the summer of 1993. Antonio Angles, called 'Europe's most wanted man' and said to be a master of disguise, could be anywhere. And is certainly very dangerous. It has been established that before the triple killing he had been imprisoned for abducting and torturing his girlfriend and had spent time in a psychiatric hospital.

United States
Dorothea Puente

The sixty-four-year-old white-haired grandmother who had been convicted of killing a number of her tenants was on 14 October 1993 sentenced to life imprisonment at Monterey, after a Los Angeles penalty jury returned deadlocked 7–5 against the death penalty. Mrs Puente ran a boarding house in Sacramento catering for the homeless and alcoholic underclass whom she subsequently killed for their disability and welfare benefits cards and then buried beneath the flowerbeds in her garden.

Aileen Wuornos

Another of America's most celebrated serial killers joined Jeffrey Dahmer as a star of the small screen when the idiosyncratic film-maker Nick Broomfield assembled the remarkable study 'Aileen Wuornos – The Selling of a Serial Killer'. 'Lee' was, you remember, the highway hooker who, not content with taking her clients' money, robbed seven of them of their lives as well. In January 1992 a jury found Wuornos guilty of a sample charge of killing fifty-one-year-old Richard Mallory, her first victim, and she was eventually sentenced to death. And so the woman who had become known as the 'Damsel of Death' entered Death Row and history.

What very few people knew, or were particularly interested in at the time, was that Aileen Wuornos had been first befriended and then legally adopted by an evangelical born-again Christian named Arlene Prall, aided and abetted by a bizarre latter-day hippy lawyer answering to the name of Steve Glazer, whose answerphone message apparently begins with a few rousing choruses of Bob Marley's classic *Get Up, Stand Up*. Between them, and for reasons at first best known to themselves (but which became apparent later), Arlene and Steve persuaded Aileen not to contest the conviction. Needless to remark Ms Wuornos, now facing the implementation of the death sentence, has had time to consider the strength of her commitment to 'meeting Jesus sooner', and rather regrets taking this advice.

The relationship between adoptive mother and daughter is to say the least strained. Not that this has prevented Arlene from capitalising on her daughter's notoriety in a big way. Indeed so offended was Broomfield that he engaged in verbal fisticuffs with Arlene, accusing her of being 'mercenary' and deceitful. She is reported, for example, to be taking a one-third cut on a paperback book on the case. Certainly, as Nick Broomfield discovered to his cost, Arlene charges a hefty fee for interviews, and Steve, when he can be persuaded to talk for less than a fistful of dollars, waxes enthusiastic about selling film rights to Lee's execution. Broomfield, with his lovably hillbilly approach to sound and camera (both pieces of equipment he lugged around the whole time on his shoulders) also exposed a degree of exploitation among police officers who have been approached with various film contracts. In short, the footage disclosed a cynical collection of money-grubbing backstabbers compared with whom, as one journalist put it: 'The serial killer seemed almost saintly.' Max Davidson, reviewing the film for the *Daily Telegraph*, agreed: 'She [Wuornos] was by some distance the most likeable person to appear on the programme.'

But what of Lee Wuornos herself? Would *she* talk to the camera? Of course, said Steve Glazer rubbing his hands – for just $25,000! With the cool ruthlessness of somebody with nothing to lose, Broomfield beat him down to $10,000. Even then it was not plain sailing; actually getting to see Aileen was not without its problems. Having humped the heavy hand-held camera and bulky sound recorder (for economy, the film-maker was acting as his own sound engineer as well as cameraman) up to the prison, Broomfield found that Aileen could not make herself available because her laundry hadn't been done. It looked as if our intrepid reporter had been foiled once again. But that is to reckon without the Broomfield stubborn persistance; and it was well worth it. Having clearly charmed the lens with a smile described by Jennifer Selway in the *Observer* as: 'Not so much a goofy, vulnerable Julia Roberts sort of smile, more of a Katharine Hepburn laser-launch, the sort she uses to let Spence know that he is the one', Aileen gave a sparkling interview with more than a few robust comments about her new 'family'. Much talk was devoted to Lee Wuornos' insistence that she is innocent of murder. Not that she is saying she didn't kill those men but, she claims, it was self-defence, the last resort of a prostitute who is being attacked by a vicious client. None of this was new – that was the defence that Aileen's counsel put so eloquently at trial – but it did reinforce demands made by several observers of the original investigation and trial for a review of the case. Adding his own voice to theirs, Nick Broomfield concluded: 'I hope that a proper inquiry will follow and a decent retrial.' Meanwhile, it looks as though serial killers as capital assets are here to stay.

Appendix 2
Mass Murder Update

Introduction

For an introduction to, and a psychological analysis of, mass murder, the reader is recommended to the recently published *Encyclopedia of Mass Murder* by Brian Lane and Wilfred Gregg (Headline, London, 1994). Since that wide-ranging study was delivered to the printer and since the last similar update in the 1994 edition of *Murder Yearbook* a number of significant acts of multicide have occurred which supplement previous accounts. So prevalent has mass killing become that frequently only the scantest of information is available from the world's press – often we cannot even trace a multicide's name.

Although it is a fact that the majority of these incidents take place in the United States, the period 1993–4 saw mass murders in England, Germany, Finland, Australia, Sudan, Niger, Tajikistan and China.

Perhaps the case that most caught the British imagination (via the ever-ready tabloid newspapers) was the arson attack on a cinema club catering for homosexuals in east London in which eleven people lost their lives, and in doing so reanimated the whole debate on pornography and violence.

Case Studies

WHEN DREAM TURNS TO NIGHTMARE
The Case of the Dream City Cinema Fire

Imagine this nightmare; being trapped by fire in a confined space crowded with other people . . . all possible escape routes are already blazing infernos and the heat is unbearable, burning skin and flesh until they almost melt . . . utter chaos, and the thick choking black smoke, so hot it burns the lungs as it coats them with soot. Those who do not die from multiple burns or asphyxia are crushed to death in the screaming panic to find an exit.

On the morning of Sunday 27 February 1994 this nightmare became a reality. At around 5.15 a.m. the Dream City, a private cinema in east London, exploded into flames, claiming the lives of seven people and injuring twenty more. According to the London Ambulance Service, a fleet of twelve ambulances manned by paramedics gave medical assistance at the scene of the disaster and ferried the injured to local London hospitals. Six who were being treated at nearby St Bartholomew's were suffering 50 per cent or more burns; a further three had sustained serious lung damage through smoke inhalation, and one man had a fractured pelvis after jumping from a window. Other casualties were treated at Guy's and the Royal London, and some with more serious injuries were transferred to the specialist burns units at East Grinstead and St Andrew's Hospital.

Although the first firefighters arrived at the scene within minutes of being called, the flames had taken hold so rapidly that the fire had spread through all four floors of the building. Ken Emsley, station commander at Euston fire station, and one of the first on the spot, gave his impression of the sight as: 'Chaos. One of the most horrific incidents I have attended in thirty years of service.' About fifty firefighters grappled with the double problem of quenching the fire and rescuing panicking survivors whose only means of exit was through windows. Ken Emsley recalled: 'We had a ladder pitched at the second floor and about twenty people were trying to get down it at the same time – which obviously made the work of my men very difficult.' In fact, the fire took such a grip that it was still smouldering four hours later. A less 'authoritative', less 'official', but far more graphic picture was painted by Mrs Valerie Martin, a nearby resident who was quickly on the scene helping emergency services care for the injured: 'The fire started in a passageway by the video and cinema and it seemed almost immediately to shoot up through the building and through the roof . . . The fire took hold within seconds, it was like a fireball exploding. The fire brigade were great; they got people out on stretchers and on fireman's lifts from the ladder very quickly . . . People were all over the floor, some of them badly burned on their neck and arms. One man I saw was delirious. They [the paramedics] were pumping people's hearts to resuscitate them . . . There were people sitting in the gutter groaning. Most of them seemed to have burned hands; they were all in a daze and didn't seem to know what was going on. I helped one guy. He seemed to be aged about twenty-three, his head, neck, arms and back were burned. As the ambulancemen were giving him oxygen he moaned that he wanted to lie down. Steam was coming from him like he had been in a microwave. The firemen brought other people out on stretchers but I couldn't say if they were alive or dead . . .' In fact, in those first hours six victims were found dead; one more died later in hospital, and by 17 March the toll had risen to eleven.

So far the newspapers had, rightly, concentrated on reporting the tragedy itself and the strong police suspicion that they were dealing with an arson attack. Although the charred hulk of the building was not yet cool or safe enough for fire investigators to make a full examination, the fire-raiser theory was given some substance by the witness Valerie Martin, who reported that she had seen two youths 'standing on the other side of the road, laughing'; she described them as being eighteen to twenty-two years old. On the following day arson would be confirmed.

However, another aspect of the case was also about to emerge. The press – or certainly some sections of it – were going to turn the story – or certainly some sections of it – into an unseemly attack on homosexuality. The first indications could be seen in the report in the *News of the World* beneath the headline '7 Killed in Porn Cinema Inferno'. It printed a paragraph 'overlooked' by other papers: 'Some of the injured were carried out naked . . . it is unlikely that they [the firefighters] would remove a victim's clothes because that could make their injuries worse.' The implication was clear.

By the following morning, Monday the 28th, these twin strands were competing for press attention. For a start, forensic fire experts had established beyond doubt that the blaze had been deliberately set using an accelerant – petrol. Which dovetailed neatly with information given by the sales assistant at the Clerkenwell Road service station less than a quarter of a mile from the Dream City cinema club, that some time between 5.00 a.m. and 5.30 a.m. – that is to say the time the fire was started – a man had bought a red plastic petrol container. The salesman could be sure because it was the only container of its kind he sold that day; the purchaser had then put £2 worth of petrol in it and made off in a hurry. The man was described as white, aged between thirty and thirty-three, slightly stooped, with dark hair and wearing a dark jacket. This was almost certainly the same man who was seen carrying a red container in St John Street. Police were also following up information that a man had been thrown out of the club following a fight just before the fire.

Meanwhile, the public was learning a lot more about the Dream City cinema club – not least that it was unlicensed. The previously named New City Cinema

Club had opened in 1990 in the premises of a former massage parlour. The club charged members £6 to watch videos which had been pirated from the Danish satellite pornography station Red Hot TV. If they liked what they saw, punters could buy a copy of the tape for £20 to prolong the experiences in the comfort of their own home. The club had two viewing rooms – not large enough to be dignified as 'auditoriums', each containing a few rows of seats and a large monitor screen. There was also a reception area where people could 'meet' each other. As it was all but blacked out, this spot was reputedly used for some quite intimate meetings. Although all the victims of the fire were middle-aged men the club was not exclusively homosexual; in fact, according to one long-standing member, it had started off strictly heterosexual but increasingly absorbed the requirements (and cash) of the gay scene. Towards the end it became almost exclusively the haunt of homosexuals who, between the hours of midday and just about any time in the morning that there were punters to entertain, were fed a diet of so-called hard-core gay pornography. Another member, speaking to the *Guardian* newspaper, was reported as saying: 'Lots of people were very bold. Some of them even took a bag and took off some of their clothing. A couple came in women's clothing, some in leather, some in very short shorts. If you saw a bulge you fancied, you just grabbed it. Others would join in. Mostly it was at the back. It was all sorts, a real cross-section. There were foreigners. There were skinheads. There were leather boys.'

So there it was. From the horse's mouth, so to speak. The *News of the World* had been right: 'Some . . . took off some of their clothing'. Worse: 'A couple came in women's clothing'! Good copy indeed for any newspaper which cared to exploit it. 'Gay Porn Club Victims Died in Dresses', screamed the *Sun*: 'Some of the dead and injured, all males, were transvestites watching hard-core gay movies. Several murder victims found in the shell of the Dream City club wore wigs, dresses and high heels.' Ah! those sobering words: 'murder victims'. So it was more than just a sex romp put on for the benefit of the tabloids. Somebody must have realised that, whatever the circumstances may have been, this was one of the most horrific cases of mass murder the capital had ever seen.

One of the major difficulties facing the investigation was directly related to the circumstances, however. Survivors of the fire were proving very coy when it came to helping the police with their inquiries. Some were even refusing to give their names to hospital staff, and were instead using such soubriquets as John Smith and John Brown. One nurse commented: 'They are not co-operating at all. It means they have had hardly any visitors. It is an extremely peculiar situation which we have never come across before.'

Meanwhile, a beleaguered Islington Council was facing some very uncomfortable questions about its control of safety in unlicensed clubs, and in particular cinema clubs, which came under the 1985 Cinemas Act. And MPs were making demands that the Home Secretary force all clubs to observe fire safety rules 'as a matter of utmost urgency'. Mr David Young, Labour member for Bolton South-east insisted: 'There has got to be a review of fire regulations to see that there are inspections in all the areas where people come together, even if in very small numbers and for whatever purpose. If owners of these clubs are not compelled to take this action, then not only do they put their own members at risk, but they put other members of society at risk. There must now be an urgent review of fire regulations to ensure that nobody is allowed to slip the net.'

For their part, detectives were following the only lead

they had – the report that just before the fire was started a man with a Scottish accent was ejected from the club after a fight. And it was a Scotsman who was taken into custody after he walked into Walthamstow police station, east London, at 5.00 p.m. on the evening of 28 February. As police continued their inquiries, the thirty-four-year-old man of no fixed address was transferred to Islington police station for further questioning. On 3 March 1994 the Scotsman was named as David Lauwers, a tailor's cutter; the following morning he was remanded in custody at Highbury Corner Magistrates Court. It will almost certainly be the last the public hears about the inquiry until David Lauwers appears at the Central Criminal Court, probably in early 1995.

Not so the controversy over unlicensed private clubs. In the wake of Lauwers' arrest there were some unfortunate revelations about the Dream City club. Local residents and businesses had already made numerous complaints to both the police and the local council about the activities that went on there, but little had been done. The cinema itself was traced to a company named Jest Lark, and a prosecution planned over the admittance of non-members was delayed because the owners could not be traced. Instead, one of its managers was fined £230 in 1988 for operating an unlicensed cinema; he also collected a four-month suspended sentence resulting from a police prosecution under the Obscene Publications Act. In 1990 a second manager was fined £100 for operating without a licence, and his projection equipment was confiscated. More worrying still, perhaps, was that the club itself invited the fire brigade to make an inspection and after some minor alterations the brigade found that the precautions were adequate and the club was given a fire certificate. However, there were no fire escapes or stairs at the back of the building, leaving the rickety staircase to the street as the only means of escape in the event of a fire. It has also been claimed that some form of exit existed on the floor above the cinemas in what once had been a video shop (pornographic of course). Unfortunately some of the more sexually active members had begun to colonise the area for the purposes of sex, and the doors had been boarded up.

Despite the obvious loopholes in the law, and despite the horrific incident at Dream City, there is still no adequate legislation to control private clubs. It is known that there are at least two similar establishments in the same district as Dream City – will one of those be next?

I'LL KILL YOU IN COURT
The Case of Erwin Mikolajczyk

Fifteen miles to the west of the German city of Bonn is the small town of Euskirchen in the state of North Rhine–Westphalia. Like small towns anywhere, Euskirchen has its modest courthouse to process local offenders, and its only apparent gesture to the rise in crime is a small modern redbrick extension to the old court. As such legal establishments try mainly petty criminals – the more serious crimes being sent on to Bonn – the security, if not exactly lax, is not particularly strict either.

The sort of offender that comes before the judge at Euskirchen was personified by thirty-nine-year-old boilerman Erwin Mikolajczyk. Mikolajczyk had first appeared in court charged with an assault on his then girlfriend. It was a comparatively minor offence (except to the victim), and Mikolajczyk was ordered to pay a fine of 7,200 Deutschmarks (about £2,800). He appeared for a second time on 9 March 1994 to hear the result of his appeal against the sentence. It was rejected, and Mikolajczyk, cursing loudly, stormed out of the court a clearly disappointed man, a not uncommon occurrence. What could not be foreseen was the scale and savagery of his revenge.

A few minutes later, Erwin Mikolajczyk walked back into the courtroom brandishing a pistol and carrying a black rucksack. Before he could even press the emergency bell to alert the security officers, the thirty-one-year-old appeal judge, Alex Schaefer, fell dead with a bullet in his neck; without pause the gunman turned his weapon on two lawyers, shooting them dead. Court officers and observers threw themselves behind or under anything that looked solid enough to stop the force of a madman's bullet. One official jumped through an open first-floor window just as Mikolajczyk pulled the rucksack from his back and detonated the powerful bomb inside. The force of the blast was sufficient to hurl his dismembered body down into the street below along with the glass, debris and blood-stained law-books that the explosion had blown out after him. Among those left dead by the explosion were Mikolajczyk's girlfriend and his mother; a further eight at least were seriously injured, including a child, and many more sustained minor cuts and the effects of shock.

Little clear information has yet emerged about Erwin Mikolajczyk's background. It is thought that he came from the former East Germany and, via Bonn, settled in Euskirchen, where he lived with his mother. Vaguely reported facts also indicate that Mikolajczyk fitted a common profile of the mass killer – he was a gun-fanatic who became an enthusiastic member of a local gun club, and it is said that police searching his home took away with them an assortment of firearms, ammunition and explosives. One survivor noted that when he first came into the court, Mikolajczyk was wearing combat-style uniform and boots and, incongruously, a string of garlic around his neck.

One report which could not be verified, and was not

taken up, at least by the British media, was an article headed 'Killer's Kinky Wellies', which went on to reveal that Erwin Mikolajczyk had a collection of '140 pairs of sexy wellies'. By all accounts this multi-coloured footwear represented a record of his sexual exploits as each pair bore a name and a date. When all is said and done, though, such goings-on are fairly harmless compared with the souvenirs collected by other killers – after all, Jerry Brudos used to keep the dismembered feet of *his* victims in the deep-freeze so that he could dress them up in black stiletto-heeled shoes!

THE MAN WHO 'LOATHED WHITES . . . AND ASIANS . . . AND CONSERVATIVE BLACKS'

The Case of Colin Ferguson

It was 5.33 on the evening of 7 December 1993; rush hour on the busy Long Island commuter rail system – the largest in the country. Nobody had paid much attention to the rather bulky black man who had boarded the express train at New York's Pennsylvania station carrying a paper bag; not until the train was just outside Garden City station, when the man later identified as thirty-five-year-old Colin Ferguson opened his paper bag and pulled out a Ruger 9mm semi-automatic handgun and opened fire, apparently randomly, on his fellow passengers. Methodically, Ferguson walked up and down the third carriage of the train shooting and reloading as he went; screaming passengers in total panic tried desperately to escape – by crawling from that carriage to the next, or throwing themselves under seats; some simply knelt and prayed. Finally the gunman was overpowered by three passengers who wrestled him to the floor and snatched away the gun. In a spree which had lasted just over three minutes, four people lay dead, nineteen more suffered bullet wounds, one fatally, and two passengers suffered crush injuries. A survivor later told journalists: 'I heard "pop, pop, pop!" My first thought was that someone outside the train was shooting . . . then I glanced up and out of the corner of my eye I could see someone making a slow back and forth motion with his hand. That's when I realised there was actually someone in the train shooting people. I just crashed to the ground. I ducked down behind a partition. I didn't want to make eye-contact with him. He was standing at the door at the end of the carriage and was shooting. He was holding the gun waist-high – it looked as if he had both hands on it. He was shooting people point-blank. When he finally stopped, I ran the length of the car to the opposite end. People piled on top of each other trying to get to the door. Then he went into another round of shooting.'

Although the killings had at first seemed random, it was observed later that Ferguson had only shot white or Asian people, no blacks; it was a fact that would prove significant in the light of what was later learned of Colin Ferguson's possible motive for such gratuitous violence. Notes found in Ferguson's pockets after his arrest, and others recovered from his Brooklyn bedsit revealed that he had nurtured an irrational hatred of white people, 'rich Chinese' and 'Uncle Tom Negroes and rich black attorneys'.

Colin Ferguson was born in Kingston, Jamaica, in 1958, and following the sudden death of his parents he emigrated to the United States. He married, but was divorced by his wife in 1988, a blow from which, according to friends, he never recovered. Subsequently bad grades forced him to quit New York's Adelphi University. Although Ferguson had never been arrested or had a record of mental illness, his oddball racial prejudices were well known. His landlord recalled Ferguson telling him: 'I shouldn't be living here; I should be living in a mansion.' Apparently he was convinced that the only thing holding him back from his rightful position at the top was white people. Not that he had much time for those blacks whom he considered 'non-militant', and after he had been mugged by two black men, Ferguson took to carrying a gun around in a paper bag. Things went from bad to worse; following an injury at work he was refused compensation, then his landlord asked him to vacate his room after getting sick of Ferguson taking five baths a day and keeping all the other residents in the building awake at night by chanting mantras about 'all the black people killing all the white people'. Ferguson thought he had suffered enough . . . next day he shot up the Long Island commuter express.

Colin Ferguson has been charged with four counts of murder in which it was said that he behaved with 'depraved indifference to life'. One of the prime exhibits at his forthcoming trial is certain to be the scrap of paper found in his pocket. Scribbled at the top is 'Reasons for this', followed by 'The sloppy running of the #2 train. It is racism by Caucasians and Uncle Tom Negroes. Also. The false allegations against me by the filthy Caucasian Racist female on the HI line.' This last reference was to an earlier incident when a woman complained to the police that Ferguson had harassed her on the subway. However, other observers had commented that far from being a victim of racism, Colin Ferguson is a 'paranoid madman'. Which interpretation of his psyche prevails will be up to a jury to decide at some future date.

By April 1994, Ferguson, the man who hated just about everybody, came up with a novel if slightly preposterous line of defence. Through his attorney, Colin Ferguson announced that his shooting spree had been the direct consequence of 'black rage' – in other words, white racism had turned him crazy: 'It is necessary to see the torment he was going through as a racial victim to see what drove him to this action.' It is not as silly a move as it may seem (racial defences as well as racially based appeals against the death sentence have been notoriously unsuccessful); the celebrated lawyer William Kunstler accepts that his client is a very unsympathetic figure – hated by many blacks as a 'crazy', feared by whites and Asians because . . . well, he kills them, so there is little chance of a truly fair and unbiased trial. The only possibility seems to be to recast Colin Ferguson as a victim. This tactic was used with spectacular success by the attorneys defending Eric and Lyle Menendez (see page 111) when they were transformed from greedy, cynical familicides into tragic youngsters who had suffered their parents' constant abuse.

That there is still a long way to go has been emphasised by an incident that took place at Nassau County Correctional Institute in Long Island. Ferguson found himself in the same prison as the white serial killer Joel Rifkin; the two entertained an almost instant mutual dislike which, as can happen, crystallised racial tension within the penal institution – black prisoners rallied behind Ferguson and the whites behind Rifkin. One of the results was that Colin Ferguson was recently attacked by a white gang who severely beat him, breaking his nose and doing considerable damage. It was reported in one newspaper that a guard at the prison observed: 'If he [Ferguson] wants to use black rage, then this is a test of white rage.'

THE MAN WHO HATED INDIANS
The Case of Michael Stevens and Earl Figley

It was headlined as 'the world's bloodiest feud' which, although it certainly wasn't, made a very strong crack at the title. What caught the imagination of the media and their public was the bizarre method of slaughtering five members of the same family – parcel bombs, usually the staple of political terrorism, were sent to five locations, and their detonation timed meticulously.

6.00 p.m., Tuesday 28 December 1993 A courier delivered a brown-paper-wrapped package to the home of Pamela Epperson and her boyfriend Richard Urban. The couple took their 'gift' into the kitchen, ripped off the paper exposing a metal toolbox, and lifted the lid. The resulting explosion ripped apart the house at Snug Harbour, Rochester, killing both Pamela and Richard; neighbours heard and felt the explosion, one describing it as sounding like 'a supersonic jet'.

6.30 p.m. The second explosion rocked the offices of Armored Motor Services of America at Cheektowaga, near Buffalo. Of three men who had stayed behind to work overtime, Robert Fowler, one of the company's owners, and John O'Donnell were killed and another colleague was injured. As horror and bewilderment swept through the small community of Cheektowaga, another quiet town was about to go into mourning.

7.00 p.m. A parcel arrived by taxi at the home of the late Robert Fowler, his wife Eleanor and son Jonathan. The house was set on fire by the explosive device and Mrs Fowler was killed instantly; Jonathan was saved from the wreckage badly injured. By now the police had realised that this was unlikely to be a series of random killings; it was clear that the Fowler family were being targeted (Pamela Epperson was Eleanor's daughter). This frightening scenario was confirmed when guards at the Lakeview Shock Facility prison refused to accept a parcel delivered in an official US Mail truck addressed to Scott Kemp – Eleanor Fowler's son-in-law.

7.30 p.m. At his home in Hogansburgh near the northern border of New York State and Canada, William Lazore became suspicious of the parcel that had just been delivered by courier, and opened it from a distance with a garden rake – it saved his life, but left him with grave leg injuries. William Lazore is Eleanor Fowler's brother.

7.35 p.m. An increasingly desperate police force, now it had found a common link, was preoccupied with *averting* disaster; and with just minutes to spare officers raced to the home of Lucille Fowler and Scott Kemp in time to prevent Lucille becoming another victim of the mad bomber. Just fifteen minutes later another team intercepted the parcel that had been addressed to Scott Kemp and disabled it.

While an as yet unidentified killer was still on the loose, forensic explosives experts were working on the clues available from the lethal devices. The conclusion was chilling; the parcel bombs were the work of an expert. Although they were home-made, they were of highly sophisticated construction, with the explosive packed inside metal boxes to ensure maximum 'shrapnel' injury. One expert claimed: 'The structure of the bombs showed a working knowledge of explosives.' Such a person could be very difficult to snare unless he made that one vital mistake. Other information gleaned from the bombs was that they were all identical, and had been sent in boxes bearing the name of the Liberty Iron and Metal Company, based in Erie, Pennsylvania.

All this new information would prove useful, but detectives still felt their strongest lead would lie in the background of the decimated Fowler family. It proved to be so, and a truly bizarre picture began to emerge.

Robert and Eleanor Fowler were regarded around the small community in which they lived as ordinary hard-working folk – he at Armored Motor Services of

America, she at home in West Valley, Buffalo, with her family. Fifty-six years of age at the time of her death, Eleanor had two daughters from her previous marriage – Brenda and Pamela, who had been killed by the second bomb, at Rochester. When Eleanor separated from her first husband, the girls retained their father's name. Pamela married and became Mrs Epperson and then separated and began a happy relationship with Richard Urban. When Eleanor married Robert Fowler, some years her junior, they produced two children of their own, Jonathan, who miraculously survived the explosion which killed his mother, and Lucille who had set up home with prison guard Scott Kemp, both of whom had been saved thanks to quick-thinking police officers and prison guards. The final casualty was Eleanor Fowler's sixty-two-year-old brother William Lazore.

Despite the various separations, the Fowlers' extended family seemed as close and friendly as any normal family. Except for Brenda. Brenda had taken up with a convict named Michael Stevens – bad enough in close communities like those in which the Fowlers lived, but when her daughter actually married Stevens, the shame became too much for Eleanor, and so a family feud began which was to end in a bloodbath. And as Brenda was pushed further and further from the family, so the bitterness grew like a cancer.

Tongues have a habit of wagging at times like this, and it was not long before Brenda Stevens was taken into custody; police spokesmen were openly using words like 'revenge', 'vengeance' and 'reprisal' – they also kept in mind the greatly more practical point that, with the rest of the family dead, Brenda stood to inherit. Besides, it seemed just a mite fishy that she was the only one not to receive a 'package'. In the end Brenda Stevens was questioned but not charged. Instead Michael Stevens was arrested and charged along with an accomplice, Earl Figley, whom he had met in jail. The two men face multiple murder indictments plus the federal charge of transporting explosives (the dynamite used to manufacture the bombs) across state lines from Tennessee to New York State – an offence which carries the death penalty.

Although detectives were cautiously announcing that 'The motive is unclear, but it is probably something like vengeance,' an eager public had only to wait until the following morning for the sordid details. The problem for Michael Stevens was that his girlfriend's family were Indians – 'redskins'. Imagine, a tribe of injuns trying to turn his own woman against him! It is a well known phenomenon that once they have a general grudge against the world, the multicides generally find a scapegoat on which to pin that resentment. In Stevens' case it was Brenda's Mohawk family. Pamela was a particular target for his anger – she even wore native American jewellery and brought *his* son Mohawk clothes! Which was typically irrational – after all the mother of his son was Brenda, Pamela's blood sister and so sharing a common native ancestry. Matters came to a head when the family, including Stevens got together over the Christmas holiday to talk over constructively the future of his son. Michael Stevens, as usual, became angry and abusive, though it was only when he began making death threats that he was thrown out. A few days later he was mailing out bombs.

Speaking before the arrests were made, local police Superintendent Constantine observed: 'This is crazy. In my opinion, the whole world is crazy.' One thing is sure, the lawyer who prosecuted Stevens in a minor fraud case is on record as saying: 'This guy is weird. He was a few pickles short of a barrel.'

Updates in Brief

Australia

26 August 1993

An unnamed fifty-three-year-old man went on a shooting spree in a block of apartments in the Sydney inner-city suburb of Burwood, killing two men. The gunman then climbed back into his truck and calmly drove to a take-away food store in neighbouring Redfern, where he shot the owner in the head at point-blank range. Police cars and a special helicopter caught up with the killer back on Burwood Road, one of the city's busiest commercial streets where he was loosing off a shotgun at early-morning commuters. As passers-by leapt for the safety of the shops a troop of armed police officers cornered the gunman and cut him down with serious gunshot wounds to the legs; he was later reported to be in a serious condition in hospital under police guard.

Both police officers and witnesses were inevitably reminded of the massacre in Strathfield, not far from Burwood, in August 1991, when a part-time cab-driver ran amok with an automatic gun and machete killing seven people.

2 March 1994

As a parcel bomb ripped the insides out of Australia's National Crime Authority, a police officer died, another person was seriously injured and three people were slightly hurt. Since it was detonated at the peak of the morning rush hour, it was a minor miracle that the cascade of debris and glass that tumbled down from the skyscraper's twelfth floor on to commuting office staff did not turn the event into a massacre. It was not difficult to see why the NCA had been selected as a target – after all, it had been set up specifically to provide a robust opposition to organised crime and corruption in Australia. And despite such attempts at mass murder as the 2 March parcel bomb outrage the Authority is determined to continue its work.

China
20 May 1993

A Reuter report gave news of a mother living in Peking who, anxious to give birth to a son, went to visit the local 'wise man'. His suggestion was that the woman poison her three daughters as a sacrifice – which she did.

England
Spring 1993

Another violent psychopath inevitably compared with Dr Hannibal Lecter was twenty-year-old Ian Warby. A self-confessed admirer of both 'Hannibal the Cannibal' and the Marquis de Sade, not to mention Ted Bundy and 'Night Stalker' Richard Ramirez, Warby proved singularly ineffectual as a multiple killer – indeed it emerged at his Old Bailey trial in the spring of 1993 that he was so 'weedy' that he asked his father to accompany him to see the movie *Silence of the Lambs*.

However, Warby's background had shown him worthy of at least one lengthy spell in a psychiatric prison hospital after threatening a schoolteacher with a knife, threatening to kill a young girl who was a neighbour of the Warbys and committing robbery. In 1991 he was released, unsupervised and against medical advice,* on to the streets of Witham, Essex, where he indulged himself in a diet of violent video films and books on serial murder. Then on 12 October 1992 Ian Warby, now

* See also chapter 'Released to Kill'.

calling himself 'The Outsider', left his parents' house armed with a sheath knife and a claw hammer – he had told a friend that he wanted to 'kill with relentless horror and obscenity and make as much mess as possible' and dreamed of 'a spree like Hungerford'. Over the hours that followed, Warby injured a young schoolboy and an elderly man with the hammer, slashed the face of Gary Wheeler as he sat in his van, and attacked a young woman and her baby, but he was chased by Gary Wheeler and his passenger Robert Ellis. The two men caught up with Ian Warby just as he was stabbing forty-two-year-old Marilyn Malster while she sat helpless in her wheelchair. Wheeler, Ellis and Ms Malster's nursing companion overpowered Warby and turned him over to the police.

When his case initially came up for trial at Chelmsford Crown Court in 1993 he denied the five charges of attempted murder, but put his hand up to three counts of wounding with intent to cause grievous bodily harm. The miracle was that no one died as a result of Ian Warby's warped desire to 'reap vengeance on a world he thought was against him'. One reason was, of course, that he was improperly armed for an act of mass murder; had he, like his hero Michael Ryan, had the benefit of sophisticated semi-automatic firearms, then he would indeed have been capable of re-creating the Hungerford massacre. As it was, this pathetic youth was convicted as charged and sentenced to life imprisonment. After the judge and jury were treated to Warby's innermost fantasies – that he would chew off his victims' lips, stitch their broken mouths up with needle and thread and hammer nails into their kneecaps, Mr Justice Henry, observing that Ian Warby was 'guilty of indiscriminate, mindless, motiveless, morally chilling attacks for kicks with no vestige of remorse', sentenced him to spend at least eight years in prison before he could expect a review of his case. The judge had earlier rejected a plea to send Warby to a psychiatric hospital because, according to medical opinion, he was considered 'an untreatable psychopath'.

27 January 1994

Statistically, mass murder within the family unit is the most common form of multicide, and in the category of 'familicide' the prevalent syndrome is murder followed by the killer's suicide. Early on the morning of 26 January 1994 angler Barry Kay was trekking to his favourite fishing spot along the secluded lane running beside the river Ancholme when he came across the parked Ford Granada. The hosepipe leading from the car's exhaust told the fisherman everything he needed to know. Within the hour police officers from nearby Hibaldstow, Humberside, were confirming his worst fears. Inside the fume-filled vehicle were the bodies of a middle-aged man and three young girls; above the dashboard a suicide note. They were later identified as fifty-two-year-old chef Ian Lazenby and his daughters Princess Heidi, aged nine, Kelly, six, and Rachel, just two years old.

To detectives investigating the deaths, the story was a familiar one. Mr Lazenby had suffered an acrimonious separation from his wife the previous month on grounds of his alleged drunken violence. While legalities were being pursued, he was reluctantly given access to the children. It was established that Lazenby had collected the girls on Saturday, promising to take them to the zoo at Marwell and return them to his wife's care on the following Monday morning. Instead, Ian Lazenby drove his daughters the 250 miles from their home in Portsmouth, Hampshire, to Humberside where he had relatives. On Monday Lazenby phoned his wife to announce that he was at Grimsby and would not telephone again. Sylvia Lazenby, pregnant with the couple's fourth child, applied for and was granted what is called a 'safe deliverance order' compelling her husband to return the children to their mother's custody immediately. This order was circulated to police forces nationwide; it was already too late. On Tuesday evening Ian Lazenby was turning the family car into an execution chamber.

28 January 1994

It was a tragic coincidence that at the time Ian Lazenby was slaughtering his offspring, another aggrieved father was planning the deaths of his. Within twenty-four hours of the Lazenby incident a telephone call brought firefighters rushing to a blazing car near the National Watersports Centre outside Nottingham. When the fire had been extinguished the officers were appalled to find the remains of four people inside the vehicle, too charred for recognition but from the evidence the bodies of one adult and three children. Later police officers from the Nottingham Tactical Support Team organised the removal of the burned-out Ford Orion and its grisly contents to a police workshop, where it was met by a Home Office pathologist. Although no details were immediately available, fire experts suggested that the intensity of the blaze was consistent with one of the victims – presumably the adult – having doused the car with petrol before setting light to it.

26 May 1994

In 1976 Kulwinder Kaur Bahia arrived in England from India; she was aged five. When she was eighteen years old Kulwinder entered into the by no means uncommon process of an arranged marriage and settled with her husband and mother-in-law at Smethwick in the West Midlands; their neighbours were Mrs Bahia's married sister-in-law and her four-year-old son. Kulwinder Bahia in time gave birth to the couple's first child, a daughter. In common with most males of their culture Kulwinder's husband was disappointed that he had not produced a son – or rather it was his wife's *fault* that she had not given birth to a male heir. Unsurprising, then, that when the Bahias' second offspring also turned out to be a female, tongues began to wag. Subsequently, Kulwinder was reported as claiming: 'They keep picking on me. There was a fight and they pulled my hair.' 'They' were the other female members of the family.

By November 1992, Mrs Bahia had suffered enough. Following constant alleged abuse not only from her mother-in-law but from her husband, she went to the shops and bought a kitchen knife and a can of petrol. Then, on 7 November, taking a lunch-break from her job as a machinist she visited her sister-in-law Surinder Kaur Dhandwar and stabbed her forty-six times; after that she stabbed Surinder's four-year-old-son Avtar to death, and went home to change out of her blood-stained clothes. After her husband had returned from work, bathed and slipped down the road to the pub, Kulwinder pushed a knife sixteen times into the body of her sixty-year-old mother-in-law, put the dead woman in a plastic bag and dragged it across the road to join her other corpses. By comparison, destroying the evidence was simple. Kulwinder Bahia simply doused the house in petrol and set light to it.

When Mrs Bahia faced the jury at Northampton Crown Court in May 1994, she was not denying that she had killed three members of her family, only that she had *murdered* them. In other words, through her attorney, Kulwinder was advancing a defence of diminished responsibility, effectively a plea of guilty to manslaughter. And that was the way the jury saw matters for, on 26 May 1994, twenty-three-year-old Kulwinder Kaur Bahia was sentenced by Mr Justice Tudor Evans to be detained 'without limit of time' under the Mental Health Act at Reaside Clinic, Birmingham. It was argued in her defence that Mrs Bahia had been suffering from post-natal depression after the birth of her second child – a girl.

17 June 1994

It is seldom appreciated when cases of multiple murder are reported by the media quite how many victims an incident leaves in its wake. Of course there are those very observable victims, the individuals who have prematurely lost their lives. There are the bereaved relatives unable to make any sense of their loss because there *is* no sense to it. And we must never forget the killer's own bewildered family, who for the rest of their lives will be asking 'Why?', 'Where did we go wrong?' Then there are the hidden victims, the forgotten ones: onlookers forever haunted by the violence of the moment, wondering whether there was anything they could have done, should have done; the emergency services, called in to untangle the dead, the dying and the wounded; and the law enforcement officers – ordinary men and women, much like you and I, only braver – policemen and women whose unenviable job it is to confront violence and sometimes death.

One of the most tragic pieces of news to be reported in 1994 was the death by his own hand of thirty-year-old Christopher Larkin. In 1987, when gun-fanatic Michael Ryan cut a swathe of death through the Berkshire village of Hungerford, Chris was PC Larkin. Having joined the force as a cadet at the age of sixteen, Larkin was one of the first officers on the scene of the massacre, where among the victims he found the body of a friend and colleague shot down by Ryan. According to Mr Larkin's mother Kathleen, her son became very depressed, spent hours lying in bed and began to drink heavily, something he had never done before Hungerford.

The former policeman was found in his fume-filled car at a country park near Wellingborough. Although the coroner Anne Pember recorded a suicide verdict, she added that Christopher Larkin was clearly seriously affected by the massacre; perhaps, then, the former PC Larkin should really join the ranks of those 'killed on duty'.

Finland
20 April 1994

An unnamed Finnish soldier, armed with a semi-automatic assault rifle and a crossbow, killed a middle-aged couple on the streets of his home-town of Kotka and later shot dead another man. Reports via Finnish radio said the man had been firing 'like a maniac'. Later information revealed that the killer had deserted from his garrison in nearby Hamina taking the rifle with him; he was due to appear in court on the day following the killings on a charge of vandalism.

Germany
10 May 1994

A former British soldier named Steven Bladen was reported to have gone berserk when his lover threatened to leave their home at Schwuelper, a village near Hanover. Thirty-five-year-old Bladen, who was trained as a marksman with the Rhine Army, shot dead Saskia Jebok and then her mother before turning the 9mm revolver on himself. Friends of the couple said that Steven had been acting strange since losing his job at a local leather factory.

Niger
11 January 1994

A brief wire report claimed that a former psychiatric patient had walked into a school at Maradi, close to Niamey, and beaten four children to death with a club; he also killed a woman who tried to stop him.

Sudan
5 February 1994

At the mosque in Omdurman, fifteen miles north of Khartoum, a stronghold of the strict Ansar Sunna sect, three masked gunmen burst in on worshippers spraying them with machine-gun bullets. Ten men and two children were slain and a further seventeen were wounded.

30 May 1994

In Khartoum itself, a fifteen-year-old girl was being held by police, accused of murdering five children. The victims, aged between three and twelve, had all been strangled. According to one report, a further nine children have been reported missing and the bodies of some of them have also been found.

Tajikistan
8 February 1994

According to the Interfax news agency, twelve people, including four children, were killed when a man threw grenades during a wedding celebration at Kulyab in the former Soviet republic.

United States
16 May 1993

Four men and three women were shot dead at Carillo's night club in Fresno, California, on the night of 16 May

1993; two other women were seriously wounded. Although Fresno is generally regarded as 'a nice little town', the club was recognised as a trouble-spot. Two known criminals, described as hispanics, had earlier been thrown out of Carillo's and it is thought that the blood-bath was a revenge attack.

1 July 1993

The law firm of Petit and Martin occupy the thirtieth to thirty-fourth floors of a forty-nine-storey high-rise office block on California Street in the centre of San Francisco's business district – not exactly mass-killer territory. But on the first day of July 1993 a lone middle-aged gunman carried out a massacre leaving at least nine people dead as he rampaged through offices and corridors. The man, said later to have gone to the lawyers to make a deposition, was carrying two Uzi automatics as he roamed purposefully through all four floors shooting anything that moved. One survivor recalled: 'I heard the alarms and ran out of my office, smelling smoke. I saw bullet holes in the walls and ran straight back . . . I was terrified.' As to the heavily armed police teams called in to track the killer through the labyrinth of corridors and offices, they were at the same time picking their way over the dead and wounded in an attempt to snatch a killer crazily out of control. On the thirtieth floor they did; after straffing the three floors above the gunman was confronted with his Nemesis in the form of armed security guards. Like many before him and certainly many after, the Petit and Martin gunman turned one of his weapons on himself.

9 July 1993

Alan Dorris, having shot three people in a bar in Jackson, Mississippi, drove the ninety miles to Greenville and killed an elderly woman and her son. Dorris then put the barrel of the gun into his mouth and pulled the trigger. Just hours later he was recovering from serious, but not life-threatening, injuries to the mouth. While Dorris was being patched up and processed, another man, indicted as an accomplice to the shootings, was charged with the three killings. Thirty-one-year-old Michael Laney had earlier gone to the police voluntarily, though at the time of reporting it was unclear how he was connected with the Jackson murders.

14 October 1993

Nineteen-year-old James Buquet was a dedicated weight-lifter and, like many committed bodybuilders, had been devastated when a knee injury prevented him from pumping his regular dose of iron in the local health centre; in his case the Family Fitness Centre at El Cajon near San Diego, of which Buquet, a former drug addict, had been an enthusiastic member for some three months.

At lunchtime on Thursday 14 October 1993, Buquet drove to the centre in his Datsun car. First he circled the car park for some minutes before jumping out and shooting dead a man standing outside the building, then he blasted his way in through a window. In the gymnasium, James Buquet fired wildly in all directions with a 12-bore shotgun. Witnesses described his actions as 'crazy', shooting people in the head and all the time laughing; as terrified bystanders were screaming and begging for mercy, Buquet just kept on shooting. At one point he stood over a victim's body, reloaded his gun and fired repeatedly into the corpse. Three women died in the gymnasium and two elderly men taking part in a senior citizens' work-out were injured.

Suddenly, James Buquet stopped firing; he left the club, got in to his Datsun car, put the barrel of the shotgun under his chin and pulled the trigger. Police investigating the quadruple killing were unable to find any motive, though they were able to discount rumours that Buquet was involved with one of the slain women. Furthermore, although he had once spent time in a drug rehabilitation centre following chronic marijuana and LSD use he had, according to a friend of the family, been off drugs for about four years. However, another man who knew Buquet said: 'He was one of those kinds of guys you don't want to cross. He always had an angry look on his face. If you saw him coming down the street you wanted to cross the road and get away from him. He was just a bundle of anger and looked very tough.'

And that, as it stood, was the brief and unremarkable if bloody life of James Buquet. It was what emerged in the aftermath that would grip the imagination.

During the investigation into Buquet's background it was discovered he had once written a thirteen-page essay about a fictional mass killer as part of a creative writing course at a college in El Cajon. The piece described the activities of a character named Natas (Satan spelt backwards!) A. Bishop, who believed that he could give some meaning to his own life by robbing others of theirs. In the essay, Buquet wrote: 'Natas had these thoughts a lot. They would come and go along with his depressions. God, how many times had he thought about this? At night it was the last thought he had. The one that put him to sleep. In fact, he didn't feel right at night unless he thought about killing.' The reality was that the fiction had an uncomfortably consistent similarity with Buquet's own killing spree: Natas uses a 12-gauge shotgun to kill at least ten people in a fast-food restaurant. The essay describes Natas preparing for the killings 'with the ice of a serial killer going in for the prey', and sets out the murders in detail, particularly describing how one woman was shot in the face: 'The pellets hit her face and it became nothing more but a red pile of glob with thin hair and blood drops rinsed through it.' This reference was chillingly reminiscent of Buquet standing over one of his own victims and firing shot after shot into the body. Buquet's piece of fiction concluded by insisting that society was full of 'robots', and that he would one day show the world what life was really all about by murdering them.

In a curious postscript, two weeks after James Buquet's killing spree, sixty-two-year-old Gordon Newman, a recluse and long-time resident of El Cajon opened fire on people in the street below his second-floor apartment window; a woman and a nine-year-old child died and five others were wounded. The shooting ended when Newman's apartment inexplicably burst into flames and he was found dead inside. The reason for the spree? None really, except that Newman was known to hate children and noise.

2 December 1993

A lone gunman opened fire in a crowded Los Angeles benefits office claiming the lives of three people and wounding six; he then shot dead a police officer with a bullet to the head. Thirty-three-year-old engineer Alan Winterbourne targeted only staff of the office, sparing other claimants which seemed to confirm that the attack was motivated by Winterbourne having been unemployed for eight years. The killer fled in his car pursued by a police vehicle; after being surrounded, Winterbourne cut down officer Jim O'Brien before himself dying in a hail of police bullets.

17 December 1993

Two people were killed and four injured in the third major shooting in the small town of Hugo, Oklahoma, in twenty-four hours and the fourth in the same week. The gunman drove into a car park in the centre of town and loosed off a semi-automatic rifle apparently randomly; he then got back in the car and drove a short distance before shooting himself.

January 1994

A bizarre family murder involved one Brandon Teena, an apparently popular twenty-one-year-old described by his many girlfriends as 'a dish' and 'a hunk'. What the residents of the small town of Humboldt, Nebraska, did not know is that Brandon Teena was in fact a woman named Teena Brandon – even 'his' local girlfriend testified that: 'We dated for a week and I believed he was a man. He never gave me any reason to suppose otherwise.' Then, unfortunately for Brandon, he was taken into custody and charged with forgery offences, and the cat was out of the bag.

Two men said to have learned of the strange double life are twenty-two-year-old John Lotter and Marvin Nissen, twenty-one; they were by all accounts not so well pleased at having been fooled and set out to teach Brandon a lesson. Lotter is currently charged with kidnapping and sexually assaulting the victim Teena Brandon and both men are accused of the first-degree murder of Brandon, his last girlfriend, Lisa Lambert, and a twenty-two-year-old friend, Philip Levine. A detective investigating the killings said later that Brandon always dressed, talked and walked like a man; he added: 'This is a small community. You don't expect this sort of thing.'

15 February 1994

Marcus Muriel Thompson, a twenty-six-year-old employee with the Tulsa, Oklahoma, branch of the fast-food chain Wendy's Hamburgers, had arrived early for his shift and because of the lunchtime rush had been asked to start work earlier. This did not make Thompson a happy man, especially as he had been refused a pay rise. So he decided to get even in his own way.

While the restaurant was full of children, Marcus Thompson walked in with a .38-calibre handgun and shot and wounded the manager and five other people before walking out and calmly giving himself up to armed police officers. Three of the teenage students were among the injured. One survivor was reported as saying: 'We were at a back table and didn't get out . . . He started shooting my friends, then he came to me and held the gun right in my face and said: "You better be awful lucky." Then he asked me if I believed in God and I said yes. He said: "The [ammunition] clip is out," and walked towards the front.' Of the injured, one was shot five times in the stomach, another was in a serious condition with a bullet wound in the head, the others were said to be stable.

15 March 1994

Another disgruntled employee who had been sacked from an electronics plant in Santa Fe Springs, California, went back to the factory and killed three former colleagues and wounded two before turning the gun on himself.

5 April 1994

At Versailles, Indiana, a man who offered a defence that evil spirits drove him to kill five of his relatives was sentenced to prison terms amounting to 240 years. Under Indiana state law, George Hardebeck will have to serve a mandatory half that sentence; it was not reported how old Hardebeck was, but it is extremely unlikely he will make it.

23 May 1994

Two men walked into an Indianapolis restaurant and held twenty-five hostages for six hours before being flushed out by police assisted by SWAT teams and a helicopter. The gunmen entered Danny's diner just before lunchtime, and although they allowed some of the captives to leave, when the gunmen finally surrendered they left one man dead and four people wounded, one a four-year-old child who was in a critical condition after suffering gunshot wounds to his face.

More True Crime from Headline:

THE NEW MURDERERS' WHO'S WHO

150 YEARS OF NOTORIOUS MURDER CASES

J.H.H. GAUTE & ROBIN ODELL

'A must for all crime buffs' ***Sunday Express***

'Gruesome, fact-packed . . . compulsive reading' ***Daily Mirror***

The most comprehensive book available on murder, written by leading experts in the field, THE NEW MURDERERS' WHO'S WHO is the fully revised and updated edition of the true-crime classic, THE MURDERERS' WHO'S WHO.

Fascinating, macabre, revealing, THE NEW MURDERERS' WHO'S WHO shows the state of the art in murder:

- **Over 500 cases, of which 100 are new, amongst them the Yorkshire Ripper, Dennis Nilsen and Kenneth Bianchi (the 'Hillside Strangler').**
- **The latest developments on existing cases such as the Moors Murders and the Kray Twins.**
- **New, rarely seen before, illustrations.**
- **A fully revised bibliography containing over 1,000 reference works.**

For professionals and experts and armchair detectives alike, THE NEW MURDERERS' WHO'S WHO – don't leave home on a dark night without it.

'Perhaps the most valuable single volume ever published on murder' Colin Wilson

TRUE CRIME/REFERENCE 0 7472 3270 9

More True Crime from Headline:

THE JACK THE RIPPER A TO Z

FOREWORD BY DONALD RUMBELOW

PAUL BEGG, MARTIN FIDO AND KEITH SKINNER

THE JACK THE RIPPER A TO Z

– the most comprehensive book ever written on the enduring mystery of Jack the Ripper.

Compiled in encyclopedic format by three of the world's leading experts on the subject, THE JACK THE RIPPER A TO Z provides completely up-to-date, fresh and unbiased accounts of the many theories as to his identity. It also describes all the main suspects (including the hitherto unidentified police suspect, Michael Ostrog), giving details of the policemen, politicians and innocent bystanders caught up in the case. It provides a wealth of topographical detail and social background which put the crimes into their proper historical context – thereby helping to explain why they created such a sensation at the time and why they continue to exert such a fascination over a century later.

'This book has to be the anchor of future Jack the Ripper studies' – Donald Rumbelow, author of *The Complete Jack the Ripper*

TRUE CRIME/REFERENCE 0 7472 3676 3